ANOINTED MOMENTS

Everyday Miracles While
Transforming Two Schools,
Thousands of People,
And a Dog Named Blue

DAN HORN

www.DanHornBooks.com

Printed in U.S.A. for delivery within United States.
ISBN: 978-1496069771
Cover design by Howard Anderson (www.HowardAnderson.com)

DEDICATIONS

Anointed Moments is dedicated to the many boys, girls, women, and men — and families — who have been hurt by our Catholic Church over the decades. This book is for each one of you.

Additionally, the anointed moments described within these pages would not have been possible without the profound spiritual teachers I've had along the way. It is impossible to list them all, but here are some who have had the most impact on my life, in the order in which I met them:

My mom, Aldene Horn
Reverend Douglas Albert
Marianne Williamson
Monsignor Lloyd Torgerson
Father Ken Deasy
Father Dennis O'Neil
Father Mark Toohey
Sister Joan Faraone
Don Miguel Ruiz
Sister Clare Fitzgerald
Louise Hay

And finally, to Pope Francis…although I haven't met you yet, I've been waiting for you all my life!

CONTENTS

FOREWORD

Miracles are hard to come by in education these days. *Anointed Moments* chronicles a passel of them, centering around two Los Angeles schools where one humble and incredibly optimistic and energetic man with a vision for what a true "Catholic" education could be, teamed with teachers, students and parents alike to transform these once deeply challenged, about-to-fail institutions into schools of national distinction.

I didn't meet Dan Horn until January of 2010. Still, without knowing it, I was becoming aware of his work simply by driving past St. Genevieve High School not far from where I lived. You only needed to be an occasional passerby to notice the changes that were taking place at St. Gen's over time.

Back in the 1990s, I saw fewer and fewer students make their way in the mornings to this once-prestigious school on Roscoe Boulevard. Not only that, those who were attending didn't seem to be walking with the same pride that had once characterized the St. Gen's student body. Much of the news coming out of the school was also less than positive, and eventually I, like many others, heard rumors that St. Gen's might close.

And then right around 2000, things started to change. I'd see more kids on the Boulevard making their way to and from St. Gen's, some proudly wearing letterman jackets while others just walked with a renewed sense of purpose. Students seemed to be getting the old St. Gen's swagger back. One day I drove by to see a huge banner over the entire entryway: "St Genevieve High School — a National School of Character." I didn't know what it meant, but I figured it had to be a good thing: call it a "transformation affirmation."

Flash forward to January 2010, when principal Dan Horn invited me to take part in the school's Character Education Program. I was delighted to accept, unaware that I was about to experience the transformation that had taken place at St. Gen's firsthand. It was an evening I'll always remember.

A welcoming committee of students met me at my car. There was nothing shy about any of these individuals: firm handshakes, unwavering eye contact and a genuine interest in making me feel instantly at home. It was clear that they loved their school and they wanted me to love it, too.

It was in the faculty lounge — where I enjoyed a dinner with the St. Gen's faculty and staff — that I first met Dan Horn, or Danny, as he quickly became known to me. There was just something about him that made me feel I'd known him for years. Over our meal, he shared some of his insights and the efforts it took for him and his team to turn a failing school into a national model for character education in just a few years' time.

But talk is one thing. Actions are another. And it was after dinner that I first realized how deeply ingrained "character" actually was in the St. Gen's students, as well as in their parents. It was 7:00 p.m., already dark out, when it became evident to me that school was still in session. And that the students and teachers who had just completed their afternoon classes were now making their way to the gym for my presentation. Walking among them, I encountered hundreds of clearly happy, well-dressed, and motivated students shouting words of welcome and encouragement.

It wasn't until I arrived at the gym, however, that I became aware of the hundreds of parents also waiting to greet me and hear what I had to say. This was no run-of-the-mill high school assembly, in other words, but rather, it was an opportunity for me to share my thinking and my experiences with an entire community. Nor, as I would later learn, was tonight's assembly an occasional event. St. Gen's Character Education Program gatherings were a monthly occurrence.

Prior to my taking the stage, there was a school prayer and all the students stood to sing. And sing they did! In all my years of taking part in school events, I'd never heard young people sing with such obvious enthusiasm and joy. Truly, it was as if the heavens had opened with song.

And then it was my turn to speak. Often in high school assemblies there is an undercurrent of whispers as students who wished they were elsewhere expressed their frustration. There was no such undercurrent at St. Gen's as hundreds of students — and their parents — listened attentively, then asked thoughtful questions.

Figuring that my evening was over after I answered the last question, I was absolutely stunned when the entire audience blessed me and prayed for my ministry to leave the world a better place. The ring of students sitting near me on the floor suddenly stood as one, surrounding me as they were joined in song, and then in prayer, by everyone else in the room. To say that I was both inspired and thankful would be an understatement. It was for me an anointed moment.

In the pages that follow, Dan Horn shares a number of other such touching and often life-changing stories from his years as principal at St. Genevieve High School in the San Fernando Valley, as well as from his nine-year tenure as principal of St. Thomas the Apostle elementary school in the Pico-Union District of Los Angeles.

I believe you'll find these special anointing moments as powerful and affecting as I did, and will feel refreshed and heartened by your reading.

— Edward James Olmos

PREFACE

You may have noticed that this book is partially dedicated to people who have been hurt by the Catholic Church. Throughout history, our Christian church communities have done more good for the world than we can possibly imagine. However, there have been some in various ministries that have corrupted the power and trust they have been given. In fact, I have been personally disappointed and affected by the corrupt values of some of my church colleagues and superiors in a number of instances. Those stories, however, are for an entirely different book.

Instead, I've chosen to concentrate on the many blessings I have received throughout my career as a Catholic school principal. I have been blessed with an ability to lead, and I have chosen to lead with a spirit of love and kindness for those with and to whom I minister. By doing so, and by being in a perpetual state of spiritual growth, or at least by acknowledging the desire for growth, I have experienced more than my share of encounters with the divine presence of God. I was looking, and not only found God, we actually met face to face.

I suppose the same may be true for anyone who is looking. That is a key part of the message of *Anointed Moments*: are you looking? And if not, why not? I have been at the receiving end of experiencing God's power, light, and love because I wanted — and asked for — a front-row seat. I have discovered that God's divine love for us is evident all of the time, even in tragedy.

I hope you enjoy reading about some of the anointed moments of my life. Be blessed.

Chapter 1. Conversion

Moving to Los Angeles in the fall of 1986, I had one goal: to be a movie star. Small-town Pennsylvania boy, I was 25 years old, wide-eyed, as they say, and had the feeling the city was just waiting for my arrival.

Prior to moving, I was told that once I got to Los Angeles I would need to have some headshots taken: eight-and-a-half-by-eleven black-and-white glossy photos from the neck up. Once I had the headshots, I would need to get a list of casting agencies and the approved agents from the Screen Actors Guild, and begin my ascent to stardom by sending my picture and acting resume to everyone on the list. I had been warned about the crooked agents who would tell naïve actors that in order to be represented they would have to use a certain photographer. It was a ruse. The agent and photographer would then split the fees. I was too smart to fall into that trap. Not only was I college educated, I had been a teacher for three years, was living on my own, and was ready for the big city as well as the big screen. Danny Horn, my screen name and alter ego, would outsmart them.

To avoid the Hollywood con artists and have agents and directors eagerly awaiting my arrival, I decided to have my headshots taken in Virginia, where I was living prior to my move. I scoured the Yellow Pages and found just the right photographer. During our phone conversation, he convinced me that not only was he experienced and knew exactly what I was looking for, he would lower his regular price because he knew that I would soon be incurring moving expenses. He told me to bring several different shirts and sweaters; we set a date, time, and wow…it felt like I was already making progress in my showbiz career.

The fact that it took him a while to answer the doorbell to his studio, that he wobbled a bit, that his speech was slurred and his eyes were glassy all registered, but did not faze me. Even when he spilled a little beer on one of my favorite shirts, I did not question my selection of him. Creative types, I thought. Belching, and then wiping some beer from the corner of his mouth with his wrist while his hand tightly clasped the Miller's can, he studied my face and body quizzically. Then, his head bobbed a bit unsteadily as he announced, "I have just the thing." What did that mean, I wondered?

Reaching into a tiny makeshift closet, he said, "You're a young Don Johnson type. Miami Vice is very big." He pulled out a lavender t-shirt with the sleeves cut off and the word "HOLLYWOOD" emblazoned across the chest. Don Johnson, I thought. Hmm, this guy, although inebriated, really seemed to know what he was doing. Next thing I knew, I was dressed in the sleeveless t-shirt holding a prop pistol; at least I think it was a prop. I never thought to ask if it was real. In retrospect, it may have been as loaded as he was.

Not only did I send out the horrible headshots to dozens of agents and casting directors, but as a follow-up, I had the picture of me holding the gun looking oh-so-serious made into postcards on which I wrote catchy phrases like "Represent me...or else!" Of course this was pre-Columbine and 9/11; I shudder to think what would happen if someone did something like that today.

Needless to say, I spent two years falling into every trap, succumbing to every scam, taking useless classes, and spending every cent I was making. I was working at a myriad of part-time jobs, ranging from gopher and delivery person to hotel concierge, houseman, and tour guide. I had no health insurance and never knew from one day to the next how much money I would be making. However, it was the first time in my life that I was living irresponsibly and totally independently and I loved almost every second of it. After two years, I still wasn't ready to give up on my acting aspirations, but I was desperately ready for some steady income.

When I read the help wanted ad for principal of a Catholic school in the *Los Angeles Times*, I found the answer to my prayers. I had been a certified English teacher for three years in Pennsylvania and Virginia prior to moving to L.A. One of the many part-time jobs I'd had since arriving in California was being a substitute teacher whenever I could get a gig that didn't interfere with an audition or daytime acting class. I knew what principals did: not much, at least I thought that at the time. And if I were principal of the school, whose permission would I need to slip out during the day to make an audition? Mine. Whose permission would I need to leave early to get to an acting class on time? Mine. And when the big break came...who knew, maybe I could still earn my principal's salary while filming; it all seemed highly possible.

Although I didn't get that particular job, I now had a game plan for bringing in some steady cash while still pursuing my dream, which, by the way, seemed to be taking a lot longer than I'd bargained for.

Over the next two years I worked as a full-time teacher, first in a Catholic elementary school, and then as an English teacher and an English-as-a-second-language teacher at what was in the 1980's one of the most notorious inner-city high schools in Los Angeles: Fremont. I became somewhat desperate to find another position. Although I always found teaching to be satisfying, neither of these two teaching positions was fulfilling enough for me to want to settle in and stay. If anything, I was feeling a bit resentful that I was now limited to late afternoon auditions and evening acting classes. The fact is, after taking numerous acting classes and having been in L.A. for several years, I still had not secured an agent and most of the auditions I went on were open casting calls where anyone was free to try out. As much as it hurt to admit it to myself, my ultimate goal of becoming a professional actor seemed less and less realistic. There are things we know about ourselves but sometimes find difficult to admit — to ourselves let alone to anyone else. In my case, I was coming to the conclusion that I was not good at the craft of acting. Most of the time, when I did get in front of a casting director, my voice would shake or my knees would reveal how nervous I was. I knew that I was largely fooling myself. I knew that I didn't have the "fire in the belly" that so many thousands of others around me obviously had — those who were so determined that they were able to keep going, keep pushing, even in the face of incredibly demoralizing comments from acting coaches and casting directors. Perhaps, I thought, my goal was only a temporary one. Perhaps I was meant to do something else with my life.

In January of 1990 I received a letter from the Department of Catholic Schools at the Archdiocese of Los Angeles. The letter was signed by Sister Margaret Ann Nowacki, director of personnel. I remembered her. When I'd interviewed with her two years earlier for a principal position, she'd told me, "I think you should go and sell used cars, young man." It seemed more an endorsement of my gift for salesmanship than her assessment of my leadership abilities. Now her letter asked if I was still interested in becoming a principal in the archdiocese. I believed the New Year was blessing me with one last opportunity to have a steady income and still have the freedom to pursue agents, and go to classes and auditions during the daytime. I immediately called and left her a message that I was indeed interested. Within two weeks Sister Margaret Ann called to let me know she was going to forward my resume to pastors who were looking for principals, and that I could expect to receive some calls for interviews. I waited awhile but didn't receive any calls, so I took some initiative and began knocking on doors of parishes whose elementary schools I'd heard might have openings for principals. When one pastor saw how young I looked, he practically closed the door in my face. Another pastor asked how I would deal with parents of students who did not attend Sunday Mass. He described a situation in which one child's father, who was traveling for business and was out of town on weekends, might not be attending Sunday Mass. "How would you deal with that?"

"I wouldn't," I responded. "That's none of my business."

In my mind I was shouting, "NEXT interview please." I have a feeling the priest was as well.

Then I got a call from Father Dennis O'Neil, pastor of St. Thomas the Apostle School in the Pico-Union District of L.A. He invited me to come for an interview. Dressed in my one and only suit, I rang the bell of the craftsman-style house on Mariposa with the sign in front reading, St. Thomas Parish Office. Behind the security door, I could see a receptionist begin to get up from the desk when a male silhouette appeared quickly in the doorway; I could see a priest's collar.

"I've got it Sonia," said the priest who stood ramrod straight, and mechanically put out his hand to shake mine, like a schoolboy greeting his own principal. While his initial greeting seemed oddly deferential, it was much preferred to the immediate brush-off I'd received at the first school where I'd interviewed. He was in his late forties, about my height, 5'10", with dark hair that was thinning and beginning to gray.

"Are you Dan Horn?" he inquired. Before I could say anything, he answered for me, "Well, of course you are! Other than me, there are no other white guys around here today, especially dressed the way you are. Are you ready for your interview?"

"Yes sir, I am."

"Then let's go over to the rectory dining room. I have a committee that wants to ask you some questions," he said, leading me to the larger house next door. For the brief moment I stood in the parish office reception area I noticed that it was filled with adults and children, as was the front porch. I had no idea what they were waiting for. Even those who appeared exhausted perked up when they saw Father Dennis. There was a chorus of *Padre. Hola. Padre! Hola! Buenos Dias, Padre Dennis."*

"You've probably figured out by now that I'm Father Dennis O'Neil, the pastor of this place," he said with both humility and pride.

The committee was comprised of various parish group leaders. They sat around a large dining room table and left places at both ends for Father Dennis and me to sit. Some of the committee members only spoke Spanish and their questions had to be translated along with my responses. To my surprise, Father Dennis provided all the translation, easily flowing between the two languages. At one point, when one of the Spanish speakers seemed to be at a loss for a word, Father Dennis simply filled in the blank for him. About an hour passed, and the sun was beginning to set on the neighborhood. Father Dennis abruptly thanked everyone and announced that he and Dan were going to take a walk.

Oh good, I thought, as the room was getting a little warm and I liked to walk, especially in places I've never been before. "We can continue our conversation as we walk," Father Dennis said. I was holding my cards close to the vest. Never would I admit that I had ulterior motives for wanting to be principal. It would be months later before I learned, however, that Father Dennis also had ulterior motives for that walk — and for interviewing me in the first place.

At the time, drug deals were taking place in the neighborhood, right out in the open. Seeing a potential customer, dealers would often chase a car down the street, attempting to get the driver's business before a competitor. Vagrants would lie on the sidewalks drunk, sometimes passed out, sometimes having fallen into a neighbor's front yard. The Playboys, one of L.A.'s largest gangs, ruled the streets, and some of the buildings were covered in graffiti to lay claim to their territory.

As Father Dennis and I walked that day, I was struck by the unlikely sounds of chickens clucking and roosters crowing, which set a stark contrast to the sophisticated downtown skyscrapers that loomed just a few miles away. I felt saddened by the first-floor windows on some of the apartment buildings having been partially or entirely bricked over. Father Dennis stopped in front of one apartment building. "See this window? The landlord bricked it up to stop bullets from entering during drive-by shootings," he explained. "They just leave room at the top for some air to get into the apartment." I shook my head in astonishment. "You see that park next to the school?" he asked me.

"Yeah, it looks pretty nice," I said.

"It looks nice now, but it took us almost two years to get that park cleaned up. Dealers used to sell drugs all day long in that park right in plain view of our students." Normandie Park was a small patch of land that housed a baseball field, some basketball courts, and a few picnic tables.

He shared poverty and crime statistics with me. "The corner we're approaching, Fedora and Pico…it has the most drive-by shootings than anywhere else in the city. Our parish is working to change that." All of the houses in the area were small single-story dwellings with tiny front lawns, most of which were tenderly cared for and had beautiful flowers and neatly trimmed bushes, seeming to exude pride. "Several of these houses have numerous families living in them. Same with the apartments in these buildings," he pointed out.

"Really? The homes look barely large enough for a single family," I said.

"They squeeze into them. There are families that even live in some of these garages."

As we walked, we passed young and middle-aged men dressed in the Playboy uniform of khaki pants and white t-shirt, short hair slicked straight back, some with hair nets. Whether they sat on the front steps of the apartment buildings or stood in groups, they all watched us closely and almost everyone said "*Hola!*" or "Hi, Padre!" as we passed by. Some reached out to shake the Father's hand, and most seemed glad to see him.

They all seemed to know Father Dennis and those who didn't certainly recognized the white collar, and they showed their respect. They also seemed curious about the guy he was with. Although I was 29 at the time, I looked about 20, still had chubby cheeks and some baby fat, along with blondish hair, and green eyes — in other words, very much the gringo, dressed in an ill-fitting suit, nodding my head, waving, and greeting everyone along the way. I did not realize it at the time, but I was taking — and passing — a test. Father Dennis' motive for the walk was to see if I would grow afraid or become intimidated by the neighborhood. I'm not sure what he expected me to do or say but he certainly didn't expect me to smile at everyone, greet them, attempt to speak Spanish with them, and enjoy myself, as I clearly was doing.

Prior to the tour and to him sharing the neighborhood statistics with me, I didn't know enough to be intimidated. That was a good thing. Perhaps I wouldn't have gone for the interview at all had I known these things ahead of time. In the years to come, numerous teaching candidates failed to show up for an interview with me only to call later to say they weren't interested once they learned where the school was located. Although I had seen people exhibit prejudice while I was growing up, my mom used those experiences to teach us kids that we were like everyone else and that we should accept everyone.

So, I enjoyed that walk with Father Dennis, and it was obvious. We were two men, each with ulterior motives.

During our walk, as I learned a lot about the tiny school and its parish, I began to think of a future in which I might be able to help meet the needs of students at this school more than one in which there would be any real possibilities for me in the acting world.

The school, I learned, was over eighty years old and had always had a nun as principal. Most recently, two nuns had worked as co-principals, but they had been fired by Dennis O'Neil. There were serious divisions among the teachers, the parents, and the pastor. The majority of families living in the area surrounding the school were from Mexico and Central America, mostly immigrants or first-generation Americans, almost all of them Catholic. The relatively small area was the most densely populated neighborhood west of the Mississippi River. There were 6,000 families registered as parishioners and countless others who attended church but were not registered. St. Thomas the Apostle parish was baptizing approximately 1,200 babies a year, and between 500 and 600 children from the parish would make their first communion annually. There were a large number of marriages and funerals. Every Saturday there were three to six weddings, several sometimes happening simultaneously. The funerals were most often the result of gang-related violence. This church, I was beginning to see, was the beating heart of the neighborhood, providing undeniable hope to its otherwise hopeless citizens. It was the social, spiritual, and emotional epicenter for thousands who immigrated in search of better lives. As we walked, I felt something building inside me telling me that perhaps this was what I was being called to do.

When we returned from the walk it was dark, and Father Dennis saw me to my car. By the time I reached my Hollywood apartment, I was hopeful that the committee would choose me to be the school's principal. Although I'd originally schemed that being principal would allow me to sneak away from school for auditions or the occasional acting class, it now occurred to me that this leadership role would itself be very satisfying. After hearing from Father Dennis about the community of St. Thomas the Apostle, I actually was now feeling guilty that I'd considered going there under somewhat false pretenses.

As the days passed, any ulterior motive I had arrived with at the door of the St. Thomas parish office had now completely vanished. The more I thought about the school, the neighborhood, Father Dennis, and the committee, the more I found my desire to be principal growing. I promised myself that were I to be offered this job I would immerse myself in it, learning what I could from those already there and hoping that I would be able to bring something of my own — an open-minded and creative approach to education, perhaps. I would work to inspire the teachers to think and go beyond the textbook, to help students discover who they are, and more importantly, who they are meant to become. Most schools and many teachers tend to quash creativity from the moment they insist that students color within the lines. I would encourage them to create their own lines. And while I would throw away the red pens so students wouldn't feel as though their teachers had bled over the errors, I would encourage teachers to be colorful in their teaching, as well as in grading and encouraging the positive contributions of students.

I found myself thinking about that school community and their needs in every spare moment. Then, I was struck by a humbling thought. I needed them. Fate had turned the tables on me. If only that committee and that priest would trust that a young guy with only five years of teaching experience and no graduate credit in anything could mend the divisions and provide leadership for good quality Catholic education, I would accept the position and work toward success with every fiber of my being. I developed a "fire in the belly" feeling that I had never felt before. For the week following my interview, I prayed and hoped that this priest, Father Dennis, would see in me what I knew I had within me — the grit and determination to make St. Thomas School succeed.

Waiting was excruciating. I experienced one of the longest weeks of my life. It was now seven days since I'd met Father Dennis and the committee. I returned home from a long day attempting to teach English at Fremont High School, hit the switch on my answering machine, and heard, "Dan, this is Father Dennis. We at St. Thomas the Apostle parish would like you to be our school's principal. Call me when you get this message."

Needless to say, I was thrilled. But at that point, I could never have imagined all the lessons I would learn at this tiny school and from this man offering me the job, Father Dennis. And little did I know that when Father Dennis offered me the position, it was not because he sensed the fire in my belly or noticed the passion in my eyes. In fact, it was not until my first year at the helm was complete that I discovered the truth as to why Father Dennis had hired me.

After my first year as principal, enrollment was full, we had a waiting list for the coming year, and morale among students, staff, and parents was palpably high. Everyone seemed to be looking forward to the next school year. It was the end of June and the parish was having its annual fiesta in the church parking lot. Dennis invited me to come taste his favorite fiesta treat, a turkey sandwich from the El Salvadorian booth. Sliced roasted turkey atop a savory roll called a *bolillo*, the sandwich was garnished with watercress and a fresh-made salsa — it was delicious. The next day, Dennis would be leaving for a month in Alaska, his favorite spot on earth. As we ate our sandwiches, he told tales of his years in Alaska as a pastor in Ketchikan. He fondly recalled losing all sense of time while fishing during the almost night-less summers there. He would often be stunned to look at his watch while out on a fishing boat and discover it was two in the morning. His enthusiastic descriptions made me yearn to visit there one day.

Finishing up my sandwich, I expressed my gratitude. And I finally told him my little secret, that when I'd arrived for the initial interview, I'd been hoping for an easy gig where I would still be able to pursue my acting career. I admitted that all of that desire was behind me now, and that in being principal of St. Thomas School I had discovered a joy I never knew I could experience. I told him that I realized he had taken a big chance on hiring someone like me, with no administrative experience and no academic preparation beyond my bachelor's degree. "Apparently you saw something in me that others had not seen before and I want you to know that I'm very grateful for that," I told him. It was a brutally honest moment for me, one that I hoped would bring us closer.

Dennis had a rather ferocious eating style and was not concerned about polite table manners; he was the kind of eater that most cooks dream about serving, but not cleaning up after. He had never stopped eating while I was opening my heart to him and he continued to eat while saying, "Well the truth is, Dan, Sister Margaret Ann and I never expected you to last. We thought you would surely fail."

"Sister Margaret Ann, from the Department of Catholic Schools?" I asked, somewhat stunned.

"Yes, I had gone to her for help. Things were so bad here that we thought that whoever became principal this year would fail big-time. So we decided to pick someone who was young and hopefully resilient enough to dust themselves off and go on to become principal somewhere else. Sister suggested I interview you."

"You're kidding me," I said trying to digest what I was hearing.

"Then our plan was to hire a principal for a long stretch after the community had their blood," he said laughing and dripping salsa down his face and neck. "We never expected you to make it to year two. You should probably take that as a compliment," he said, still laughing heartily.

It was that kind of blunt honesty with a little calculating spirit thrown in that I always liked and enjoyed about Dennis. I suppose I deserved it; after all, I had shown up with my own ulterior motive. Shame on both of us.

St. Thomas School deserved a dedicated and diligent principal. I deserved a chance to show that good leadership does not necessarily come from experience or by taking classes. In the end, although we took the sneaky route to get there, both St. Thomas School and I got exactly what we deserved.

Danny Horn

I wrote on the back of these postcards, "Represent me...or else!"
Can't imagine why I never heard from any agents.

Chapter 2. Getting Ready

It was only after both Father Dennis and I signed my first contract that I actually read the job description. Most of it was generalities; however, one of those generalities made me choke on the Mountain Dew I was drinking at the time: *"The principal is the religious and spiritual leader of the school."*

I should have expected something like that, but I had not. It caught me completely by surprise. For a few brief seconds I began to panic. For the remainder of the day I considered whether I had made a mistake.

Was I up to this task? Of course I wasn't. I had no idea how to quote scripture, and most of the time was pretty turned off when I heard others do it; it often seemed so pretentious to me. And prayer? Oh, was I going to be in trouble! I remember once volunteering to lead prayer at one of our family Thanksgiving dinners with almost twenty relatives and friends. Our family only prayed together on Christmas Day and Thanksgiving. It was traditionally the "Bless us O Lord for these Thy gifts, which we are about to receive from Thy bounty through Christ our Lord, Amen." It was easy enough for almost all ages to memorize, and my aunts, uncles, and cousins were all comfortable saying it together.

However, much to the chagrin of most of my family members — all of us cradle Catholics — when I was in seventh grade in Catholic school, I started attending services at the church right next door to our house, the Protestant Grace United Church of Christ. The minister and his wife were practically members of our family and it made sense to me to check things out. I immediately loved it. At their services, unlike at our Catholic Masses, people actually sang, and sang joyfully. The sermons, delivered by

Reverend Phil Saylor, a grandfather figure to me, were thoughtful and powerfully delivered. Plus, I sat next to Mrs. Dorothy Saylor, a Mrs. Claus-looking woman, heavy-set, with long, flowing white hair, and a laugh that could make a statue crack up. I felt very special attending that church. I could understand the devout Catholic members of my family finding it disconcerting that I was attending a Protestant church, but found it contradictory that it was equally upsetting to those who did not attend Mass. Almost every prayer I heard at my Catholic school and during Mass was something written by someone else that was either read or memorized. We were never taught to pray from our hearts and say exactly what was on our minds. What a change it was for me to hear prayer that was pure, thought up at the moment, and coming right from the minister's heart. It inspired me.

On that Thanksgiving in 1974, as my mom was taking her place at the table, giving the unofficial signal that it was time to eat, I blurted out, "I'd like to lead prayer if that's all right with everyone." My uncle Bobby, my mom's brother, said, "Sure, well go ahead then, let's go, food is gettin' cold."

"Let us bow our heads in prayer," I began. A sigh came from my brother Bobby, "How long is this going to take?" I ignored him. "Dear Father God," I continued, "thank you for this day, for this gathering of friends and family." I could hear someone giggle; my head was down. It could have been grandma, but I'm not sure. Then I heard someone else snicker, then another. My heart was racing from embarrassment; they were starting to laugh at something I was attempting to do with true feeling. Better wrap it up before it gets crazy and they start to say things during the prayer. "We also thank you for the food we are about to eat and for the hands that have prepared all this delicious food. Amen." Phew. Done! There were about 15 of us gathered around the table. Our alcoholic neighbor Ann, who'd arrived intoxicated, gave me a wink and a thumbs up, and we began to pass the serving bowls. When I had volunteered to lead prayer, of course everyone expected the standard prayer before meals. When I began to pray words they were not expecting, it stunned most of my family members, and they did what people often do when they feel uncomfortable: laugh. And I did what most kids do when they feel as though people are making fun of them: get out of that situation as fast as possible. I vowed never to pray that way again, at least, not in front of my family. I vowed to stay small and not embarrass myself like that again. Even Jesus learned that you can't be a prophet in your hometown.

As the years went by I continued to attend Grace Church, even years after my beloved Rev. and Mrs. Saylor retired and moved away. I became even closer with the new minister and his family; he was younger and had kids who were around my age. I loved visiting with them at the parsonage. They often invited me to stay for meals. I marveled at how easily prayer came to Rev. Albert's children, Phil and Kris, both younger than I was, and how respectful their parents were when their son and daughter prayed.

When I first started attending Grace Church I also attended Catholic Mass on Saturday night, a new rule that allowed the Saturday evening Mass to count toward Sunday obligation. It is a sin in the Catholic Church to miss Mass on a Sunday. By the time I got to Catholic high school, I was completely bored by Sunday/Saturday Masses at our parish and decided to break the third commandment, *Thou shall keep holy the Lord's Day*. Although I was attending church weekly, it was not Catholic, so in the eyes of the Catholic Church, my lack of attendance at our Catholic church was considered a sin...and each week I was racking up the same sin. To make matters worse, in seventh grade I had decided that confession was no longer for me after two confrontational experiences with priests, one in which I was lectured at in a harsh tone and the other in which I felt like I was being interrogated. There was nothing to stop me from communicating directly with God, I reasoned, so I cut out the middleman and stopped going to confession. Instead, I confessed silently each week with the congregation at Grace United Church of Christ.

Both of Grace's ministers, who had lived next door to us, made me feel that I was part of their family. And although I attended Catholic school for twelve years, I never quite felt part of *that* family. Sunday Masses were boring. Our elementary school Masses were mostly boring with the exception of an occasional "Folk Mass," which had folk music thrown into the mix. Our Masses at high school were geared more toward younger people and I enjoyed them, but they were held only a few times a year.

Back then, priests were greatly respected and there was an abundance of them. At our home parish of Sacred Heart there were typically four or more priests in residence to minister to the large Catholic congregation in our town. There was also a second Catholic church in Jeannette. Ascension Church was primarily built to serve the large Italian population in our town. With approximately 10,000 residents, our small town had two parishes and plenty of priests to minister to the needs of the large Catholic community. I would guess that any boy growing up Catholic in that day and age at least gave thought to the possibility of becoming a priest. I know I did. The nuns used to encourage it.

As a boy, I began to study the priests of our parish. Although my father died when I was six, I don't remember experiencing any outreach or compassion from any of our parish priests. It was a time when very few women were single mothers. My mom went to church every day and sent all three of her children to the parish school, yet I can't recall a single time when any of the priests of our parish ever dropped by or attempted to minister to our family. Instead, I remember them being quite distant. One seemed angry most of the time, and I have a memory of witnessing what I would consider a nervous breakdown of another one of the priests. We were at recess one day and this priest was looking down at us from where he stood on the balcony of the rectory dressed only in his white t-shirt, something that was quite unusual for a priest back then. As we were lining up to go back to class, he was shouting to us, "Satan frees the slaves, Satan frees the slaves..." I can still hear his voice trailing off as we went into the classroom. I never saw him again.

By seventh grade I knew that the life of a priest was not for me. After years of observation, I had witnessed too much unhappiness in that line of work. The "calling" that the nuns talked about was clearly not heard by me.

Religious life became quite puzzling to me as a boy. Although there were some nuns who were kind, caring, and sweet, I also experienced more than my share of the bitter kind of nuns. I can't blame them. In the eyes of the church, they were low on the totem pole; the boys in the white collars were the ones who were in charge. The good sisters were not always treated well, and it was only natural that over time, some of them would become angry and bitter. It was a shame, though, that they would remain in teaching long after their caring ways were no longer evident.

These early observations would serve me well in my future. They led me to some clear conclusions. As I grew older, I became quite certain that the God I came to know wanted me to be happy. Although I came to believe that we are all "called" to serve in some capacity, we are called to serve in ways that are unique to our unique selves, and most of all, we are called to love and to be loved.

Now it was years later, and I had just signed a contract that made me a Catholic school principal. In the hours and days following my reading — and choking over — the job description at St. Thomas, I recalled as a youngster seeing the sisters whacking my friends with a ruler or threatening a paddle. I remembered the irony: they would teach us about Jesus and his love for us, then beat or berate one of us. Didn't Jesus love my classmates and me? It took a few years for me to realize that it was Sister who didn't love us. It took even more years before I realized that Sister most likely didn't love herself very much either, and quite possibly hated the life she had dedicated herself to; she probably had nowhere else to go.

When I read the job description again, I remembered the hours, days, and months that followed my father's death and then my grandfather's sudden death. I recalled the lack of interest by our parish priests for our little family and my devoutly Catholic mother, now a young widow with three young children who had lost both her husband and her father within four months of each other. Recalling these memories, I looked anew at the once daunting line of the job description. This time, I did not choke. Instead, I stared at the words — *"The principal is the religious and spiritual leader of the school"* — with a newfound confidence.

I did not possess the same devotion as the priests and nuns who had led my Catholic schools and those who, until now, had led St. Thomas School. I would not be able to quote scripture or have the same knowledge of Catholic doctrine that the decades of nuns and priests who came before me had. What I possessed was something else. I knew that what I shared in common with most people was a desire to be accepted and a desire to be loved. I knew instinctively that the most effective way to lead spiritually was by example, and I knew I would work harder than anyone else who had ever served in that role to do just that: to be a daily example of a loving and caring leader, someone who would strive to make a place at the table so that every teacher and student would feel as though they belonged to something special, a community in Christ.

By the end of my reflection, I had not a single doubt that I could build a faith community. Most of my life I had been a student and a seeker, not so much for religious information, but for spiritual growth. For many, the religious formation is important. For me, however, the most important elements for growth and education for any individual are the formation and the nurturing of the spirit. Our spirit is the very core of who we are. It is our spirit that becomes one with the particles of the universe after our bodies have decayed to dust. I came to the realization in those few days that if I set a goal to make the nurturing of the spirit my highest priority, then education would be possible. I realized that if teachers and students feel cared about, then teaching and learning become authentic and powerful.

In my adult life I have found myself surrounded by spiritual teachers. A teacher friend in Virginia shared his Buddhist beliefs with me. When I told him I was moving to California, he said, "If you're moving there, you have to look up my two college friends who live in Venice Beach; they're both great guys." Craig Udit, Jim Fleming, and I forged friendships that last to this day. They were among the first California friends I ever had. Jim offered me a place to stay until I got settled in Los Angeles and I lived at his apartment for three months. His kindness in allowing a stranger to move in with him meant so much to me.

Upon moving 3,000 miles from home, I did become a little homesick, and after passing St. Monica Church, only a few miles from where I was staying with Jim, I began attending Catholic Mass once again. It felt like home. Thankfully, the church was much livelier than the Catholic experiences I'd had in my youth. Although I invited Jim to attend Mass with me, he respectfully declined. A few months younger than I was, Jim seemed so much wiser and he definitely possessed a zeal for life. He had lots of friends and a job he enjoyed. I became curious about his spiritual life.

Jim introduced me to Marianne Williamson and the life-changing *A Course in Miracles*. The course is a self-study curriculum designed to help students achieve a spiritual transformation. It provides practical lessons and applications for the practice of forgiveness in everyday life. Having just arrived in Los Angeles to attempt a career in show business, which can be detrimental to anyone's self esteem, I, with no steady income, was in a rather high state of anxiety most of the time.

"Dude, relax," Jim would say. "Look where we're living," he'd continue, pointing to the Pacific beyond the living room window.

"I know, I love it," I'd quickly fire back. "It *is* beautiful here."

"Take time to enjoy it. What's the point of being here, not just California, but in this life, if you don't take time to appreciate what's around you? Don't be one of those people who moves to L.A. and gets so caught up in trying to break into show business that you don't enjoy your life."

"I know, I know," I'd say. "I *am* enjoying it." Then Jim would laugh, "C'mon, let's go down to the beach and grab some burgers."

This scene played out in numerous ways until I started to really "get" it. Jim didn't realize it, but he was as much an influence on me as Marianne Williamson was. I'm glad I had the opportunity to be a student of them both.

One of the greatest influences on my life was my mother. She grew up in the coal-mining town of Yukon, Pennsylvania, where much of the entertainment was watching their neighbors and listening in on the party-line telephone. She was, and remains, a paradox to me. While she was accomplished in her studies as a young woman, joined clubs, and played on her school's basketball team, her clear and ever-present message to her own children was that we should not be too bold with our choices for fear of embarrassing her. You might say she had a "what will the neighbors think?" mentality. That concern always puzzled me. I understood it, but rarely capitulated. Even early on in my life I realized that to live to please neighbors, or even family, was to live in a way to please others, which rarely makes people happy; it is a way for people to stay small in their own hopes and dreams.

"Hey mom, guess what? I'm running for president of the student council," I announced to her one day during my junior year of high school. "Do you have any tips for my speech?" "Just don't say anything embarrassing," was her response. Then, another time, I told her, "I got a role in the musical; I'm going to play Schroder in *You're a Good Man, Charlie Brown!*" "You don't have to sing do you?" she asked. "Yeah, I have a solo part." "Oh God. I'm not coming," she said. But she was there.

Of course, that was the key: not so much what she would say, but what she would do. I was far more influenced by her example than by her words. In high school, she was an honor roll student and then pursued a degree in nursing during the 1940s. Although some of her elders growing up were quite bigoted, she herself didn't see color and instilled in her children the belief that everyone is equal. She was one of the few people in the hospital where she worked who befriended a lonely gay orderly. He was an outcast in our town and she was his ride to and from work every day. When the very first AIDS patient, a prisoner, was admitted to her hospital, most nurses refused to enter his room. Not Mum; he was her patient. She took care to wear a mask and gloves, to protect *him* from any germs *she* may have been carrying. In the mid 1980's in small town America, that was quite a statement.

Her prayer life was private. She prayed on her knees each night until recently only because it had become too painful for her to remain on her knees so long. On the morning following my father's death from throat cancer, she knelt beside my bed and gently imprinted on my six-year-old brain that during the night the angels had come and taken my daddy to heaven. Although I can recall the tears streaming down her face, she would not allow that moment in my life to be tragic or terrible. She made it beautiful. To this day, I do not fear death or what may or may not be on the other side. In her own way, quite naturally, she taught me that life is eternal…the angels had come for my Dad so he could go live in heaven! How powerful is that?

In many ways, my mum was ahead of her time. However, like all parents, she had her faults. After my father died, she tended to withdraw from the world. She worked, paid bills, and became a news junkie. Many of my memories are of her behind a newspaper. She became disinterested in the day-to-day lives of my sister Mary, the oldest, my brother Bobby, and me. But she seldom seemed unhappy and never depressed. Content. That is about the best word I can think of to describe her. She was a widow at 38 and made it clear almost from the moment of my father's death that he was the love of her life and there would never be another. She meant it. I recall a painful Saturday when I was 9; most of my friends were busy with their fathers. She was at her make-up table doing her hair as she prepared for church that evening. I cried as I said, "Why won't you get a boyfriend? I'm the only kid who doesn't have a dad. Please find me a father!"

She got up from her chair and came over to her bed where I was sprawled out bawling. "Get up and come over here," she said matter-of-factly, indicating for me to sit on the side of the bed. I obeyed.

"Your father is the only man I will ever love," she told me plainly. "Do you understand that?" I nodded. "I know it hurts not to have him around. It hurts me, too. But there will never be another man in my life."

She was ahead of her time, yes. Smart, you bet. But very much on the shy side, and God forbid if we did anything to embarrass her. Try out for a team, but don't expect her to be cheering at your games. Run for student government, but be prepared for the dread she'd feel at the thought of one of us having to give a speech. She never really held any of us back, but she definitely did not encourage us to do anything other than to keep the house clean. Now, all three of us rebel by not being good housekeepers — the running of the vacuum cleaner is definitely not a top priority in any of our lives. However, all three of us do remember well the lessons of acceptance and unconditional love, and we three use those lessons daily — my brother and sister in the raising of their children, and I in the education of other people's children.

My spiritual journey was profoundly influenced by the teachings, both positive and not so positive, by the Benedictine priests and nuns who were so much a part of my life. The Catholic community of Greensburg Central Catholic High School, where I spent four years was also a great influence on my life. Perhaps even more influential were Rev. and Mrs. Saylor, along with the Albert family, who followed in their footsteps, at the Grace United Church of Christ.

My spiritual life took a new and exciting path once I moved to Los Angeles and began to experience the weekly teachings of Marianne Williamson, who eventually introduced her classes to the works of Louise Hay. Louise is a metaphysical teacher and one of the founders of the self-help movement. Today, many other new and established authors are published by Louise's own company, Hay House. Louise is a practitioner and teacher of self-affirmations, something that would become a regular part of my own teaching once I became a principal.

Marianne and Louise became the first in a long line of spiritual teachers who helped me to complement the teachings of Catholicism, which I, in turn, shared with the hundreds of students who would eventually be part of the educational journeys on which I helped guide them as their principal.

So the man who was now reflecting on his new job description in April of 1990 was a very different human being from the grown boy who had arrived in Los Angeles in September of 1986. Although I still had a lot of learning to do, my experiences and teachers along the way had prepared me to serve as a leader, especially as the spiritual leader of my new school.

Although I was not among the ordained, had never taken religious vows, and did not wear religious robes or a white collar, I had not a single doubt that I had been made ready. I stared at that phrase one last time and read it aloud:

"The principal is the religious and spiritual leader of the school."

I put down the job description for the last time. I was ready to lead!

Where do I sign?

First year principal Dan Horn with kindergartners and eighth graders posing across the street from St. Thomas School. The neighborhood has come a long way since then.

Chapter 3. Our Father, Dennis

In saying "yes" to Father Dennis' offer to become principal, I had no idea that I was embarking on the adventure of a lifetime.

After I signed on the dotted line, he took the contract and signed below my name, now making it official. As he wrote his signature, I noticed the crookedness of his cursive handwriting. By now, I was overjoyed at the prospect of becoming principal at this school. I could hardly contain my excitement. After the signing of the contract, I left the parish office and sprinted the block to the school. I wanted to look at it with a fresh set of eyes. It would now be "my school." I knew I would always remember the way it looked on this beautiful, sunny California Saturday morning.

What I didn't realize, what I had no idea of, was how important the relationship between the pastor and the principal of a parish school is. Although I was eager to become the boss, I didn't realize that Father Dennis' role in the school could enhance my success or assure my failure. It would be months before I realized that not only would this relationship be crucial to my future as principal there, but that I had indeed been very fortunate to have signed a contract with a man who would become more than a boss, more than a priest, more than a mentor. While at the time I simply noticed the way in which he wrote his signature, I guess there was no way I could have known that I was signing a contract with a man, Father Dennis O'Neil, who, aside from my mother, became the greatest influence on my entire life.

Dennis had an interesting way of not only teaching people but of influencing them as well. He was simply very comfortable in his own skin. I don't think there is any more attractive trait in a human being than confidence and enjoyment in being who one is. Dennis loved being Dennis. He was one of the few priests I've met in my life who truly loved being a priest. He loved his life. Very much an extrovert, Dennis loved being with people and would throw himself into a crowd.

He taught me to think on my feet as well as plan for the unexpected. Early on in my principalship, when Dennis was scheduled to address the parent group or meet with a disgruntled parent or archdiocesan official, it was common for him to simply be a "no show" or a "too late, they've-already-gone show." Usually he would be involved in something that he felt took precedence over what I had him scheduled for. Sometimes he was simply so engaged in what he was doing that he would lose all track of time. Or perhaps he had double- or triple-booked himself, or a parishioner in need may have stopped him along the one-block route from the rectory to the school. Sometimes he just forgot to check the little calendar that he kept in his black cleric's shirt pocket.

He taught me to have patience. At first I would become frustrated and sometimes even express my frustration to him when he didn't show up for an event. But he had a way of taking my anger from me. "Dan, it was an old lady who is facing eviction from her apartment," he'd say. "I really wanted to address the parents tonight, but I couldn't turn my back on her, she was crying and needed my immediate help."

I often learned that my frustration about my needs not being met paled miserably in comparison to the needs that Dennis saw as priorities. Soon enough, I learned to schedule him at the end of the night's agenda, but not count on him to show up at all; and if he did show up for an event, I'd let him speak the moment he walked through the door. Most important, I learned not to get bent out of shape if he didn't show, even if it was for an irresponsible reason. One time, for example, he didn't show up for a meeting with the committee that was visiting about accreditation of the school. The next day he whispered, "Dan, as I was on my way to the meeting, my jogging buddy Michael pulled up next to me in a van with several other friends. They wanted to take me out for pizza because they knew it had been a long time since I had a day off."

"Are you serious?" I asked in disbelief.

"How could I say no? They were already here and had planned this for me."

"I hope the pizza was good," I responded.

"Oh, it was," he laughed. "It was delicious!"

The accreditation team met with him a day later. Was it a big deal? After a year of working with Dennis, I learned that not much amounted to being a big deal.

He taught me to see humor where most people could not. During a hot Sunday morning Mass with a packed church, standing room only, police sirens were blaring from the neighboring streets through the open windows and doors of the church, which lacked air-conditioning. The police helicopter was making a wide circle overhead; although it could not be seen from inside, the reverberations told the congregants the copter was getting closer to our church, which meant that whomever they were chasing was also coming closer. As Dennis was proclaiming the gospel in Spanish, his voice became louder and louder in fruitless attempts to drown out the helicopter, which by then sounded as if it was about to land on the roof. As Dennis finished the gospel and moved to the front center of the church to deliver his homily, a member of the notorious Playboys gang came running through the front side door of the church, pushing away the crowd that partially blocked the doorway. Dashing across the front of the church as fast as his feet would carry him, the gang member said, "*Lo siento, Padre,*" (I'm sorry, Father) before reaching the exit on the opposite side of the building. Two armed police officers followed in hot pursuit, both obviously Catholic, judging from the fact that they both took time to stop in front of the altar and bless themselves by making the sign of the cross prior to making their own frantic exit through the same door that had been used by their suspect. Without missing a beat, Father Dennis said, "*Si quiera le hiceron a la iglesia!"* (At least they made it to church!). His statement was followed by thunderous applause and laughter, and it was a good minute or so before he could commence with his sermon. I marveled at the ease with which the community reacted to this situation. I imagined how the same scenario would have played out in the church I grew up in or, for that matter, at most suburban churches. Most likely there would have been panic or a lock-down.

Not only did Dennis teach me to not sweat the small stuff, he also tried to teach me to not sweat the big stuff, too. When he visited the school one Monday morning, I asked him why one of his eyes was black-and-blue. He somewhat happily recounted an incident that had occurred the day before when he was preparing for one of his Sunday Masses. The sacristy, the room where the priest prepares and dresses for Mass, was always full in between Masses. It often reminded me of backstage at a rock concert with groupies attempting to get a glimpse of their favorite star or to secure an autograph. While preparing to go onstage, or I should say, preparing to say Mass, Dennis would greet as many of the congregants who competed for his attention as possible. He would hear their problems, accept their invitations, and bless the various items they would bring, among a myriad of other requests he would attempt to satisfy. He explained that an older woman had asked him to perform an exorcism on her adult son who was standing next to her and making strange noises. He had just finished putting on his alb when he turned to meet the son. Before Dennis' arms were at his side, the man sucker-punched him straight between the eyes. Dennis fell to the floor, out cold. Dumbfounded by this story, I asked, "How long were you out?" He responded, "Long enough to make me ten minutes late for my Mass."

Dennis taught me not to be an overbearing administrator who gets so caught up in the rules that you

and your charges don't have any fun. It was commonplace
for Dennis to take large groups of students camping. He
would come to the school and enlist a number of teachers to
accompany him as chaperones. It was not unusual for those
teachers to return only to swear that they would never help
Father Dennis chaperone another trip. They were, after all,
Catholic schoolteachers who were trained to be risk
managers and to be constantly on the lookout for possible
danger to their students. That was hard to reconcile with
their experience on the camping trips, where after telling
ghost stories and serving Coca-Colas to the kids, Dennis
would depart for his tent, oblivious to the fact that the kids
were now jacked up on sugar and fear. He left it to his fellow
chaperones to stomp out the little fires that the kids would
set in the woods or to deal with their sugar-induced behavior.
To make matters even worse, Dennis snored louder than
most, indicating to the others that he was enjoying a sound
sleep while they struggled to get their charges into their
tents.

Dennis also taught me to multitask before it was
fashionable to do so. One Saturday evening when we were
holding the eighth-grade dinner dance, Dennis was
scheduled to present awards to some of the students. As
usual, he was very late. I approached the church and could
barely get through the crowd that was blocking the doors for
the 8:00 p.m. Saturday night Mass. I poked my head in so I
could gauge how much longer he might be. Once inside, I
saw not one, but three brides and three grooms, and Dennis
in the middle of the marriage vows. Without a clue as to why
three couples were being married late on a Saturday night, I
returned to the dance to present the awards for Dennis.
When he finally showed up I mentioned that I thought it was
supposed to have been the regular Saturday night Mass. He
said it was. I said it looked as though three couples were
getting married. He said they were. I said I didn't
understand. He laughed and said, "They showed up with
their marriage licenses and were ready to be married, so I

did it during the Mass." "Can you do that?" I asked. He said, "Sure! Marry 'em, bury 'em, why not? It's Mass!"

He taught me to stay calm. Shortly after my arrival, the church completed a renovation. Within a week of the church opening its doors after the renovation, an arsonist broke in during the night and set the church on fire. I was horrified. Dennis was calm. "We'll get it fixed; we did it once, we can do it again."

After a group of satanic taggers covered the school building, benches, basketball backboards, and much of the ground with satanic images, Dennis' advice was to not get excited.

When the building was burglarized or a dead body was discovered in the driveway of the school, Dennis said, "Yeah, that's probably gonna happen once in a while. There's no use getting excited."

Most of all, Dennis taught me to allow myself to be changed by the experience of ministering there. Dennis loved the St. Thomas the Apostle community. He too, had been a white boy sent there not knowing a word of Spanish. By immersing himself in the language as well as the issues and needs of his flock, he became fluent in a year's time. It impressed me that Dennis knew the name of every student in the school. The fact is, he possessed an uncanny ability to remember people's names as well as their personal stories. He made it his duty to personally interview every new family coming into the school. His photographic memory allowed him to know where they lived, what country they had come from, the names of other family members, and any issues the family faced. He provided counseling to families and individuals when they needed it. He helped to educate the community on ballot issues that affected them, and was a community leader on immigration issues. Dennis helped people who were homeless find shelter, and those who were out of work find jobs. Following the massive amount of looting that took place after the riots of 1992 in and around our Pico-Union neighborhood, Dennis appealed at Sunday Masses to those who had taken advantage of the situation and urged the congregation to return stolen goods to the parish office, no questions asked. The police department took dozens of truckloads of returned items in the week following the riots.

Dennis taught me to bring out the best in the people I hired by trusting them to do their jobs. He trusted the parish leaders he appointed, including me. Under Father Dennis' leadership, I was transformed into a leader greater than I ever imagined possible.

Following Dennis' lead, I allowed myself to be loved. That is what happened to me. I not only fell in love with that community, but eventually, I let down my guard and realized that with the great challenges that existed every day, I was also being loved by a community where sometimes love was all they had to give, and for me, that was the greatest gift anyone could have given.

At times he was lenient, lax, and laughable, but most of all, this great man with the smallest of egos was not just our pastor...he was — to thousands, including me — our father, Dennis. To me he was and will always remain, the pope of Pico-Union!

Father Dennis O'Neil delivering a homily at a school mass

Chapter 4. Godspell

We plow the fields and scatter the good seed on the land…
— "All Good Gifts," from the Broadway play, *Godspell*

Our fields were the classrooms and corridors of an eighty year-old, recently earthquake-retrofitted building. Our fields were the park next door, from where the eastward wind would carry our way the smell of burning marijuana being smoked by gang members, or the sometimes stench of urine or feces from some of the homeless folks who slept there.

Our land was the blood-soaked streets and sidewalks of Pico-Union, Los Angeles, where so many people had lost their lives to murder by gang members, who either saw no value in life or who sought revenge.

Our land was the cracked sidewalks along Mariposa Street, where we would pass the graffiti-covered drug house with the withered drunken soul lying in an ironic peace as we made our way to the open doors of St. Thomas the Apostle Church.

Our land was a downtown neighborhood that had become the modern-day Ellis Island to thousands of immigrants arriving from Central and South America.

A sweet and petite young college freshman from Mount St. Mary's who loved to dance dropped by one day to offer to help plant the good seed in our fields by volunteering to teach classes to our potential dancers. I liked her and said yes, fully expecting that like so many others with good intentions, she would quickly grow nervous about the neighborhood and find some excuse to stop coming. Instead, she grew roots.

Impressed by her fortitude and persistence, I introduced her to a dramatic and dramatically devoted new teacher and old friend of mine. He was an excellent kindergarten teacher largely due to the fact that his previous career had been acting, and the little kids instantly took to his creative teaching techniques and animated storytelling. He had appeared on Broadway and had a broad way himself of exposing our students to the arts that seemed to appeal to youngsters of all ages.

The dancer, Colleen, and the actor, Joe, clicked.

Within months of commencing an after-school dance program, Colleen and Joe announced auditions for a full-length musical. Students in fourth through eighth grades could audition; however, it was made clear that actors would need to learn every line, every lyric, and every dance step. No short cuts. Considering that the majority of students went home and spoke only Spanish and that their reading of English often proved challenging, the idea of memorizing lines in English was a tall order. The parents were largely immigrants or first-generation Americans. Many of the moms were maids or seamstresses, and the dads were typically gardeners, cooks, or factory workers. We had a smattering of parents who were teachers, police officers, or other professionals, but they were the minority. For most of the parents, a "play" was a quick vignette performed by their child's class at Christmas time lasting only minutes and ending with a Christmas carol; a full-length play was something they — and their children — had never experienced before.

Joe and Colleen announced that their first joint production would be *Godspell*. It was fitting because there are few solo parts and none of us knew how many singers we had in the school. Plus, if we were going to begin a tradition of musical theater in this particular community, starting with a show that was based on the Bible seemed like a really good idea. What began as a lark swiftly turned into an exciting adventure, which in turn became a transforming chapter in St. Thomas School history.

Although Joe and Colleen were opposites in many ways, they shared a love of the arts and they attracted the interest of almost 100 students, who auditioned for what quickly became prized roles. I was excited at the prospect of our students having this opportunity, and made time to sit through much of the audition process. I would occasionally hear Joe whisper to Colleen, "She's got good instincts for that role, you should see if she can dance," or something similar. Colleen might say something like, "I can tell he's got rhythm just by how he walked onto the stage." When one young lady struggled with reading some lines from a sheet of paper, Colleen did something brilliant. Knowing that this particular student was right for the part, Colleen instructed her to memorize the page. "Come back tomorrow and we'll try it again." The girl beamed knowing she would have another chance. The next day, she not only had the lines memorized, she now was able to act out the part, having already committed the words to memory. Although reading may have been a daily struggle for her until then, her reading of the script became important to her because she had the opportunity to become a character on stage.

In so many elementary school classrooms, students are asked to simply read words on a page. By providing students with a purpose — and eventually an audience — their motivation soared. Having been given an opportunity they never had before, students now had the motivation to read, study, and memorize lines, lyrics, dance steps, and stage cues. Instead of the goal being simply to put on a show, Joe and Colleen had a shared goal of helping to discover and unleash potential.

Once the cast was selected and the rehearsals commenced, Joe, the director, and Colleen, the choreographer, had high expectations. At times, the atmosphere was tense. If students did not come prepared, they were questioned about their dependability and were often chastised. Neither adult was receiving any compensation for the additional hours they were devoting to this project. Both of them came prepared for rehearsals, which lasted a minimum of two hours each weekday, and as show time approached, an additional four to six hours on Saturdays. Although the actors were elementary school students, the adults were determined to provide as professional an experience as possible. Sometimes the reprimands the students received caused them to cry or would result in the intervention of a parent. However, no student quit and no one was asked to leave the show. Although the regimen was at times grueling and the atmosphere tense, the camaraderie that existed among cast members provided plenty of nurturing.

As their principal, I could clearly see changes in each one of the participants. They were growing and responding positively to their developing talents. I realized that they could also see and feel themselves changing.

Maricela was a shy, pudgy girl who had gotten the role of Joanne, a rather outgoing and bawdy character. This was definitely not typecasting. Maricela's mother had come to Los Angeles from the mountains of Oaxaca, Mexico. Maricela was the youngest of four daughters; their father was absent from their lives. The four daughters and their mother shared a one-room apartment not too far from the school. In order to pay a very low, negotiated tuition, Maricela's mom sold tamales and corn in front of the church, made clothes to sell, and cleaned houses. She wanted a different life for her daughters. As the weeks of rehearsals turned into months, Maricela was developing a wonderful stage presence. And best of all, she could sing! This shy girl could really belt out a song. The daily affirmations she received from her fellow actors as well as from Joe and Colleen were helping to bring her out of her shell to stand deliberately and confidently center stage.

Jesus would be played by…"Wait a minute Joe, did you say Adolfo?" I asked incredulously. "That's what he said," responded Colleen with a broad smile, enjoying the fact that I was in a bit of shock. Adolfo was a troublemaker, the kind of kid I wasn't sure would even be around for opening night in four months. He had been receiving far too many second chances for his bad attitude. His grades were a problem because he often refused to study. Getting additional help from teachers didn't seem likely because his attitude was so sour and none of them really wanted to help a kid who seemed to be sabotaging his own education and future. I was shocked that he'd auditioned, and shocked that Joe and Colleen were willing to gamble on Adolfo's iffy reliability. But, hey, I'm a believer in what theater arts can do for a person. I know the effect that the arts had on my own life, so I figured, let's give it a try since everyone else was willing.

As the opening date of the musical approached, Joe and Colleen were obviously proud of the experience they were about to offer our community. Joe stayed for hours after school prior to going to a second job waiting tables each night. Colleen had sought out some donations to help with costumes and a very limited set, and she'd also secured the use of the stage at Mount St. Mary's College downtown, not too far from our campus. Both Joe and Colleen had put more than hours into this show, and it meant more to them than simply a show. As the months progressed, they had front row seats to changing lives.

While Joe and Colleen were growing somewhat nervous as the opening of the show approached, the actors began lamenting the fact that they soon wouldn't have rehearsals to look forward to anymore. As often happens with professional theatre, they had formed a tight and loving ensemble, proud of the gift they were about to give, but sad for the impending final curtain.

Our cast and crew were overjoyed knowing they would perform on the stage of a college campus. However, I realized that since the college was a few miles away from our campus and some of our parents did not own cars, some of our students might not get a chance to see the show. Since so much time and work had been put into this show, I requested that Joe and Colleen consider doing the show for the kindergarten through eighth grades on our own tiny stage. They agreed.

Our school's small auditorium was about the size of two large classrooms with a stage at one end. White it was a tight fit, the room could accommodate all 315 students sitting on the floor, with their teachers in chairs. Everyone squeezed in even tighter to allow the 10 or more curious moms who had volunteered to help in our cafeteria that afternoon. Although the eight-foot high windows were covered in black butcher paper, the bright California afternoon sun squeezed through the sides so no one was really fooled into thinking it was nighttime. However, when the lights went out, there was that heightened sense one experiences when it feels like something special is about to happen; and it did.

The students, from the five-year olds to the fourteen-year olds, were mesmerized. They were witnessing musical theatre, and for the overwhelming majority, it was their first experience with this art form. No one fidgeted or left to use the bathroom. They sat and they watched. Kids under 10 always have to use the bathroom during assemblies, at least one or two. But now, no one budged. The students laughed when they were supposed to laugh, they clapped when it was time to applaud, and they were quiet when they were meant to be quiet. There were live musicians and live actors. Spellbinding!

I loved the show. However, I loved the show that was happening around me even more. Little ones sat uncharacteristically still on the floor, ignoring the usual temptations to play with their peers who were sitting shoulder to shoulder. Some little ones' mouths fell open as they watched in wonderment as the big kids in the school performed for them. The older ones sat cross-legged, many of them supporting their chins with their fists. The one thing that they almost all shared was a stare; they stared at the stage, attempting to follow the story and wondering what would happen next.

My curiosity and physic energy had me thinking that many of those youngsters watching so intently were probably wondering how the actors could remember so many lines. I knew they were impressed when they heard their own peers and classmates harmonize. I knew that many in the audience were wondering if, given the opportunity, would they be able to perform that well, too? My guess was that, as they were being entertained, many of the young minds wandered to a place where they wondered, would I have that kind of confidence and ability? After all, those talented actors on the stage receiving all that applause were part of us! I sat watching the faces of our students knowing that some of their lives were changing right there and then.

Pride was evident on the faces of the teachers. For some, it was a light-bulb moment. After all, how could that particular student — or that one — have struggled so much with reading when she was in fourth grade — or he was in fifth — and only one year later, not only read but memorize and act in an entire play? Amazing!

How I also enjoyed watching the reaction of those few parents we were able to squeeze into the room. The fact is, most of them could not speak or understand English. But while they may not have understood what the children were saying or singing, they laughed when everyone else laughed, applauded when the songs were finished, and felt, perhaps, an even greater sense of pride in our school — and in our students — than any of the teachers or I did. Although these parents loved our little neighborhood school, the dream for many of them was that their children receive the tools to take them out of this neighborhood. The sound of the music, the singing, and the applause signaled to those parents that their children were receiving exactly what they, as parents, were hoping and working so hard for.

I myself realized that I was witnessing the lives of those children on stage being transformed before all of our eyes. We were more than just an audience; we were the vessels through which these young actors would become more confident. We were their community, and like most members of any community, we look for acceptance there. What our student actors found was adulation.

Once on stage, Maricela, became a young woman far away from Pico-Union. She was a star, off in a world of her own. Hundreds of faces sat staring at her, listening enthusiastically.   Almost all the students appeared delightfully startled by her beautiful singing voice.   She became her character, bawdy, outgoing, in control. Onstage, the young woman Maricela became someone most of us were meeting for the very first time. Perhaps Maricela was meeting her for the first time as well.

An ear-to-ear smile kept appearing on my face as I watched that troublemaker Adolfo become the character of Jesus Christ. As I recalled the times we'd almost expelled him, I marveled at now seeing him push back his demons to pull out his inner-Christ. His performance was so convincing that it seemed impossible that the compassion and love he currently was exuding did not reside somewhere inside the real Adolfo.

I glanced around the room at his teachers who had largely experienced Adolfo as a problem for them and even more so for himself. It is always so heartbreaking to see students with potential for success choose the path of self-destruction. Without question, this young man had definitely been on that path. Students like that were attractive to the Pico-Union gang leaders, who were always looking to recruit the kids who needed to fill a void in their lives. Now, by becoming part of the theater experience known as *Godspell*, Adolfo seemed to not only have filled whatever void he may have been experiencing, he filled it enough to become his better self. For the last few months of rehearsals, Adolfo had not been sent to my office. His teachers had been reporting more effort and an improved attitude. Now, on this day of performance, we could all see what had been capturing this young man's imagination and taking him in a new direction.

Then came one of the dramatic moments toward the show's conclusion: the final moments of Christ's earthly life. The cast sings a hauntingly beautiful rendition of "By My Side," while Adolfo, as Jesus, prepares to depart:

> *Where are you going?*
> *Where are you going?*
> *Can you take me with you?*

For my hand is cold
And needs warmth
Where are you going?
Far beyond where the horizon
lies.

This is one of the most serious and moving moments of the play. This is the moment when the former Adolfo, sitting in this same audience, would have found a way to take the attention from the stage, probably by getting others to laugh — and most of the older students knew that this serious part of the show would have been his cue. Instead, there he was, standing at the front of the stage, all hearts with him. Just prior to his crucifixion scene, he turned from the cast and looked out over our heads into the distance. I studied his face. What was he looking at? There was vulnerability in his eyes, an uncertainty, and maybe even a little fear. Yet his gaze said to me that he was seeing something we could not see. Just before he turned to go to his cross, I could see something in Adolfo he had most likely discovered weeks earlier. In the last few seconds of his performance, Adolfo showed us, his community, the face of Christ.

Postscript: They plowed the fields, known as our classrooms, they scattered the seeds of theatre arts and they reaped a crop that survives to this day. *Godspell* cast a spell of delight in our inner-city pocket of Los Angeles where there is often so much gloom and doom. *Godspell* breathed some life-altering breaths into students and helped them to discover talents and reveal dreams. *Godspell* began a tradition of musical theater for the community of St. Thomas the Apostle School. It is a tradition that continues to this day.

The cast of our production of Godspell,
including Adolfo, who played Jesus
and Maricela, who played Joanne

Chapter 5. Tears of a Tattooed Padre

It's funny how sometimes in life the answers to our problems can become problems themselves. It's just as funny — and, perhaps, leads to a better outcome — when the problems we face sometimes become our greatest opportunities.

One of the many problems I encountered upon arriving at St. Thomas was that the two nuns who were co-principals prior to my arrival had been fired by Father Dennis, and they were bitter. Therefore, the kindergarten class had not been filled, nor had the empty spots in the other grades. Some families had moved away and others were fearful about re-registering their children in a school with a seemingly uncertain future.

A Catholic school depends largely on tuition to stay afloat. If enrollment is not healthy, the school cannot always pay its bills. Since the tuition at St. Thomas was relatively low, approximately $800 a year in 1990, it required all of the 35 desks in each classroom to be filled. Considering that kindergarten families paid higher tuition than all other grades, I would face a giant deficit if those seats, in particular, did not get filled. I spent my first few weeks at the school pondering how to begin filling all the empty seats. It seemed to be a daunting task.

No students had been tested or accepted into the incoming kindergarten class. I was told that the previous administration had put out the word that the school might close the next year and had encouraged current families not to re-register. Therefore, there were numerous vacant seats in each grade. However, once we began to advertise, many of the faithful returned to register their children. Additionally, swarms of new, hopeful families arrived, hoping for a spot for children in various grades. As it turned out, we would soon have a long waiting list.

In only a few weeks, Monica, my newly hired secretary, a force of a woman from Chile, began telling me that parents were coming by looking for me after receiving their waitlist results or their denials. Looking for me? I must have seemed nervous, because Monica, a couple of generations my senior, who affectionately referred to me as Danny, quickly assured me that they just needed to hear from *el jefe*, (the boss) that the decision was final. She reminded me that they were stopping by in person because we currently had no phone. One of the other challenges that first summer was the fact that the main school building was being retrofitted to make it safe for earthquakes. Therefore, Monica and I were working out of a bungalow in back of the school, which was normally used as a computer lab for students during the school year. We spent the entire summer working out of a room that had no phone or fax, long before the days of wireless telephones or Vice President Gore's announcement that he'd invented the Internet. It would be only days before the scheduled first day of school that the staff and I could move back into the school building; it was like moving from one century to another.

The sacrifices that so many of the parents made to have their children attend a Catholic school were at times simply beyond my comprehension. Immigrant and first-generation American parents by and large worked at low-paying jobs, many working two or more jobs to support the family and pay the tuition. I was soon to become aware of entire families living in crowded apartments, garages, or in even harsher living conditions. When I had interviewed for the position of principal two months earlier, I'd heard the stories of the neighborhood during my interview and the walk that followed with Father Dennis. Now, I was meeting the families personally.

During that summer, the difficult realities these families faced began to set in as people often came to the bungalow looking to speak with me. Those who came had no trouble recognizing me from the descriptions going around. Monica told me that word had gotten around to look for the "blonde boy." Sometimes people would see me walking to the parish office or out to lunch at a local eatery. At the time, there were very few *gringos* (slang for white person or foreigner) walking about Pico-Union. And when I did sit down to talk with the parents, it was rarely just a conversation between them and me; most of the time, Monica had to sit with us to translate. In fact, one of the apprehensions I had about joining the school was the need to have most of my conversations with parents translated. The pastor, Father Dennis, had assured me that it only took him about nine months of working in the community before he was fluent in Spanish. I, on the other hand, was there for a total of nine years and still only speak about nine words of Spanish.

However, not speaking Spanish turned out to be a blessing, in many cases. For example, if a person became angry and yelled, pounding the tables or desks, I was able to hear what they said through Monica, whose translation defused the emotion. If a parent I was speaking with began to cry, I could hear the content through Monica's steady translation rather than getting too caught up in the emotion. Plus, Monica and I quickly formed a mutual admiration society. She became protective of me, and there were times when, after a parent had made an obviously angry statement directed at me, Monica, in a rather scolding tone, would address the person in Spanish. Prior to Monica providing me with a translation, I would often hear the parent say *lo siento* to her, and I quickly learned what those words meant (I'm sorry). Monica had a power to her presence, and although she also was new to the school, it appeared that she immediately garnered the respect of this community of parents and guardians. I began to realize that the respect I ultimately received from so many Spanish-speaking parents in our community was due to the fact that Monica would not allow them to speak to me in hostile tones or in a rude manner. I sensed that there were those who were apt to condescend or take advantage of me due to my young age. Monica became my protector until I had some history there and my work could speak for itself. Monica quickly became a mother figure to staff and students alike. Possibly old enough to be my own mother, I respected her as if she was. Our relationship grew closer by the day; she was someone who was both nurturing and trustworthy. She was far smarter than I was but never let me know it. It would be years later until I realized just how brilliant she actually had been. I never could have been successful at St. Thomas if God had not sent me an angel in the form of Monica for my first two years as principal there. It was sad for all of us, though, that after only two years at the school, she and her husband relocated to Texas. Although Monica's time with us was short, her influence on me remains strong today.

Once the school year was underway, the constant stream of parents did not stop. Parents of children who had been placed on a waitlist continued to drop by for the first five or six weeks of the school year hoping that a spot would open up for their child. I was stunned that even prior to the Christmas holidays, there were those who came to apply for the 1991-92 school year. By January, we were accepting applications for the next school year.

Months later, during the early spring of 1991, I sat at my desk staring out the window at the old convent that sat about 25 feet from our school. It was originally built to house the nuns who used to staff the school. One of the reasons so many Catholic schools have closed or are struggling today is that they neglected to foresee a future without the nuns. Since the inception of our Catholic schools in the United States, whenever a parish built a school, they automatically built a convent, too. The nuns were cheap labor. They lived in community in the convent; they ate together, lived mostly in tiny cubicle bedrooms and, for the most part, lived lives of poverty. As a result, the Catholic schools were able to charge a nominal tuition, often subsidized by the parish, enabling the largely immigrant communities the schools served to afford the relatively low cost of the education provided. I can remember my mom paying a book rental fee of just $12 per year for my own and each of my siblings' Catholic elementary schooling. As the number of nuns dwindled, the schools were forced into hiring lay teachers. For decades, the salaries of the lay teachers in Catholic schools were paltry in comparison to the already low wages of their public school counterparts.

One of the first things I did as principal at St. Thomas was look for ways to offer bonuses to teachers, whether a small cash bonus at Christmas or Easter, or perhaps a bottle of wine or a ham for a holiday. Eventually, once I was able to, I began to raise salaries with the goal to not merely become competitive with the salaries of our public school counterparts, but to surpass them.

Because I valued teachers and spent countless hours hiring the best possible staff, our school very quickly became a hub for good teaching and learning. Most people could feel it the moment they walked in the door. When teachers are happy, students usually are happy, and there is energy in a school — a positive energy that attracts more positive energy.

There were guest speakers, educational field trips, art and music classes, and most of all, teachers excited about their jobs. Our teachers would arrive early and stay late in order to tutor students in groups as well as one-on-one. They would meet with parents when necessary and sometimes call even when it wasn't necessary; teachers sometimes would even call to tell parents about good grades or good news in the classroom. Teachers who spoke Spanish would translate for those who did not, whenever necessary. When there was an event involving parents and teachers, all of the faculty would almost always be present. From the get-go, the teachers and I agreed that although our students faced some extremely challenging circumstances due to conditions in the neighborhood and the poverty of many of the families, we at school should be compassionate without lowering standards or grading out of sympathy. We agreed that if a student was getting an A in a fourth-grade math class at St. Thomas, that same student should be able to transfer to any other school in the city and receive the same grade. Our standards were high and we maintained them. However, to get students to reach these standards often required more effort and creative planning than in most other schools. During my first year I was incredibly fortunate to be able to attract a talented and dedicated faculty and staff, which, each year after that, continued to grow only stronger.

Now, as I sat staring out the window at the convent, I was not wondering how to fill seats. Instead, I imagined a bulldozer crashing into the convent roof and tearing apart the walls. I imagined it hauling away the initial debris to come back again and again until it reached the concrete foundation, which would allow us to build another building in its place, so that we could add an additional classroom for each grade. I also imagined much needed facilities like a library and a larger meeting space for our students, parents, and the parish groups who used our building immediately after classes let out until late each evening.

One of the main reasons that so many parents wanted their children in Catholic schools was the perception — which in many cases was a reality — that Catholic schools were safer than the public schools. Most of the Catholic schools in the area had waiting lists, including ours. However, the first year of my tenure, I had an unusually young and energetic staff, who implemented exciting lessons, and students became very excited about the school. When we began taking applications for the next school year, our number of applicants for every grade was higher than the other Catholic schools in the area. My teachers and I soon realized that we would be turning away a very large number of families, enough students to possibly fill three or four more classrooms for each grade.

I also discovered that there was insatiable demand for meeting and storage space among the myriad parish groups. The parish was home to more than 6,000 families at the time. Many of those attending Mass each Sunday were not even registered. If permitted, that little school building most likely would have been in use 24 hours a day to accommodate all of the meeting needs. There simply was not enough space.

During that first year I would witness several serious arguments among parish group leaders. In almost every case, the cause was a lack of space or the need to share the limited amount of soil and mortar. The fact that only five people lived in that convent building, which was vacant throughout the day, began to gnaw at me.

As time went by, the demand for meeting space at the school continued to increase. After playing referee between two parish group leaders who were arguing over use of the auditorium or a prized closet space in the basement, I would sit back in my desk chair, fuming, looking out at the convent with perhaps a nun or two sitting on the patio enjoying their peace and quiet; I knew they were paying less in rent for that beast of a building than I paid for my small one-bedroom apartment in Hollywood.

I decided to begin the conversation. At first it was just a conversation between some of the teachers and me, then extended to Father Dennis, and eventually grew to include the new assistant superintendent. I would use the same line with each person I talked with: "Imagine what we could do with that convent building space if it were empty." I would then elaborate. "That's a big building for just five nuns to be living in. The rent they pay does not help this community as much as if the community were able to make use of all that extra space." I continued making my case. "We could put three new classrooms for the first, second, and third grades on that second floor. The first floor could be turned into a large library and a faculty meeting room and lounge. Then we could raise enough money to build a brand new building attached to the renovated convent, which would include classrooms for the other grades as well as a large, all-purpose room."

The assistant superintendent, a nun, smiled at me during this, our first time meeting one another. She was gently and cautiously encouraging. "It's a great vision, Dan. But first of all, you have to be careful about the Sisters who reside in that convent. There have been examples right here in our archdiocese, where Sisters have been evicted from their convents with very little notice. Considering how these Sisters have staffed our schools and parishes for years, some of them have been very hurt by this sudden rush to push them out so the parish can take over the school."

Oh my God, what was she thinking? Yes, I wanted to renovate, and yes, if possible, I'd like to begin tomorrow. However, I knew that raising the necessary money for such a project wouldn't happen overnight, and I attempted to assure her that I believed there would be plenty of notice given to the good Sisters next door.

"Have you thought about where you would get the money to do such a project?" she inquired.

"No, I was first hoping to garner your support and find out what process would be necessary to begin a fund-raising drive," I explained.

"Well, my guess is it will take a lot of money for a project like this, Dan," she said. "Plus, you're brand new here; you haven't even gotten your feet wet. You should also know that we have 231 other elementary schools in this archdiocese, and many of them are getting older and are in need of repair. You're lucky because St. Thomas just received some dollars to help with the retrofit project. I don't know if people will be ready to give to St. Thomas again with so many of our other aging facilities needing attention."

Although I did not admit it, the reality was that I did not have a clue as to where the money would come from. I only had commonsense economics. It was obvious to me that we were offering a valuable product in a neighborhood where it was most needed. I knew that a lot of people with means had to care about the education or lack thereof in our inner-city. It seemed obvious to me that the way to attract money was to attract the attention of those people to our reality and to our collective dreams for the future.

One day in the spring of 1991, I read an article that said Notre Dame Academy in Los Angeles had received a National Blue Ribbon School of Excellence Award. I had never heard of that distinction before, but it sure as hell sounded impressive. After a little research — remember, no Google yet! — I requested an application for Blue Ribbon Schools from the United States Department of Education. I was getting excited.

I kept thinking that if our tiny school in the inner-city, graffiti-covered, gang-ruled neighborhood could capture a title like that, not only would it bring pride and hope to the entire community, it would distinguish us from the other 231 Catholic elementary schools in the Archdiocese of Los Angeles. I truly believed that it would distinguish us enough that people would come forward; I believed that people would approach us asking how they could help us achieve our dream.

When the large envelope arrived, I tore it open wildly. Foolishly, I had imagined a process involving some narrative responses that I could do on my own. I would complete the application and not tell anyone that I had applied. My rationale for this was two-fold: one, I imagined how excited everyone would be when we received notice that we, too, had become a National Blue Ribbon School of Excellence — it would be a wonderful surprise; and two, I didn't want to get people's hopes up if we did not win.

My own naïve hopes were dashed as quickly as I had torn open the envelope. I could hardly believe my eyes as I leafed through the daunting application. There were approximately 20 pages of precise instructions. Part of how the schools would be judged had to do with how many members in the community participated in the writing and research of the document — so much for keeping it private. It would need to be signed by the superintendent of schools. Research about the neighborhood was required, complete with recent statistics regarding ethnicities and socio-economics. There were dozens of questions that had sub-questions in order to help you precisely answer each of the larger questions, which covered every aspect of school life, from the curriculum to the school plant. They were the kind of questions that would naturally generate at least a hundred pages of narrative — the problem was, there was a limit of just 30 pages, including specific font and margin-size requirements. Feeling frustrated and defeated, I threw the application on a shelf, out of my line of sight. It was simply too much work for an already over-worked and underpaid staff. Plus, I was still concerned about raising the hopes of our entire community and then not winning. It was not worth the risk.

As much as I loved my first year at my new school, I was frustrated by the helplessness I felt about not being able to expand the good work the school and parish were doing for the community. It continued to gnaw at me. Before I knew it, spring had arrived and it was time to begin processing the many student applications for the coming year. The first step in the process was testing the applicants.

Silvia, our kindergarten teacher, was an immigrant from Argentina. She had a personality as fiery as a chili pepper. She was petite but tough. In the fall, Silvia had given birth to twin girls. She worked the entire day prior to leaving for the hospital to give birth to the twins, took off only a few weeks afterwards, and was then back at school to teach her class of 38 five and six year olds. This was her first experience teaching kindergarten. In her home country, she'd taught at the university level. She was a natural with our kindergartners. The aide we hired for her was a wide-eyed young man fresh out of high school named Junior. Junior was born and raised just blocks away from the school. Junior, who had been an altar boy for Father Dennis, came highly recommended by the priest. All of Silvia's kindergarten students were now reading and all had passed the first-grade entrance exam. This meant that she would have at least 35 vacancies to fill for the new year. She approached me with a reorganized and more efficient way of testing incoming students than we had used previously. She would test on Saturdays and involve some other teachers in the testing so we could see large groups of students at once, which meant we could provide our decisions earlier than before.

On one particular Saturday as testing was taking place, the parents waiting anxiously outside the kindergarten bungalow — some sitting on benches, some standing nervously near the bungalow — I noticed a man staring at me as I approached. He made me nervous. Although he looked younger than I was, I assumed he was one of the dads waiting while his child was being tested. He wasn't wearing the typical gang wear of the neighborhood, but he pulled his white socks up almost to meet the hem of his jean shorts, and his tank top revealed shoulders and arms completely covered in tattoos ranging from Our Lady of Guadalupe to various people's names. I tried not to look too long, knowing that a stare from me could be greeted by a challenge from him.

There was something about his slicked-back hair, goatee, and "don't mess with me" attitude that said gang member to me. While dropping off the copies I had made for Silvia, I whispered to her, asking if she knew who the guy with the tattoos was. She pointed to a distracted little boy who seemed to be having difficulty following the instructions being given to him by the teacher's aide. "His father," she whispered.

I breathed a sigh of relief knowing that the tattooed man had a legitimate reason for being on the campus. On occasion throughout the year, a gang member or two would wander onto campus taking a shortcut to the park next door or looking for an out-of-the-way place to smoke a joint. Now, walking back to the main building, I watched the man discreetly. He continued to stare until my back was to him. He asked a woman near him a question in Spanish and I heard her reply, "*el director*" (the principal). Apparently, he was also questioning my presence on the campus.

The little boy did not pass the test. I heard that his mother came in and requested that he be tested again. Silvia agreed to have some students come back for another test, although we had another overflow class of 39. The archdiocese required 35, which is a large number for a kindergarten. Silvia took an additional four students, insisting that she and Junior could handle that many. She also had talked me into the idea of going from a half-day kindergarten to a full day like the rest of the grades in the school. This was during a time when most kindergartens only did a half-day.

The tattooed man's son did even worse on the second test. Silvia was convinced that the boy was not ready for kindergarten. Both the young mother and father spoke Spanish and of course that is what the little boy spoke. Even with Silvia providing directions and questions in Spanish, he was not prepared academically or emotionally, especially for a rigorous full-day schedule.

My prior secret worry soon became reality. When I entered the school one morning the following week, the boy's father was in our waiting area just outside the main office. He gave me the same penetrating stare he'd displayed earlier as I now walked through to get to my office. I nodded as I passed by but did not look to see if it was reciprocated. Instantly I knew why he was there. My stomach churned. Monica immediately followed me into my office telling me she had already spoken to the man and informed him that the kindergarten class was full and there were many students on the waiting list who *had* passed the test. She also sensed my hesitation and said that he had very respectfully asked if he could have just ten minutes of my time, and promised he would not take longer. I asked Monica to tell him to wait a few minutes and I would see him.

I dashed out the rear door of my office, from which the man would not see me depart, and went straight to the kindergarten classroom. Telling Silvia that the father with the tattoos wanted to meet with me personally, I asked her to tell me the reasons the boy was not ready for kindergarten. She provided me some sound explanations and told me that the diversity of learning backgrounds in her class this year presented great challenges. She had already accepted 39 for the coming year, and said that if we had two kindergarten classrooms, it would make it easier to accept more struggling students because we could devote more time to their needs. With a single classroom, it would not be fair to her, the other students, or the students in question. During the previous eight months, I had grown to respect her opinion and ability greatly. I knew her well enough to know that if she had a hint that the boy could be successful, she would have taken him.

A few minutes later, I sat uncomfortably at the conference table in my office attempting to provide an explanation through Monica that would give the boy's father some satisfaction. He sat directly opposite from me with Monica in between. With both of his elbows resting on the table, he supported his jaw with both fists, his black eyes staring directly into mine as Monica spoke. This time, I would not look away from his stare. Although I felt extremely intimidated, I was determined not to show an ounce of it. Attempting to look calm and be firm in my decision, I stared straight into his eyes as Monica translated my words to him.

For a brief moment, he sat silently and I could see his chest pumping faster as his breathing increased its speed. I braced myself for an outburst.

I was definitely not prepared for what happened next. I watched as his steely eyes began to well with tears. He continued staring at me as tears rolled down both of his cheeks, rolling past a tattoo of a tear marked on his face. Suddenly his fists hit the table hard as both Monica and I sat silent and still. He began to speak loudly in Spanish, his voice in anguish. To say I was stunned would be a gross understatement.

Monica immediately translated: "Sir, I'm begging you." Not taking his eyes off me, allowing his tears to land on the table and his forearms, he continued in Spanish as Monica calmly translated. "I've made mistakes in my life. I do not have a high school diploma." Although Monica's voice was steady, when I looked at her as she translated, she did not look back at me. She now had tears rolling down her face, too.

As the man continued in Spanish, Monica reached for some tissues, lifting her glasses and wiping her eyes, and gently placed the tissue box in front of the young father whom I now looked at through a different set of eyes. My eyes had remained dry until Monica's next translated sentence to me. "I've been to jail and I want my son to have a better life than I did."

Now the three of us were crying together, the father feeling the pain of his past while Monica and I felt the pain of this moment, knowing we could not help him.

"Monica, please tell him how sorry I am that we cannot accept his son at this time, that I truly wish we could," I said. "Let him know that I can provide a list of some other schools and we can make some calls for him to see if they have openings."

As Monica finished her translation, the man pulled a kerchief from his pocket and firmly wiped his eyes, said something in Spanish, and left my office with a pool of his tears on the conference table.

I was stunned that he left so suddenly, and Monica reached over, put her hand around my wrist, and said, "Danny, he said to thank you for your time and that he will not bother you again."

When I asked why he didn't want us to help him find another school, she replied that he was ashamed that he had cried in front of us. "It's okay," she reassured me. We offered to help him find another school. We can't help everybody who needs it. It's okay."

As she got up from the table, I sat looking at the drying tears and the rays of sun beaming in on the table. In the sun's reflection on the table, I could see an open window on the second floor of the convent next door. As soon as I wiped the tears from the table, I looked for the application to become a Blue Ribbon School of Excellence. I put the application down where I had just wiped away the father's tears and, as I once again leafed through the pages, this time I was determined that when we won, we would paint a giant blue ribbon around the school for everyone to see. I wanted all of Los Angeles to know of the greatness of this school. We would indeed win this award and we would build a new building!

I never saw the man with the tattoos again. And although it took from 1991 until 2010, both of the goals I set that day would be achieved. The first one didn't take all that long. In 1993, I proudly accepted the Blue Ribbon at a White House ceremony only months after President Clinton took his oath of office. As promised, I had a giant blue ribbon painted on the building to help tell the story of our proud community.

The second goal took a little longer to achieve; and although it was long after I'd left St. Thomas, a new building was eventually completed. And while the giant blue ribbon we painted on the building in 1993 is no longer there, for years our students proudly looked to it as they saluted the American flag each morning. That ribbon helped to raise the funds to build the new building on the campus of St. Thomas School, because when people far and wide heard our story, they came forward and helped fulfill a dream born from a father's tears.

Chapter 6. Blue Ribbon Rumble

What did he just say? I don't know if many of you out there have a reaction that's similar to mine upon hearing something negative.   If during a casual conversation someone says something negative, prejudiced, or simply annoying, I usually give that person the benefit of the doubt, thinking that perhaps I misheard. However, after the same person voices the same opinions more than once, I realize that I may have a friend or an acquaintance who is ignorant or possibly bigoted.

In 1990, when I assumed the principalship of St. Thomas, I was both happy and proud to do so. However, it often struck me as inconsiderate and mean-spirited that when I mentioned to various individuals what I did for a living and where my job was located, it was not unusual for people to say things like, "You're kidding? I wouldn't work in that neighborhood if I got paid twice as much as what I already do," or "I try my best not to drive east of La Brea, and when I do it is always on the freeway."

Every time I heard statements like these, I was stunned.   Eventually, I found the voice to simply say to people, "I love where I work," or "You ought to visit; you have the wrong impression." I discovered that our fears of the unknown often cause us to judge randomly and sound stupid.

I also discovered that there were many who were willing to do just what I suggested and come to visit; they then had their eyes opened to a world they'd never imagined.   Just behind the mental barriers and walls they had erected around a perceived "bad neighborhood" lay a vast array of cultures blending amongst themselves, placed there largely by circumstances beyond their control.

Was Pico-Union a dangerous neighborhood? You bet. However, there also existed, if one was willing to look, so many families who were committed not only to each other, but also to their churches, their country, and to the education of their children. Pico-Union was, and continues to be, a neighborhood filled with inspirational people, whose lives and stories afforded me life-changing experiences that I will always cherish. I did not find the same kind of judgments being made by the people of Pico-Union regarding the people who lived west of their neighborhood. What I found in Pico-Union was by and large a spirit of love and acceptance. What I found there was a second home, which often was more nurturing and satisfying than the home I actually was living in at the time. I longed for the days of neighbors knowing neighbors and visiting with one another, dropping by unexpectedly. Instead, my apartment building in Hollywood was filled with neighbors who were largely strangers to one another. People nodded, sometimes. Many of my Russian immigrant neighbors seemed very uncomfortable with my small-town, "hey, how are you...hope you're having a nice day" greeting. Mostly, I got stared at or ignored.

When you stand in a position of knowing, it does not matter what other people's opinions are. As much as I wanted to quiet the naysayers, they were not the driving force behind my quest to make St. Thomas a National Blue Ribbon School of Excellence. Rather, it was that anonymous father, covered in tattoos, whom I had falsely pre-judged, who became the wind beneath my trembling wings and allowed me to soar into the unknown territory of the United States Department of Education's Blue Ribbon Schools Program.

I knew that earning the designation of a National Blue Ribbon School of Excellence would be incredibly positive for St. Thomas. In my mind, the story of one of L.A.'s poorest schools becoming a National School of Excellence was marketing gold. I believed it would open up doors to us that would otherwise remain closed. I believed that positive publicity would naturally follow such a designation, and the publicity would help bring in much needed dollars.

I also knew in my heart that the pride such an award would bring would be indescribable — not only to the members of the school and parish community, but to everyone in our neighborhood, which, we learned through studying the statistics for the application process, was the most densely populated neighborhood west of the Mississippi River. In my mind, even the gang members would walk taller with a Blue Ribbon School in their neighborhood; and that certainly couldn't hurt.

It was a tough application process. We began in September. The deadline was the first of November. Near the end of October, our teachers were tired of all the writing and began to complain. We had arguments regarding the content and how to word certain phrases and paragraphs. For instance, as we were rewriting the school's philosophy to provide a more current and accurate definition, some wanted to include the sentences, "To defend against the unlawful gangs that threaten our neighborhood, we have formed a gang of our own. Ours is a gang built upon love, not fear." Some staff members believed this to be too controversial and felt that we should not even mention the neighborhood's gang problem in our school's statement of philosophy. An argument over something like that easily went on for over an hour, taking up way too much time. People became offensive and offended during the arguments. There were days when not everyone on our faculty left still speaking to everyone.

The application was more than thorough; there were questions covering every aspect of school life. Every teacher and staff member was involved. We also invited our DARE (Drug Abuse Resistance Education) officer, a member of the Los Angeles Police Department, to be involved in our research and writing; he accepted. Our pastor, Father

Dennis, along with the PTA members and several other community members, also got involved. We generated over 100 pages of responses and documentation. The real challenge came in the editing process. We could only submit a 30-page report. Summing everything up in a concise manner was not only a daunting task, finding the time to edit also became increasingly difficult. We began to take entire days and hired substitute teachers to free up particular teachers who were especially involved in working on the application.

As the deadline approached, we began to burn the midnight oil. A good friend of mine, Craig Udit, an aspiring actor, also from Pennsylvania, volunteered to help us edit the beast. He was a godsend to us. Craig had the ability to rewrite our words to reflect what was actually in our hearts. After his edits, we read our revised philosophy with tears in our eyes; Craig knew how to make our work sound like poetry.

The looming deadline had been set for November 1, 1991, a Friday. I got substitute teachers for two of the teachers, Helen Villarreal and Terese Atzen, and we worked on the application the entire day doing the very last-minute edit. Craig came in about noon and we all huddled over his shoulder while he typed our suggestions at the keyboard.

About 6:00 that evening I was in Monica's office researching which post offices would accept a late drop-off and still include that day's post-mark. I could hear Craig say something with urgency and heard Helen and Terese both talking at once.

"Is something wrong?" I shouted into the adjoining office.

"Well, if you consider that the computer just froze 'something wrong,' then yes, something is definitely wrong," said a frustrated Craig.

At first I couldn't even get up from the chair. I didn't want them to see my reaction. I was angry and panicked at the same time. My head just fell backwards as I stared at the ceiling tiles and mouthed the word "SHIT" to the floor above. We all wanted to make it perfect, but I'd had the feeling that we should have allowed it to be as it was a day or two earlier. We should have mailed it yesterday, I thought to myself.

I controlled my emotions as I entered the next room nervously, sticking my left index finger in my ear to find some wax to pick at just to have something to take my attention away from a frozen computer. I keep my ears pretty clean, damn it! Nothing to scratch at there. My eyes were squinting, trying to mask any negative feeling I was having toward my colleagues for allowing this to go on too long. "What can we do?" I asked, not having a clue about those new-fangled computers. Craig was already busy attempting different combinations on the keyboard. No luck.

I had an idea. I looked up the number for St. Agnes convent a few blocks away. There was a nun there who had taught several courses in computer usage; she was the only expert I knew. I had taken a couple of classes from her and although she never seemed to like me very much, she was my only hope in this moment of panic. Since it was fall, it was already dark, which always seems to make the early evening feel later than it actually is.

"St. Agnes convent," came the voice on the other end of the phone. "May I speak with Sister Agnes?" I inquired. No response. I could hear the sounds of the phone being muffled by a hand and the voice that answered the phone saying, "I don't know who it is, he didn't say." There was more muffled movement, which I assumed was the phone getting passed from hand to hand. The new hand, that of Sister Agnes, did not cover the mouthpiece, and the sound went from muffled to clear as she cleared her throat to say in a strong and serious tone, "This is Sister Agnes."

I became more nervous. Sister was middle-aged, obese, and had the potential to be both charming and abrasive. Since she worked for the archdiocese, I innately had a level of respect for her and showed deference. It would take me a year or two more before I learned that one's title or vocation does not always mean one deserves respect, even from someone like me who was lower in the hierarchy. This night would be part of my education in that direction.

"Good evening Sister, I'm so sorry to..."

"Who is this?" she demanded before I could offer up my name.

"It's Dan Horn, and I'm calling because our school is applying for the National Bl..." As I was speaking, I could hear her hand now cover the mouthpiece while she said to her good friend, Sister Margaret Ann, "It's Dan Horn from St. Thomas. How the hell did *he* get this number?"

Maybe it was rude to call her at home on a Friday evening. But I needed help and she was the only person I thought could provide it. In an odd sort of way, I actually thought she might have been impressed that I was working late on a Friday, completing an application to become a National Blue Ribbon School. Wrong! She was mad! Truly, I think she wanted me to hear her angry inquiry to the other nun. I felt embarrassed and wanted to hang up and forget that I'd ever called that convent. Instead, I could feel my embarrassment turning to frustration; what had I done to make her mad? Her voice came back on the line.

"Yes, Dan, you were saying?"

"Well first of all, Sister, I got the telephone number from the phone book," I responded, perhaps a bit too acidly. "Your convent is conveniently listed. And second, I was hoping you might be able to provide some instruction as to how to get our computer to become unfrozen."

"No, Dan, I can't. I'm sorry you're having trouble. Good luck with figuring it out. You have a nice weekend," she almost sang as she hung up the phone!

By now, Craig was on the second phone line calling a friend of his. After what seemed like an eternity we got good news. The computer was working again. I immediately wanted to print out the application as is and get going to the post office. I was outvoted. For several hours more we kept making edits and additions, being careful not to go over the 30-page limit we knew would disqualify us. With each new paragraph we would go over the page count and have to go back and edit something else out.

Finally, it was almost 11 o'clock. With the final page printed, we went through it one more time, counting every page to ensure it was all there and in the right order. Off we went together to the post office, Craig driving in what resembled something out of a Hollywood chase scene. Now we were afraid of getting caught speeding and being pulled over, which could possibly take us past midnight. We attempted to race toward the post office without arousing any unwanted attention by police. We arrived with just minutes to spare. All of us trooped inside the post office and stood solemnly as we watched the long envelope go swiftly down the mail shoot.

That night the application did not get mailed to the U.S. Department of Education. Instead, it was mailed to the Council for American Private Education (CAPE). So many schools apply for the prestigious National Blue Ribbon award that the U.S. Department of Education asked each state department of education to review the applications, and, depending on the state's population, the local department of education was permitted to nominate a certain number of its schools to be considered for the national award. Since we were a private school, we were instructed to send our application to CAPE, which was allowed to nominate only a certain number of private schools nationwide. Once a school was nominated, its application would then be forwarded to the U.S. Department of Education, where those applications would be reviewed and then a smaller number of schools would be recommended by a review panel to receive a two-day site visit. The schools designated a National Blue Ribbon School of Excellence would be chosen from among those receiving site visits.

In the fall of 1991, Joyce McCrae was the executive director of CAPE. The application instructions indicated that we were to call if we had any questions. I wanted to be so careful and certain that we were interpreting the questions correctly that I made frequent calls. So Joyce and I had gotten to know one another and were on a first-name basis by November 1st. However, now a month would go by before Joyce and I talked again. Lord knows, I tried to be patient, but the wait to find out if we were nominated was killing me. Finally, I couldn't stand the suspense, and picked up the phone.

"Hi Joyce, it's Dan from St. Thomas. I'm really sorry to bother you, but we've only got a couple of weeks left until we go on Christmas break. I'd love to be able to share any possible good news with my staff if you have some for me."

"Well Dan, I have both good news and bad news." I couldn't quite grasp what she meant by this. Joyce continued, "Our panel nominated St. Thomas to go to the next phase of review. However, I just discovered that Congress has voted to eliminate the funding for the Blue Ribbon Schools Program."

I was speechless.

Joyce sensed my disbelief; I suppose it was my utter silence that tipped her off.

You know how so many thoughts can race through your mind in a matter of seconds? That's what was happening to me. I was wondering how I would break this news to my staff. Would the community feel like we had somehow failed? Would people be upset that I'd led them on this wild goose chase? Did we somehow do something wrong?

"Is there something we can do?" I uttered, hopelessly.

"No, the vote has already happened," she explained. "It's a good program with a relatively small budget that Congress just did not see the value in."

"I don't know how I'm going to tell people," I said.

Joyce advised, "Honey, if I were you I just wouldn't say anything to them right now. Let them enjoy their Christmas break. You'll be getting a letter from the Department of Education explaining what happened, and you can read everyone the letter. It's not your fault."

I did exactly what she said and didn't say anything to anyone...at least until I hung up the phone. Once the receiver was down, the gloves came off and I began to talk and talk and talk. I told Monica, who was in the next office with several parents, who most likely didn't even speak the language. Then I called a faculty meeting and informed the entire staff at the same time.

"We can't let this happen," I said. "George Bush dubbed himself the 'education president' and damn it, he made a contract with American educators; now he's broken his contract." The staff agreed, wholeheartedly.

As the days went by, our passion became stronger and our anger grew, at least I know that mine did. We were having the students write letters to all sorts of people — from our local councilman to L.A.'s Mayor Riordan — encouraging them to contact President Bush on our behalf. Congress had voted not to fund the program, but it had yet to be signed by the President, who, according to Joyce, would most likely sign. We wrote to our state legislators and we wrote to our representative and senators in Congress. Hundreds of students wrote numerous letters, creating what we thought was an avalanche.

Then I remembered Joyce telling me that we were the first school to learn of this plight. I realized we were probably one of the few schools, if not the only school, creating an avalanche. I knew first-hand the hundreds of hours that went into completing that application. It only made sense that other school communities would be as angry as we were. If we got the word out to other schools, they would have to feel the same outrage we were experiencing.

We had to get the word out. Back then, I had never heard of a press release. So I began calling newspapers one by one, from the *Los Angeles Times* to *The Washington Post*. I would cold call news magazines and local news channels. Sometimes I would call a particular reporter and sometimes I would begin by telling the story to whoever answered the phone and see whom they transferred my call to. Within a matter of days I'd contacted so many different media sources that my voice was beginning to become hoarse and I was beginning to lose faith that anyone with clout would care about us teachers who had been wronged by our Congress. The budget for the entire Blue Ribbon Schools Program was less than $900,000 and had been thrown in with a lot of other cuts. We at St. Thomas believed, and rightfully so, that most members of Congress had not even been aware of the fact that they had cut this most worthwhile program only after hundreds of schools nationwide had devoted so much time to completing the application. The timing was criminal, in my mind.

My impression was that most reporters were feigning any real interest or sympathy. "It's terrible that happened to your school, sir. However, I just don't think this is a story that *Newsweek* readers would be interested in."

One morning, our first-grade teacher, Lynne, came into my office with that day's *Wall Street Journal* in hand. "My husband wanted you to see this story on the front page," she said. "Jeremy thought that this writer might be someone you should contact." I did. Whoever the reporter was did not take my call. Instead, I eventually talked with young and sweet-sounding Hilary Stout. Somehow I had a feeling that there weren't that many people left to tell my story to, and unlike so many of the others, Hillary sounded sincere. Then came the word I dreaded hearing from her. "Mr. Horn, I can hear your passion and disappointment, and I don't blame you. However…"

By now, the word "however" had become like a dagger in my back. When I heard Hilary say the word, my entire body cringed and I shut my eyes in disappointment, anticipating the rest of the sentence: "…however, I just don't think it is a story of interest to the readers of our newspaper."

However…there was something in her voice that told me she really *did* understand, just not fully.

"Hilary," I said, almost pleading. I didn't care if I sounded desperate, I was. And I had an idea. "Allow me to Federal Express the Blue Ribbon application to you," I continued. "Take a look at the application, read the requirements. See for yourself the time and effort involved on behalf of school communities all across this country. To me, it reads like a contract with American educators, and our 'education president' George Bush broke the contract. If you take a look at this application and still believe it is not a story of interest to your readers, I won't bother you again."

I remember feeling overwhelmed by hope when Hilary agreed to receive the document. I also remember feeling relieved that she offered to have the *Wall Street Journal* pay for the overnight shipment; we were that low on funds!

The next morning I jumped for the phone when Monica announced that a nice-sounding girl name Hilary was on the phone for me.

"Mr. Horn, you are so right. I had no idea that the process was this extensive. Thank you for sending it; I'll see what I can do."

I did not hear from Hilary before the start of our Christmas break of 1991. I began to doubt that her bosses had agreed with her assessment. Between Christmas and New Year's Day I received a telephone call from the parish office informing me that the school had been burglarized. When I arrived, I discovered that the vandals had, among other things, taken the school's checkbook from my drawer. The bank instructed me to close the account and open a new one. In order to do so, I would have to have our Cardinal, the head of the archdiocese, sign the form to open the new account.

I had no idea how to get in touch with the Cardinal. I called our assistant superintendent, Sister Mary Elizabeth, to find out how to reach the Cardinal. I identified myself to her assistant, who put me on hold. Sister came on the line, saying, "Dan, congratulations on the wonderful article in the *Wall Street Journal!*"

I was shocked, but instantly a victorious feeling began coursing through my veins. Hilary had come through for us. She had gone to her bosses and they'd agreed. Hilary's article, dated Friday, December 27, 1991 was headlined:

"Schools Fume After Capitol Hill Snips Up Blue-Ribbon Funding"

The article began,

"St. Thomas the Apostle, a little parochial school in one of Los Angeles' poorest neighborhoods, thought it was good enough for a blue ribbon. And so this fall St. Thomas's teachers and administrators spent about 1,000 hours of their nights and weekends preparing an application for the U.S. Department of Education's Blue Ribbon Schools of Excellence Awards. Then, in late November, Congress killed the program's funding in an appropriations bill that President Bush signed..."

Since 1991, Blue Ribbon School recipients have Hilary Stout to thank, for without her, the program may very well have died without a whimper. Instead, due to her timely article, outraged citizens flooded Congress and the Department of Education with letters that quickly resulted in the reinstatement of the Blue Ribbon Schools Program, which continues through the time of this writing.

Upon returning from Christmas break, I called Joyce at CAPE to see if there had been any change in plans.

"Dan Horn, I thought I told you not to say anything to anyone," she said, laughing.

By that time, the Blue Ribbon Schools Program was on its way to reinstatement and the credit was given largely to the little school in the Pico-Union district of Los Angeles. In fact, the *Los Angeles Times*, which had originally told me that this was not a story of interest, now did a story entitled, "Blue Ribbon Schools Win Prize for Muscle", with a picture of the staff and me posing in our St. Thomas sweatshirts.

It took some time to reorganize and get the Blue Ribbon Schools Program back on track. By the time the new timetable was announced, the academic year was almost over. The 1991-92 Program would bleed over into the 1992-93 Program. Before the year ended, we received the news that the U.S. Department of Education had ruled in our favor and we became one of the finalists. Our site visit, however, would not take place until November 2, 1992.

For me, this was quite ironic. November 2, 1992 was Election Day and our "education president" was up for re-election. I said in every interview that it was a slap in the face to educators when the Blue Ribbon Program was so easily voted down after all of the hard work educators and schools had put in. Guess who wasn't getting my vote in that election!

We invited every person who had taken part in our application process to be part of the site visit. Instructions were that the DOE official should meet with our superintendent and other parties. We arranged a dinner that evening prepared by our parents and hosted in the eighth-grade classroom. The parents had removed all the desks from the classroom and replaced them with round tables for ten, which they set with tablecloths and silverware. Instead of using the bright fluorescent lights overhead, candles were lit on the tables, providing an elegant ambience.

In addition to the faculty and staff, we invited the neighboring high school principals as well as some of the neighborhood leaders, including the pastor at the nearby St. Sophia Greek Orthodox Cathedral. Although our councilman Mike Hernandez could not stay for the entire dinner, we were honored that he stopped in long enough to talk to the visiting DOE official. Before he departed, Mike asked if he could say a few words to the assembled group. During his remarks, he compared our neighborhood and our school to the ambience of the evening itself, noting that the neighborhood sometimes experienced a lot of darkness due to the gangs and the crime, while St. Thomas School was like the candles on the table, providing light and hope for the entire community. Glancing over at the visiting official, I could see that he was moved, as we all were.

That night, our visitor stayed late, joining our staff in the fifth-grade classroom as we all watched the election results until Bill Clinton was pronounced the winner of the

1992 Presidential race. We all toasted our new President, who had his work cut out for him. He was the man from Hope, Arkansas, who, just like our school, provided hope for so many across the nation.

Although we began this Blue Ribbon journey during the spring and fall of 1991, and were still going strong through Election Day 1992, it appeared as though we wouldn't receive word of the outcome until after our Christmas break in 1993. How long would we have to wait, I wondered. And worst of all, what if the answer was no? What if we didn't make the cut? My nerves were on edge.

On Thursday, December 17, 1992, my mind was far from Blue Ribbons. It was our last day of school for the year. That evening, our annual Christmas program was to take place in the school's small auditorium. We always had a huge crowd of parents for the event and some people would not even fit in the auditorium. Hoping the weather would cooperate, we would keep the front doors open so the overflow crowd of parents could actually stand outside and still see the stage during the performance. On hectic nights like these, my brain usually went into high gear with concerns about crowd control.

On top of that, I was coordinating with several of our parents, who were cooking a complete turkey dinner at the church rectory. After school, teachers would not go home. We would all go to the rectory for a Christmas dinner together with the parish priests. A little wine with dinner would usually calm all of our nerves. After dinner, teachers would return to their classrooms, where they would meet their students, who had returned from their dinners, and wait until it was time for each grade's performance. The teachers would bring their classes to the auditorium and be ready to escort their students on stage, single-file, while the class before theirs was exiting on the other side of the room. After their performance they would return to their classroom until the event was over. No matter how organized we were, there was always a level of chaos involved.

About ten that morning, Monica, with a smile on her face, announced, "Danny, telephone call from Washington D.C." I braced myself. "The Department of Education," I whispered in a trancelike state. Monica nodded, with an ear-to-ear grin. "I have a good feeling," she said. "Now you go and take the call."

I walked into my office, closed the door behind me, and sat down stiffly in my chair, staring out at the convent through the window in front of me. I cleared my throat, picked up the receiver, and said, "Hello, this is Dan Horn."

In less than a minute, I opened the door to where Monica sat, made sure she was alone, and breathing heavily in order to control my emotion, I said, "We won."

Monica stood, walked me into my office, and we hugged. What a journey it had been! Finally it was over and, in the end, we stood victorious. "When are you going to tell the children?" she asked.

I was still processing what I had just heard on the phone. In my head I was repeating what the caller had said, making sure I was not dreaming. Coming back to earth, I replied, "Tonight."

It took real strength on my part not to go running through the hallways shouting the good news. I surprised myself by not calling the diocese, my relatives and friends, or the newspapers. I wanted the school community, the kids, and the parents to know first. We received the news on a perfect day. The next ten hours, however, were some of the longest of my life.

The dinner with the faculty was tough. During the prayer and the toasts, the mention of the possibility of winning the Blue Ribbon came up time after time. The dinner conversation included people wondering when we would find out. I sat stuffing myself with turkey and mashed potatoes knowing that it would not be too much longer. Either I would burst from too much food or the desire to divulge the good news.

When dinner ended we were about thirty minutes from showtime. By the time we walked the one block to the school we could see that the crowd was already spilling over to outside the school. Cars were backed up the entire length of Mariposa Street, waiting to get into the school's parking lot. As usual, there was an event at the church that evening, which brought in another avalanche of cars, adding to the already chaotic environment of our annual Christmas program.

Once the show got underway I knew I only would have about 90 minutes more to keep my secret. As I waited, I wondered about what winning would mean to this community. In my mind, it was a huge feat that lent strong credibility to our school and our families, a bulwark against all those who looked down upon this neighborhood. But I also began to wonder if the families, some of them just worrying about daily survival, would even care about this Blue Ribbon distinction. Although we had done our best to make our students aware of and involved in the process and the eventual fight with Congress, would they really grasp the significance of what we had achieved? By the time the program was over and everyone sat waiting in their places — parents in and surrounding the auditorium, teachers and students waiting in their classrooms — I had talked myself into thinking that perhaps no one would care.

Now, it was time.

I walked to the school office, unlocked the door, used the lights from the hallway outside to light my path as I walked to the public address system where I stood alone. Parents were still in the auditorium, and students were waiting in classrooms throughout the building. I pushed the red button, which was the ALL CALL that reached every room in the school. There was an unusual quiet throughout the building; I could actually hear the click that the hitting of the button made as the sound system came on in every room.

"Parents, students and guests, before we go off for our Christmas break, I have some news to share with you," I began my announcement. At that moment I realized that so many of the parents and guests could not understand a word I was saying. Oh well, I should have thought of that sooner; I was knee-deep in it now.

There was absolute silence.

"Today our school received a Christmas gift from the United States Department of Education."

Pandemonium immediately ensued. To my surprise, they had been waiting for this news as much as I was. At once, any doubt I had about whether the community cared, or if they understood the significance of the award, was immediately erased. Before I could even get the words out, there began a rumble resembling an earthquake with a Richter scale reading of 8.0. Students in the classrooms above were pounding their feet and there were cheers erupting from the auditorium. I could hear the clapping hands of the first and second graders on our floor. Some students from the upper grades were in the hallways above cheering with delight.

Just as I'd done earlier in the day, I had to brace myself. I had not anticipated this, and I became emotional. I was thinking of the faces of these students whose parents hailed from Mexico, Honduras, El Salvador, Guatemala, Nicaragua, and Colombia. I thought of the non-English speaking parents in the gym who were having the good news translated for them by the English-speaking parents sitting near them. So many of these parents were immigrants who were making sacrifices so that their children could get a good education and have a better life.

The rumbling grew louder from the auditorium as the news was translated from person to person; my eyes fought back the tears so I would not sob as I finished the announcement. When the cheering finally died down, everyone waited for me to make it official by actually saying the words. Silence once again. Monica appeared in the room and stood next to me; her hands in the form of a prayer holding up her chin, tears in her eyes, she also waited for my words, which now came:

"As of today, the rest of the country will begin to discover what we have known for the last year. St. Thomas the Apostle School is one of 230 schools in this country to be named a National Blue Ribbon School of Excellence. Congratulations and Merry Christmas, everyone!"

Postscript: On Friday, May 14, 1993, two of my colleagues and I sat in the front row on the South Lawn of the White House and received the Blue Ribbon Award from our recently inaugurated president, Bill Clinton.   Representing the community of St. Thomas the Apostle at that ceremony remains the greatest honor of my life.

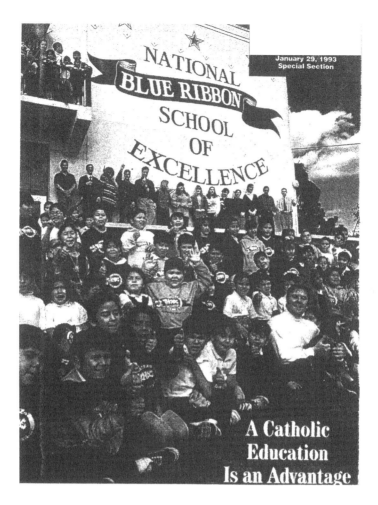

A proud school community!

Representing St. Thomas School in May 1993 was the proudest moment of my life.

Chapter 7. A Candle for the Councilman

During the hectic final days of 1992, when we were waging as much of a war with Congress that we could possibly mount to get funding reinstated for the National Blue Ribbon School of Excellence Program, one of the people we contacted for help was our local councilman, Mike Hernandez. Mike had become councilman the same year I became principal at St. Thomas School. I had never had any contact with him prior to my phone call to his office in December of 1991. He returned my call personally, and after listening to my rant about the treatment our school had just received at the hands of the United States Congress, Mike assured me that he, too, was outraged. He said that he would gladly write to both of our Senators on our behalf and would send me copies of the letters. When I mentioned my conversation with the councilman to Father Dennis later that day, he seemed surprised that Mike had called me back personally rather than one of his aides. It seemed rather natural to me, though I'd never had reason to contact my councilman prior to this in any of the places I'd lived or worked. "Dan, there are more people in Mike Hernandez's district than reside in some states," Dennis said, helping to put it in perspective for me.

The first time I met Mike in person was the evening of November 2, 1992. We were hosting a dinner party in our eighth-grade classroom so that the site visitor representing the U. S. Department of Education for our Blue Ribbon Schools evaluation could meet some of our stakeholders. We were right next door to Loyola High School and some of the Jesuit priests came for dinner along with the principal at Bishop Conaty-Loretto High School, which was a block away. Father Adams, the distinguished-looking pastor from St. Sophia's Greek Orthodox Cathedral came to represent his community, as did representatives from the archdiocese. Our faculty and staff were there along with many parents, some of whom would be joining us for dinner, which other parents had helped to prepare and which still others would serve from the kitchen located two floors below. Another group of parents had proudly worked to transform the classroom into an elegant banquet room with cloth-covered tables set with cloth napkins, silverware, flowers, and candles, which lit the room as soft music played in the background.

Father Dennis, who frequently got involved in community affairs and local politics, had gotten to know Mike over the past year. Now, as I was about to go upstairs to join the banquet, I could hear Dennis' familiar chuckle and enthusiastic conversational tone approaching my office, and then in he walked along with a rather burly Latino gentleman who was dressed in a suit and tie and had thick hair combed back in a business style. The first thing I noticed about Mike was his size, and then his rugged-looking face. He immediately reached out his hand to shake mine as Dennis introduced us, "Mike, this is our principal, Dan Horn; Dan, this is Mike Hernandez."

"It's great that you're here," I said. "Your aide called this morning to say that you might not be able to make it to our event."

"Well, I really don't have much time," Mike said, apologetically. "I've been scheduled for months to be at another event. But I couldn't say no to this; it's such an important night for this school. Plus, I've been wanting to meet you since our phone conversation last year." Mike's voice was soft, even gentle; it did not quite match his imposing appearance. At that point Father Dennis excused himself and said that he'd see us upstairs at dinner.

"You remember our phone call?" I asked, somewhat amazed, remembering what Dennis had told me about what a large district the councilman represented. Mike smiled broadly, and said, "Yes, I do. I was so impressed that a school in this district had applied for such a prestigious award. I honestly shared your frustration once I heard that Congress had cancelled the Blue Ribbon Program. I guess our letters helped, huh?"

"Our letters obviously helped; that's why we're here tonight," I responded. Mike instantly had a fan in me. He possessed an amazing memory, and genuinely seemed to care about the people in his district.

Putting his hand on my back, he leaned in and said in a whisper, "I'm awfully sorry I can't be here for the entire dinner. I wish I could. Perhaps you could introduce me to whoever is here from Washington. Then, if you don't mind, I'd like to say a few words to the group before dinner. Would that be all right with you?"

I couldn't wait to introduce Mike to our visitor, who seemed duly impressed when I introduced him to our councilman. Good for Father Dennis, who made sure to reference the fact that there were more people in Mike's district than in some states, just in case our visitor had the same misguided perspective that I'd had earlier.

Prior to his leaving, Mike picked up a glass of water and invited everyone to join him in a toast: "To this beautiful school and community. It reminds me of the candles that light this room tonight. Sometimes this neighborhood can be very dark and bear dark headlines of crime. I'm so proud to have St. Thomas School in my district because it is one of the candles that help to bring light to this corner of Los Angeles. Let us lift our glasses to the community of St. Thomas School."

After the toast, I walked Mike to the door. "This is a big night for us," I told him. "It means a lot to me that you were here and I'm so grateful for what you said up there."

"It was my honor to be here. Good luck. Let me know how this turns out, okay?

"You bet," I said shaking hands.

Heading out into the cool night air, he said, "Call me anytime."

I did…many times.

Mike was back a few months later. When St. Thomas was named a Blue Ribbon School, I kept a promise I'd made to myself and had a giant blue ribbon painted on the school with an accompanying sign reading National Blue Ribbon School of Excellence. It was two stories high and the width of half the building.

Mike too, kept his promise. Every time I called him to be with us at the school, he was there. In early 1993, we held a press conference to publicly announce our having won the award. Surrounded by students, Mike proudly stood below the large blue ribbon as he joined us in making the announcement. Remember, our goal was to bring publicity to the school; having Mike there for the event helped bring in the publicity.

Later that year, in October, we held a Blue Ribbon Celebration of Education. We invited so many people that we held the celebration outside in our parking lot in order to fit everyone in — even the church was not large enough. There were local dignitaries, including Cardinal Mahony, Bishop Ward, Superintendent Porath, and District Attorney Garcetti; newsman Tony Valdez was the host for the event. We invited Mike to be the person to represent the U.S. Department of Education and make the presentation of the plaque and flag. Once again he did us proud. In fact, Mike always said yes. Could he come speak to our parents about the controversial Proposition 187, the ballot measure seeking to limit services to illegal aliens? Yes! Would he consider coming back to talk to members of the parish on that same issue? Of course!

I had never had that kind of access to an elected representative prior to meeting Mike, nor have I since. Never have I seen as sincere a commitment to constituents as Mike had. In the intervening years, I've learned that he was among a rare breed of politician — truly committed and loyal to those he represented. I'm glad I appreciated him while we worked together, because I sure miss having someone like him now.

Several years after we'd gotten the Blue Ribbon award, I was following my typical morning routine of having the local news channel on while getting ready for school. On this particular August morning in 1997, the top story of the day was the previous night's arrest of councilman Mike Hernandez for the purchase and possession of cocaine. My heart began to beat rapidly upon hearing the news. I was not distraught over the fact that Mike had done something wrong. The fact that my heart was beating rapidly was due to my knowing what most likely lay in store for Mike. Here he was at probably one of the lowest points in his life and instead of him finding compassion and understanding from his constituents, he would most likely be facing the opposite. I had seen our society, especially our media, behave so cruelly during the darkest moments in some people's lives. My heart beat fast out of fear for my friend. With America being a largely Christian nation, it often pains me to witness how un-Christ-like we often become when people need to experience the love of Christ the most.

I wondered how Father Dennis would react to this news. Dennis definitely had a mind of his own; however, I realized that he had plenty of authority figures to answer to, from a local bishop and a vicar for clergy to a moderator of the curia and the Cardinal. By reaching out to Mike and writing a note of support, he would be representing the parish of St. Thomas the Apostle; that could very possibly get him in trouble, I thought. I placed a call to Father Dennis anyway. "Good Morning, Father," I said into the phone.

"Good Morning, Dan," he responded somewhat dryly. "I can tell from your voice that you've heard about Mike."

"Yes, it's all over the news today; you can't miss it."

"I'm getting ready to type up a letter of support from the school community and I'm going to fax it over to his office. Do you want me to write one for you to send as well?" I asked. My guess was he had not thought to send one, but hearing that I was sending one would remind him that that was the right thing to do. Dennis didn't need a reminder about what was right, he needed a reminder only in the sense that you remind someone to send an anniversary card.

"That's a good idea, Dan," he said.   "I'll write something right now. Do you have the fax number?"

As the days passed, there was more press about Mike.   He had been under surveillance by the L.A.P.D for weeks prior to his arrest. In searching his office at City Hall, the authorities had discovered residue of both cocaine and marijuana on his desk.   There also were reports about his having purchased pornographic videotapes and stories about his heavy drinking and his affinity for tequila. He pled guilty to purchasing and possessing cocaine. He agreed to seek treatment as part of a plea agreement, which meant that the arrest would not be on his record.   Not on his record?   Too late.   Journalists had already done a fine job ensuring that Mike's public record was marred for life. Yes, Mike was arrested for purchasing cocaine. However, it was not against the law to buy or watch pornography, nor was it against the law to drink and enjoy tequila. I think journalists commit a bigger moral crime when they rush to report tawdry details for the single purpose of titillating the public.

Mike was not required to resign his seat. This made a lot of people angry. I assume the angry people were those who did not like him or his politics to begin with. I couldn't imagine that people who had known him and had benefitted from his care and dedication would be angry that he was not forced to resign. Nor could I imagine that people could be so superficial that they would want someone they knew, someone who had cared about them, to suffer even more after a public and humiliating arrest.   I simply could not imagine that people would turn away from a public servant who had helped the community in so many ways at a time in his life that most certainly had to be one of his darkest moments.

Personally, however, I thought Mike should resign. My understanding at the time was that cocaine was a powerfully addictive drug and that it would take serious rehabilitation as well as a less stressful job to stay in recovery. Mike proved me wrong.

The recall effort was underway when it was announced that after a month in recovery, Mike was about to return to the council. I wondered how he would be able to successfully return and stay sober after such a short time in treatment. I also wondered where he found the kind of strength to appear before what would certainly be a nasty crowd demanding his resignation and working toward a recall. It saddened and concerned me that after he had worked so hard for the 1st Council District of Los Angeles that his "dark night of the soul" was happening so publicly, and that so many were so intent on humiliation rather than redemption. It was time to light a candle!

"The archdiocese will never go for it, Dan," Father Dennis said in reply to my request to turn this into a lesson in forgiveness, redemption, and loyalty. Our seventh and eighth graders were old enough to understand the difference between condoning drug use and supporting a friend. I was intent on putting down the religion books for a morning and putting our religion into practice. My gut told me that on the morning Mike walked into council chambers at a City Hall that would be filled with detractors and hecklers, he should also be greeted by friendly faces. And, I believed, those friendly faces should include representatives from the parish and school of St. Thomas the Apostle.

"I don't care what the archdiocese will say; I care what *you* have to say. Mike has been a friend of ours, and now is the time for us to show our gratitude. Now is our time to be there for him."

It didn't take much persuading. One of the reasons why Father Dennis and I made such a great team was that instead of just talking the talk, as so many church leaders do, we did our best to walk the walk. So many Christians in today's world are fond of the saying, "What would Jesus do?" though only rhetorically, when it benefits them. I knew that having our students attend the council meeting would bring volumes of criticism, so I did my best to diffuse some of it before it began.

I knew there would be those who would say we were "using students politically." I didn't care if that was said, I just wanted to make sure that it wasn't true. Therefore, days before our visit to the council was to occur, we began a dialogue with students. Some of the questions we asked were:

You all know who Councilman Hernandez is, right?
Are you aware of why he was arrested?
Ever know anyone who has been arrested?
Do our choices always match who we are?
Is it possible to make bad choices and still be a good person and do good in the world?
If we were to show our loyalty to our councilman by being present on his first day back at City Hall, does that mean that we are saying it is all right to use illegal drugs?

We then offered students the opportunity to attend City Hall on the councilman's first day back in office. They were sent home with a letter for parents to sign that requested the school include their child in the field trip to City Hall. The students also took home a letter explaining our objectives. We listed some of the same questions for students and parents to talk about together. Each family was free to make their own decision as to whether or not the child would attend the City Hall meeting.

There were approximately 70 students in the seventh and eighth grades combined. 100% of the parents agreed to send their children. When the students returned to school and some explained the conversations they'd had at home, it became obvious that the initial reaction from parents had been negative. Students enthusiastically reported the discussions they'd then had with their parents based on the same questions we had posed at school. Many of them had witnessed their parents change their minds as a result of their thoughtful discussion. Students went home and dialoged with parents, many in Spanish, regarding the merits or lack thereof in attending a council meeting, and they came to a mutual agreement over a matter that was highly public and highly controversial. To this day, those conversations between students and teachers, followed by the ones between students and parents and the conversion of opinions, remain among the best days of education I've experienced in my life.

When students in a Catholic school come to an understanding with their teachers and their parents regarding a serious matter of law and morality, and are able to understand the difference between condoning actions and supporting people, that is Catholic education at its finest... that's pure blue ribbon, baby! I was proud! And, I'll admit, a bit nervous.

The teachers and I had also prepared students to be somewhat media savvy. It was explained to them that journalists, while attempting to be fair, sometimes lose sight of this goal and go for the sensational in a quest for higher ratings or more readers. I explained to them that they, being children, would become a magnet for many of the reporters in the room that day. Certainly, I would not tell them that they could not respond to reporters' questions, but I did want them to know that chances were high that some of them would be approached. I was confident that the conversations they'd had with teachers and their parents had prepared most of them so that a reporter could not make them look as if they had no idea why they were there or that they'd been manipulated by the school into attending an event that they didn't really understand or want to be at for themselves. However, these were 11, 12, and 13 year olds. Therefore, I suggested that they could simply choose not to comment. It was their choice.

Downtown Los Angeles traffic, which is usually heavy, was totally jammed around City Hall. Seeing all of the news vans confirmed my hunch that this was a big story in L.A., and I took the opportunity to again advise students that once they stepped off the bus, they would be magnets for the press and that they should be prepared but not intimidated.

The council chamber was packed. We stood in the back of the room waiting for the proceedings to begin. The two teachers who were with me and I spread out and did our best to surround our students so they would not become the focus of the media's attention. I folded my arms and solidly planted my feet on the floor in a policeman-like stance, attempting to send a "don't you dare come near" vibe to anyone interested in the children.

Crashing sounds of thunderous applause and cheers met with a cacophony of boos and hisses when Mike entered the room. It seemed to be a competition between those who could out-cheer or out-boo the opposing team. Those on the positive side carried the day, eventually drowning out the negative energy. The meeting began.

The room was so crowded, I wondered if Mike would even notice us or know we were there to support him. Before long, my wonder ceased and my question was answered.

When given an opportunity to make some remarks, Mike talked about his arrest and his choice to come back to the council so soon after beginning treatment. He assured us all that he was on the road to recovery and would do his best. He began to mention individuals he saw in the room and how grateful he was for the large showing of support that day.

Then his remarks took us back to almost five years earlier, to election night in 1992. To this gathering of fellow politicians, media, detractors, and supporters, Mike recalled the night he visited St. Thomas the Apostle school for the first time. My mouth dropped open slightly. It seemed unbelievable that at this moment he was journeying back to the evening of the dinner we hosted as part of our odyssey to become a National Blue Ribbon school. It was almost incomprehensible to me that at this moment he remembered that event and was talking about the school being like the candles on the tables.

Apparently, his remarks about the candles in the dark room were something he hadn't said just for effect.

The candles? At that moment, he looked to the back of the City Council chambers at City Hall during one of the bleakest and darkest periods of his life, and he remembered the candles on the tables at our dinner. Mike remembered the little school that provided light and hope to a neighborhood that so desperately needed to be lit. I had felt fairly certain that supporting Mike on this day was the right thing for us to do; now I was absolutely certain of it. Our presence obviously meant a lot to him. Just as Mike had come to our dinner five years earlier to support us on our quest to be recognized for excellence in education, we were now there for him, during his quest for redemption. If nothing else, we had taken our turns in becoming candles, and providing loyalty and light.

from left, Dan Horn, unknown, former presidential candidate Michael Dukakis, Mike Hernandez, Father John Bakas, Father Dennis O'Neil watching play rehearsal for Godspell

Chapter 8. Reagan Style

The first time I ever met a member of the first family was in April of 1980; I was 19 years old. Well, I actually didn't *meet* the first family member in person, but it sure felt as if I did. It was an election year. Jimmy Carter was president. Forty-four Americans were being held hostage by militants in Iran, which was a major news story every day that year. President Carter pretty much sat out the primary season even though he was facing a major challenger, Senator Ted Kennedy of Massachusetts. Carter's Rose Garden strategy was that he would not leave the White House to campaign during the primary season as long as our citizens were still captive in Iran. Therefore, Rosalynn Carter did the brunt of campaigning for her husband during most of the primary season.

It was big news in our small town of Jeannette, Pennsylvania that a first lady was going to visit one of the local glass factories, Jeannette Sheet Glass, once known in town as the "Window House." During the late 1970s, the factory, which was once the world's largest producer of window glass in the world, closed its doors. It then was among the first factories in the country to reopen with its former employees as the co-owners of the company. The White House wanted to bring attention to this innovative business trend; hence, a visit from the first lady of the land. The local newspaper, the *Jeannette New Dispatch*, featured an editorial encouraging landowners to clean up their front lawns if they were along the route the motorcade would be taking.

There were fewer than 10,000 citizens living in Jeannette in 1980. It seemed like all of us were out lining the streets the day Rosalynn Carter rode through town. It was an exciting event for a town our size.

"I wouldn't walk as far as I could spit to see that Rose Carter," shouted a woman sitting in her front porch on a plastic chaise, cigarette in one hand, cup of coffee in the other. My friends and I ignored her as we found an open spot along the motorcade route. Continuing in her raspy voice, the woman said, "Her husband ain't done shit for this country."

One of her neighbors standing along the route encouraged her to join us, yelling over to her, "Get off your ass Lenore and get out here. Somethin' like this ain't gonna happen again in this town."

"No goddamn way," responded Lenore as she flung her cigarette into her yard and picked up a magazine.

"Here they come," someone shouted, and we could see police cars with lights flashing coming around the corner.

In an instant the cars were in front of us, and then came the limousine carrying Rosalynn. There she was, sitting in the limo facing our side of the street waving to all of us.. Her face was right in front of the car window and we could get a good look. And there was Lenore, just a few feet away from where I stood, her hair in curlers, wearing her housecoat and bedroom slippers, waving just as excitedly as any one of the rest of us.

Later that day, my friend Terry's dad, Mr. Pacelli who worked at Jeannette Sheet Glass, described to me how he shook Mrs. Carter's hand when she'd toured the factory. He actually giggled in his deep growly voice as he recounted the fact that she told him, "It's so nice to meet you."

"I told her it was very nice to meet her, too," he said, laughing at his own good fortune.

I was jealous. I wished I could have been there, too.

Years later, when I was principal of St. Thomas School, I walked up the driveway of the White House, past the Rose Garden, along with St. Thomas teachers Terese Atzen and Joe Neeb. We were giddy with anticipation; the three of us were representing our school at a South Lawn ceremony for the 230 schools that had been designated National Blue Ribbon Schools for the 1991-1992 school year. Instead of taking the same bus as the other attendees, we'd decided to take a cab since we were also staying at a different hotel than the others. What a stroke of luck!

"Welcome, you're the first to arrive," said an attractive White House intern, after checking our names off the list. "Please show your IDs to the man at the gate."

The three of us began walking down the driveway toward the South Lawn, when Joe started motioning toward two men, one in a suit, the other in very short jogging shorts standing under a colonnade. "They're waving at us," said Joe. We started to wave back when all at once, we recognized the two men. As President Clinton, in the shorts, and Vice President Gore, in the suit, continued their conversation, we three, in loud whispers, were "oh my God-ing" the rest of the way up to the seating area.

Looking out at the 700-plus white chairs set up neatly in rows, we kidded one another about which chairs we should sit in. We chose the first three chairs from center aisle in the first row on the right side facing the small stage, just a few feet away. As the hundreds of other educators began to file in, I sat holding the seat of my chair with both hands, smiling with anticipation. In a little more than an hour, the chairs on the lawn were full, the Marine Band played Hail to the Chief, and out walked Secretary of Education Richard Riley and our new President, William Jefferson Clinton.

Since childhood I've been fascinated with the American presidency and the first family. I was born at the very end of the Eisenhower administration; by then he was a lame duck and finishing out his final days with less than a month to go before the inauguration of John Kennedy. I have vague recollections of hearing about baby John-John, who was a little more than a month older than I was. I have clear memories of Johnson and every president and first family ever since.

One thing I've learned along the way in watching the pageant of presidents and their families is that it takes an extraordinary person to reach a position that so few men in history have held. In the more than 200 years the United States has existed, the club of presidents is one of the most exclusive in the world. Regardless of a president's achievements or foils, actually meeting one — whether current or former — is a highlight of a lifetime for most of us. NBC news anchor Brian Williams, when lecturing at the Reagan Library, commented that meeting a president is often an electrifying moment. He said that there is something almost mystical about shaking the hand of the man who has been elected president of the United States. I agree with him.

It makes sense. It takes an unimaginable thickness of skin and fortitude to be elected president in modern times. The president and his family are subjected to scrutiny and criticism that is beyond the comprehension of most of us. There is something about each one of them, like it or not, that makes them special.

I don't know what took me so long to realize the opportunity I had to meet the Reagans, but it alluded me for a while. Back when I was still pursuing acting, I took a job as a tour guide in Los Angeles. The Reagans were still in the White House, but when they moved back to L.A., their house was part of my tour. In fact, there was a great story I'd tell my tourists about their house. The Reagan home address was originally 666 St. Cloud Road in Bel Air. Nancy, however, suffers from Hexakosioihexekontahexaphobia (pronounced *hexa-koseeoi-hexe-konta-hexaphobia*), the fear of the number 666, stemming from the Biblical verse Revelation 13:18, which indicates that that number is the number of the Beast or the Anti-Christ. Therefore, prior to the Reagan's moving into the house in January 1989, the address was changed to 668 St. Cloud Road.

Then I read an article about Nancy Reagan. It stated that since November 1994 when her husband revealed to the world that he was suffering from Alzheimer's disease, Nancy periodically made appearances at the Reagan Library and Museum in Simi Valley, California. I began to type Mrs. Reagan a letter. In the letter, I told her a bit about our school. I asked her to thank her husband on our behalf for having begun the Blue Ribbon Schools Program during his administration. I explained how we had fought to save the program, and then received the award ourselves.

"Would it be possible, Mrs. Reagan, for our sixth, seventh, and eighth graders to join you one day at the Reagan Library, have a Q&A session, and have a photo taken?" I typed. I sent the same letter several times, but got no response. Then, one day I received a call from Libby Brady, assistant to Mrs. Reagan. Although it would not be possible for Mrs. Reagan to conduct a Q&A with students, she would be delighted to meet them and have her picture taken with them. Persistence paid off.

"You should go into the gift shop now, Mrs. Reagan is almost finished signing books," whispered one of her aides into my ear. "Be sure to remind her that you are here with the school and remind her about the request to take pictures."

Although nervous, I approached Mrs. Reagan and introduced myself as she looked up from her autograph table. She was wearing large glasses and looked somewhat frail.

"Hello Mrs. Reagan, I'm Dan Horn, principal of St. Thomas School," I said cheerily.

"Oh yes, I heard you were coming; are the children here with you?" she inquired while offering her hand in a greeting.

"They're all here, all 105 of them, and they're very eager to meet you and have a picture taken with you," I said. "As a matter of fact, they're waiting outside already lined up for the occasion."

"I hope the children have had an opportunity to look around the museum," she said as she rose from her chair.

"We've been here since the museum opened; they've been through every inch of it," I responded, as I held out my arm to escort her.

As she stood, her frailty seemed to disappear. She was dressed in her signature Reagan Red and began to walk with me toward the door.

"Have you had a chance to look around the gift shop? You know, there are things to be purchased here that you can't buy anywhere else in the world." I assured her that each of the students would be permitted time to visit the gift shop prior to boarding our bus.

Our students were nervous, too. Their nervousness resulted in a quiet, enthusiastic respect as the former first lady stepped into the California sun. Each of the three grades, about 35 students apiece, posed with Mrs. Reagan at the center of each photograph. As she graciously approached each group, she was met by smiles and individual hellos or hi's; she then posed for photos with the teachers and me.

When student leaders presented her with a jar of jelly beans for her husband and a St. Thomas sweatshirt for her, she graciously unfolded the shirt and held it up to her shoulders, overlaying it across her red suit so we could capture a classic photo. Known for her taste and style as first lady, Mrs. Reagan with a sweatshirt draped across her was a somewhat incongruous image, and the picture quickly became a favorite of mine. I took great pleasure in captioning that photo, "Still the first lady of style" in the St. Thomas newsletter that we sent out to alumni and friends.

It gave me joy to see our students greeting America's former First Lady knowing that when they returned home, their immigrant and first-generation American parents would take such pride in the fact that their children had experienced something that they could never have imagined happening when they entered this country or as they themselves were growing up.

As I thanked Mrs. Reagan for her hospitality, I mentioned that I had read that President Reagan still went to his suite of offices each day in Century City. She nodded.

"Do you think it would be possible for me to contact Libby around Thanksgiving so that our choir could visit him and perhaps sing some Christmas carols?" I inquired.

"That would be lovely," she said, smiling, as she was escorted by her aide and Secret Service contingency to a Town Car parked a few yards away.

Several months later our own small motorcade of cars headed straight down Pico Boulevard on our way to Century City. We were on our way to perform a short Christmas concert for former President Ronald Reagan. I knew exactly where his office building was located since it also had been part of my Hollywood tour guide route. Bruce Willis had filmed much of the final *Die Hard* movie in that distinctive Century City tower. This would be my first and only visit to the site. I was leading the motorcade of cars driven by music teachers Margarita Kleinman and Joe Neeb, and one of the student's grandfathers.

Upon arriving at the building, we had to first go through an ID check. Our small choir was made up of students in kindergarten through eighth grade. Students were dressed in various shades of red and green. None of them had ever been to a luxury office building before. As we boarded the elevator to take us to the penthouse suite of offices on the 34th floor, there was a collective chorus of oohs and aahs as the elevator lifted us off the ground and raced to the top. We were greeted by an aide and escorted to the room where the concert would take place. While we were setting up, some guests of the former president entered the room and we all introduced ourselves. The guests sat in four of the five chairs that were set up, leaving one for the former president. On the walls were photos of President Reagan that had been taken in the room we were in. There were photos of him and Mother Teresa, Margaret Thatcher, and Billy Graham, among others.

Once our singers and musicians were ready to go, a door opened and in walked a tall, handsome, and most of all, virile-looking Ronald Reagan, along with several aides. An aide escorted Mr. Reagan to each guest and loudly introduced that person to him. He wore a hearing aide, but the aide still spoke with intensity. It quickly became evident that Alzheimer's was taking its toll on the man. When one of the guests asked, smiling, "Do you remember me, Mr. President?" Mr. Reagan positioned himself to study the face in front of him and said, "No, I'm sorry, I don't."

As an aide once again explained that the gentleman had been an ambassador while Mr. Reagan was president, the former president's reply was something like, "Yes, I was president of the United States," as if he were answering a question.

Upon witnessing this exchange, I was both surprised and grateful at the same time. I was surprised that Nancy was allowing anyone to see her Ronnie in this condition. On the other hand, I understood that it certainly did not hurt him to have company and was so grateful that our students, too nervous and young to fully realize what was happening, were able to have such a moment as this in their lives. It was somewhat surreal to witness these youngsters from the inner-city of Los Angeles standing, ready to perform Christmas songs for one of the most beloved presidents in modern day history, and yet neither the students nor the man himself realized that the Ronald Reagan revered by millions was not truly in the room with us.

After two songs by the choir, the tiniest member of the school, a kindergartener name Natalie, had been instructed to walk up to President Reagan's chair and present him with a St. Thomas sweatshirt of his own. She had also been told that after she presented the gift to Mr. Reagan, Miss Margarita, the music teacher, would play "Santa Claus Is Coming to Town" on the guitar and that she, Natalie, would sing a solo to the president.

On cue, Natalie approached the Gipper. Sitting in his chair, he unfolded the sweatshirt, which read, St. Thomas the Apostle School...*Simply the best...No Doubting About It*, in reference to the doubting apostle, Thomas. Although the big man sitting in front of Natalie attempted to read aloud what the shirt said, he could not complete it. She helped him.

Natalie followed our instructions to the tee. While her tiny voice sang the lyrics, she looked straight into the president's eyes. At one point, his gaze became transfixed on this little doll-like creature, who was serenading him. They stared into each other's eyes for the duration of the song. Toward the end of the song he began to softly sing along. He looked at her as though he knew her, or perhaps it was the lyrics that captured his attention. When she finished, it was surprising that he remembered her name, as he gently said, "Thank you, Natalie." When the concert was finished, an aide escorted him over to the choir and he posed with us for several pictures.

"Weren't they wonderful sir?" a female aide asked him loudly.

"Yes they were; they were all wonderful."

"They have to leave now, so say goodbye to them," she directed.

"Goodbye everyone. Thank you for coming." And then he searched for the smallest member of the choir dressed in her red velvet dress with a large bow. "Goodbye, Natalie," he waved.

Although brief, it was a moment of victory in his battle with Alzheimer's. He fought back long enough to remember the name of a little girl who sang him a song that must have restored memories of Christmases gone by. It occurred to me while patting Natalie's head on the way to the car, that she had helped the Gipper win one for himself. And the Gipper had provided for the few of us fortunate to be in that room a Christmas memory of a lifetime.

Nancy Reagan with students

Natalie singing for "The Gipper"

Chapter 9. Upside Downtown

The third Thursday of December was always a big night in our little village of St. Thomas and Pico-Union. It was the night of the annual Christmas program.

For several years we held the traditional Catholic school Christmas program in our auditorium. Although the space was quite charming, it could not hold all the parents and friends who wanted to attend, not to mention the students. Therefore, one by one, each grade would take to the stage to sing a song, recite a poem, or express their wishes for peace and good will to all before going back to their classrooms to patiently (or otherwise) wait for the program to be over.

I'll admit, although the shows were always precious, I got bored with them and knew we could do better. After all, I was a frustrated writer and actor and thought I should put in more effort. So in 1994, I decided to start writing and directing our Christmas shows. If we used the church for the performance, we could involve every student in the school in telling one story. Since we were inner-city, I thought we could be edgier and more interesting with some of our storylines. Telling the story of the birth of Christ is nice, but there are other, more modern ways to talk about the love of Christ and the reason for his birth.

Joe Neeb and I were friends prior to his working as the eighth-grade teacher at St. Thomas. Eventually, when we began the first inner-city development office in the archdiocese, Joe became the school's first development director. The two of us began a tradition of writing the annual show together. Each year on the day after Thanksgiving, I would drive to Joe's apartment in Van Nuys. We would drink a bottle of wine or have some beers and write the Christmas program. In other words, first we'd get hammered, then we'd put pen to paper. We usually came up with ideas that afforded us a great amount of laughter, but we'd always finish the night with a full script of story and songs. *(WARNING: This method is not advised for amateur Catholic school playwrights. Do not attempt this in your own diocese!)*

Although inebriated, we always had clear goals. We set out to write something that would involve every child in the school. We wanted it to be 90 minutes or less. We wanted the show to have a modern message, one that people in Pico-Union could easily relate to. Finally, we aimed for our audience to be inspired while they laughed, cried, and finally sang along with a full heart, placing each individual on a path to his or her own personal celebration of Christmas.

Each scene of a show would typically include the students from a particular grade. The scene would first involve several members of the grade engaging in dialogue, and would then conclude with the entire grade singing a song related to their scene.

My favorite and most memorable year was 1997. We announced to the audience that instead of the show taking place in Bethlehem, the setting would be a strange, far-away land called *Upside Downtown.*

In September of 1997 I took my first overseas trip. As a boy, I'd heard about the giant clock in London called Big Ben, and had put London at the top of my "travels abroad" list. I planned my trip for the first week of September. The Saturday prior to my departure, I turned on the TV and found every channel reporting the news of the death of Princess Diana.

It was an interesting time to be in London. My first night, I had tickets to see the show *Blood Brothers* in London's West End. It was just days after Princess Diana's death, and only hours before the funeral. As the entire world mourned, the city of London was suffering a collective grief. Diana's actions on the world's stage were so profound that her sudden death seemed to turn London upside down.

Blood Brothers is about the death of two brothers, each at the hand of the other. The story begins and ends with the haunting number, "Tell Me It's Not True," sung by the character of the boys' mother:

> *Tell me it's not true,*
> *Say it's just a story,*
> *Something on the news*
> *Tell me it's not true,*
> *Though it's here before me,*
> *Say it's just a dream,*
> *Say it's just a scene*
> *From an old-time movie of years ago,*
> *From an old-time movie of Marilyn Monroe.*

As the mother in the show sings the number, the entire cast joins in. For those locals who were in this show, I'm sure it was overwhelmingly sad for them to be in this show about death while their entire nation mourned the death of their self-proclaimed Queen of People's Hearts. During the singing of that number, the cast seemed to be grieving onstage. It cast a pall over the audience, probably like no previous performances had, because the lyrics were such a parallel to what people were feeling in the aftermath of Diana's sudden death.

Thankfully, the showstopper just prior to intermission was a joyful number called "Bright New Day." This was somewhat of a surreal experience for me. Here I was, vacationing alone in a foreign land surrounded by grief. I had only been in London for a few hours when I joined this audience for a show that began and ended with a death scene.

By the time "Bright New Day" was sung, I was relieved. Permission to be joyful was granted by the cast as they sang and danced us into intermission. Wow! How grateful I was for that song. Instead of endlessly humming

"Tell Me It's Not True," I left the theatre that evening with "Bright New Day" in my head.

Back at home a few months later, as the day after Thanksgiving approached, I knew I had to find a way to work that number into our Christmas show. As the wheels turned in both Joe's and my heads, we eventually tailored the show around the song.

> *Oh bright new day, we're movin'*
> *away*
> *We're startin' all over again.*
> *Oh bright new day, we're going*
> *away*
> *Where nobody knows of our*
> *name*
> *Where we can begin again,*
> *Feel we can win and then*
> *Live just like livin' should be.*
> *Got a new situation, a new*
> *destination, and no reputation*
> *following me.*

We discovered that simply by substituting *On Christmas Day* for *Oh bright new day*, the vast majority of the lyrics worked. We decided to build the whole story around the song.

Why would someone be so glad to move from their town?

Why would someone want to begin somewhere new?

Prejudice! Our theme would be about recognizing and overcoming prejudice.

And so, *Upside Downtown* was born. It was a town where everything we know is reversed. Babies were born fully grown. As they grew older, they would grow smaller. The older you became, the smaller you became. Our kindergarten students would be cast as the old folks of the town, the elders who needed canes and had white hair. Our eighth graders were the children of the village. In *Upside*

Downtown, there were no single parents; they simply did not exist. All of the homes had mothers and fathers, and all of the mothers and fathers were small; we cast the third graders to play the parents of the town.

In *Upside Downtown,* life was simple; life was peaceful.

Then one day, a new family moved into town. The new family was unlike any other family in *Upside Downtown.* For one thing, the children, portrayed by our first graders, were small, not big. The mother of the family, portrayed by a taller fifth-grade girl, was big, not small.

The mother had no husband and she was African-American. All of her children were Latino. In *Upside Downtown,* all of the children were the same race as their parents.

Word quickly spread and the town elders, the kindergarteners, became angry and upset that this family, who clearly didn't belong, had moved into their town. They forbade their children to go near this new and unusual family. The single mother and her children were shunned. People would not open their stores to them or allow their children to play with the children from this strange new family.

Without friends, without a community, the children of the new family became very sad and felt quite alone. Their mother became concerned that she'd ever moved her children to such a cruel and mean place. The town viewed this unusual family as being so "upside down" that they simply could not allow themselves to make the family feel welcome in their normal, upstanding, and Christian community. Therefore, the citizens did what misguided Christians sometimes do: they made the new family aware of the disdain and dislike of the citizenry by treating them differently. As the children complained to the mother about the mocking they received at school, the mother understood all too well because she, too, was mistreated by townspeople as she applied for jobs and tried to go about her business.

However, she wanted her children to grow up strong and confident and to love themselves. She encouraged them to continue on and try to ignore the rude remarks and the daily bullying of their much larger peers, played by the eighth graders.

As Christmas Day approaches and none of the stores will permit the mother to shop for Christmas presents for her children, she prays for a solution to her problem. Then, she comes up with an answer. On Christmas Eve, she discovers her children being scorned in the town's square. It is then that she announces, in front of the entire town, her Christmas present to her family.

Music cue: Mother Sings:

On Christmas Day, we're moving away (her children cheer)
We're startin' all over again.
Oh bright new day,
We're going away,
Where nobody knows of our name.
Where we can begin again,
Feel we can win and then
Live just like livin' should be.

Just as it was in *Blood Brothers*, this was also a big, show-stopping number in our show. Professional musicians, donating their time, provided incredible music. Our students spent hours learning choreography to this very complicated number, which featured solos for various townspeople and members of the woman's family. The student actors joyfully sang and danced at the thought of not having to face disrespect any longer. It was a big number, carefully rehearsed, and earned the woman and her 35 children a standing ovation.

The number ends and the woman and her family go home to begin packing. But God has a surprise for this tiny village: He sends messengers in the form of 70 beautiful angels to deliver a message of love and acceptance for all, including those who are different from us. The angels enter, singing "Angels We Have Heard On High;" they are dressed in white and they're wearing wings.

Love. That is the message of God. That is the message of the manger. God so loved the world that He sent His only son! The angels inform the town that to truly celebrate Christmas, they have to find love in their hearts for everyone. How old you are doesn't matter. What color you are doesn't matter. The angels say, "Love matters. This is God's message to all of you. Love your fellow brothers and sisters."

After hearing the message from the angels, the townspeople hope it is not too late. They rush to the home of the single mother and they apologize to the woman and her children and beg them to stay. The family happily agrees to stay and everyone celebrates together by going to the town church to celebrate the birth of Jesus.

When they get to the church, all of the teachers from the town's school are there. The teachers are played by the actual teachers of St. Thomas School, who now enter the church surrounded by loving students and parents, and together they all sing, hundreds of voices as one, "O Holy Night."

If you're thinking, tough issues for an elementary Catholic school Christmas program, you're right. It was designed to be that way. Schools should make people think; we're supposed to make people — young, old, all ages — thirst for truth and justice. This was 1997, more than a decade before the national debate on immigration and how we as a country should deal with illegal immigration. However, that debate had already begun in California. Our neighborhood was a modern-day Ellis Island. Pico-Union was well known for having a mix of Mexican and Central American immigrants — some legal, many not. Many in the audience that night were quite familiar with the issues of prejudice.

Just as "Bright New Day" provided happy relief for me prior to intermission in London's West End, so it did for the audience attending *Upside Downtown* in Pico-Union. Since I'd been at St. Thomas, I'd heard dozens of stories from families who had experienced a "superior attitude" from so many who lived outside the Pico-Union barrio. I knew this play would touch them. But I also had heard some of these same families express their own prejudices, sometimes against people from one country or another, sometimes against women or gays. So I hoped that the play would not only entertain the audience, but would help the audience entertain their own prejudicial thoughts and help them overcome that way of thinking. Every single one of us, no matter who we are, deep in our hearts, feels superior to someone, looks down on something. What better time than Christmas to attempt to replace that prejudicial part of our brain with the spirit of Christ in our heart?

It was Thursday, December 18, 1997. We were in downtown Los Angeles, California, but our minds were in *Upside Downtown*, as we re-learned the message of Bethlehem. That evening in Pico-Union was indeed a holy night. Having this audience, representing many different countries and cultures, laugh together through their tears made this a holy night. Knowing that so many mothers and fathers — and extended family members — were so touched by a message delivered by their own children made this a truly holy night. It was, in fact, the kind of holy night that would have made Princess Diana Spencer, *the queen of people's hearts*, feel right at home.

A packed house for the St. Thomas Christmas program

Chapter 10.
Northern Nights and Lights of Alaska

Although I was raised Catholic and went to Catholic elementary and high school, I had never experienced a retreat until my first year as principal at St. Thomas the Apostle School. So when Father Dennis looked at my proposed calendar for that first school year and questioned, "Where is the day of retreat for the faculty?" I was too embarrassed to admit I had no idea what he was talking about.

I replied that I would add something to the calendar later in the year. He seemed satisfied with that answer, which both pleased and puzzled me. It pleased me to know I would have some time to do my research and put on the best darn retreat I could. Yet it also puzzled me since it obviously was something he cared about enough to notice and point out, but not to pin down.

I'm always somewhat amazed at how life has a way of opening doors for us just when we need them to open. Only a few months after the "when's the faculty retreat?" conversation, I received a telephone call from my friend Heather. Pretty much out of the blue, she invited me to attend a Cursillo. "What's a Cursillo?" I asked.

"Well, it's like a retreat, but it's not a retreat."

Ah, she used the word retreat. My ears perked up.

"It's something that you have to be invited to by someone who has already attended one. My brother, the priest, invited me to attend. Now I'm inviting you. It takes place over a long weekend, beginning on a Thursday night and ending on Sunday afternoon," Heather continued.

"Sounds like a long time," I said, pretty much convinced that I wouldn't go; it seemed way too long. "What goes on during all that time?"

"I don't know how to describe it, but it can be life-changing. Really. I know that sounds bizarre, but you just need to go and experience it."

"Well, let me think about it, I'll let you know," I responded.

"The next one is next weekend, and they only have them every six months or so," she said, somewhat insistently. "I really think you should go; it's quite amazing."

The following Thursday, Heather was driving me from my apartment in Hollywood to the northern tip of the San Fernando Valley; at that time of my life, I felt as if we were traveling to another state. After checking me in to my dormitory, Heather announced cheerily, "Okay, I'll see you Sunday. Good luck!"

I hadn't realized that I'd need luck, nor had I realized that she'd quickly take off and leave me on my own. The only thing I did realize was that I had no idea what to expect. And Heather was certainly right about the Cursillo being hard to describe. But I'll say what I can. There were about 30 of us, all male, with all male leaders who cooked for us, washed dishes for us, and led the weekend for us. I learned to trust and admire a priest named Father Enrique Parisi, who was there for much of the retreat. I met some other very interesting people, prayed a lot, talked about my spiritual path a lot, listened to talks, and celebrated Mass several times. By Sunday, I realized two things: first, I was having a profoundly spiritual experience; second, I'd been sufficiently inspired that I knew I could plan a splendid retreat for my faculty and staff. I got to work on it immediately.

I adapted several of the activities from the Cursillo to use on our retreat. I even invited Father Enrique, from the Cursillo, to give a talk at our retreat and to offer Mass.

Father Dennis attended and seemed very pleased. I don't think he had a clue that this was the first retreat I'd ever planned and only the second one I'd ever attended.

A memory that is clear as bottled water: shortly after we enjoyed our lunch, I noticed people looking at their watches. In Los Angeles, almost everyone who drives is preoccupied by wondering about the traffic conditions on whatever freeway they will need to take within the next several hours. At that point I knew that most people at the retreat were now likely somewhere else, at least in their heads, worrying about the time it would take them to get to wherever they were going next. The only thing that could improve this situation would be if the participants had nowhere else to be. I could see that if done well, future retreats for our faculty and staff also could be transforming, both personally and professionally.

Bam! An idea was born that transformed St. Thomas the Apostle School and, later, St. Genevieve High School, when I brought the idea with me there. I decided to model future retreats even more like the Cursillo. I realized that what really seemed to work was the commitment — the commitment of our time, the commitment to being in the same place, the commitment to growing together spiritually. I immediately began planning next year's retreat. It would be a personal and group journey of the spirit. For people who work and minister together to commit to growing together spiritually could only bring about positive results.

The following year, I planned for the first overnight retreat for the faculty and staff of St. Thomas the Apostle School. Although there were only 15 of us, it was a diverse group of people with even more diverse personalities. At our school, just like at most schools across the country, teachers are accustomed to being the boss in their classrooms. Bring two or more together, and often there is conflict. Our small staff certainly had its share of drama. Some staff members disliked other staff members; they gossiped about one another and sometimes it became just petty and mean. There were those who would gather near their cars in the parking lot and kvetch about the other members of the staff. I will shamefully admit that sometimes I joined in. I could chalk it up to human nature, but it is simply human weakness.

Big Bear, California was the destination of our retreat. Only a two-hour drive from downtown Los Angeles and nestled in the San Bernardino Mountains, Big Bear was beautiful, not too far from home, but far enough so that no one could easily make it home for the night.

People often wondered how a poor, inner-city Catholic school could come up with funds for such luxurious-sounding excursions. I had to laugh; if only they knew the details, they would more likely marvel at our creativity than envy some imagined "luxury" trip. For example, this first retreat of ours to Big Bear had 14 of us driving together in the parish van; that's certainly one way for bonding to take place. But not only were there 14 people, there were also 14-plus overnight bags, sleeping bags, a guitar or two and several grocery bags filled with snacks. Father Dennis was lucky or smart enough to point out that the maximum number of occupants in the van was 14, so he quickly decided to drive up on his own. The rest of us met early in the morning and packed ourselves into the van like sardines. When we made a pit stop, we literally had to unpack at least one-third of all our stuff in order for everyone to get out of the van.

We also hadn't realized that the nuns who operated this beautiful retreat center were militant about cleaning and keeping the place neat at all times. When we were joined by two of them for our evening Mass, we were immediately handed the vacuum cleaner before Mass to clean up after ourselves. At one point, several of us balled up masking tape to help get the finer dirt, which the vacuum had failed to pick up. Many of those washing dishes following our meal were almost brought to tears due to the number of times they were asked to rewash the pots, pans, and plates. They chose laughter instead of tears. One of the unexpected outcomes that resulted from the high level of cleanliness we were required to maintain was that the militant nuns became an outside force that actually helped to unite us. Late that night, when the nuns were asleep in their own cabin, we stayed up and laughed as we shared our own personal stories.

Our accommodations for the night were his and her cabins with bunk beds and a separate bath and shower room. It was somewhat like camping. Everyone wanted to stay up late and tell ghost stories, and in the morning, even the ladies were laughing about one of the more refined teachers opening the door to the cool March mountain evening to "stick her butt out the door to fart."

Yes, we did have some very spiritual moments, but the most important thing that happened on that first overnight retreat was the human bonding of people while cooking, cleaning, driving, primping, and yes…even farting together.

I'm not going to say that when we got back to L.A. that all the gossiping stopped and we all liked one another. I will say, however, that the amount of gossip seemed to diminish while the level of respect and caring for one another grew. Most important, a tradition was born that allowed us to become uniquely united.

After each year's retreat, the camaraderie among the faculty and staff became increasingly evident. By the sixth annual overnight retreat, there had been a palpable shift in everyone's overall attitude and spirit. That year was our second time in Rosarito, Mexico. By then, our retreats had extended into three days and two nights. On the first night, late, around midnight, someone in the group suggested that we finish an activity that we'd begun but hadn't had time to complete earlier that day. Each of us had been asked to bring four or five items that were meaningful to us. We all placed our items in a paper bag. The challenge was to go around the room, look into each bag and identify who the items belonged to based upon our knowledge of that person. We had discovered who each bag belonged to, but there were still questions about why some people identified with certain items. We had begun the process of each person explaining our items to the group, but eventually had to stop to make time for lunch and the remaining activities of the day.

It struck me as a milestone moment when every person in the room agreed to stay up well past midnight to continue what in reality was a very personal and spiritual exercise. This would not have happened in the past, when at least one person, if not more, would have balked, or made a negative comment or facial gesture to show disapproval. Instead, there was now an immediate and unanimous decision to continue the activity. It definitely said to me that we had turned a corner of some kind.

It was midnight in Mexico. Many in our group had made sacrifices to be there by leaving behind spouses, girlfriends or boyfriends, second jobs and children; one teacher left behind a newborn, another had missed a Master's program class to be there. As I looked around the room witnessing the ease of conversation, listening to the familiar laughs and giggles of my colleagues, I knew I was not the only one in the room who sensed a strong feeling of family. It reminded me of so many Christmas eves staying up late with my own family sharing memories or watching movies, and enjoying just being together. We knew that this, like so many other moments we had experienced on our retreats, was a mountaintop moment that we would remember for the rest of our lives. Another big payoff was the improved environment we each got to share back in Pico-Union. We knew that what we had created was special and we truly appreciated the teamwork that went into making excellent education possible.

During all of our retreats, Father Dennis would regale us with stories of the six years he'd spent in Ketchikan, Alaska, where he'd served as pastor prior to coming to St. Thomas. Although he adored our Pico-Union community, he loved to tell the tales of fishing late in the evening under the sunlit summer skies of Alaska. He convinced me as well as others that Alaska was the most beautiful place on earth. He was an outdoorsman. He talked about hiking and watching the bears swimming during the early spring after their months of hibernation. He described their delight in standing in the shallow waters, grabbing and devouring dozens of salmon from the plentiful schools in an attempt to add back the fat needed to survive the next winter's hibernation. Listening to him speak of the crystal clear, freezing cold waters melting from the glaciers evoked an image I had never before associated with Alaska. Dennis loved the state so much that for almost the entire month of July every year, he would invite several of his many nieces and nephews to accompany him back to answer the call of mother Alaska. He was drawn there. And as the years went by, I heard the call as well.

My childhood travel experience had been limited. It was always a huge deal for us to make the trek from Jeannette, Pennsylvania to Mayfield Village, Ohio each summer to visit our aunts, uncles, and cousins. It was less than 150 miles and my mother would always make sure she had the car inspected prior to the trip; we'd often pack lunches for what was our big family adventure. I saw an ocean for the first time at the age of 16, thanks to friends who invited me on their family vacation to Myrtle Beach in South Carolina. Just four years prior to becoming principal at St. Thomas, I drove, alone, the 3,000-mile stretch from northern Virginia to southern California. I felt like two different people. There was the Dan who dreamed of warmer climates, big cities, and knowing no one but meeting everyone, and then there was the Dan who feared the loneliness of not knowing anyone, the Dan who broke down and sobbed hard as he said goodbye to his sister the night before his cross-country journey. That trip changed me, helped me become braver, gave me wanderlust. As I took pride in crossing the border from one state to the next, I dreamed about visiting many places in the world; but I never dreamed of visiting Alaska, at least not until I met Father Dennis.

As our spring 1997 retreat to Mexico was winding down, the last few people shared their personal items from their brown paper bags and by doing so, revealed part of their own life journeys. The heightened level of camaraderie and unity we all experienced on this retreat was palpable. I knew that the next place we would journey to together on a staff retreat would be to the great frontier of Alaska. I wasn't sure how or when, but I did know why. The time had simply arrived. We were ready as a staff and as a family. Father Dennis had become much more than simply our parish pastor; he had become a father figure to most of us. And this padre had grown to love our staff as well as the great state of Alaska. It was time to put the two together!

A little more than a year later, the same group from the Mexico retreat was in the air. Juneau was our destination.

Even on this trip of a lifetime, we continued our practice of choosing humble accommodations. There were at least two in a room — Father Dennis being the exception, with a single, of course — and I think 14 of us shared one bathroom at the beautiful Shrine of St. Therese, located on a quiet peninsula on Lynn Canal just outside Juneau. We shopped for each meal and took turns showing off our culinary prowess by cooking almost all our own meals.

For this retreat, we'd waited until April to ensure that the weather would allow us to hike and tour. Our theme was nature vs. nurture, which lent itself to a number of meaningful, sometimes controversial, conversations and debates that began even months before we departed for our 49th state. On the retreat, we were together for six days. We prayed, we ate, we hiked, we ate, we sang, we ate, we toured, we ate, we drank, we ate, we played poker, we ate. Each of us received one credit at the University of Alaska after spending so much time with a land guide from the university. One day in particular we hiked nearly twenty miles. We hiked through some rugged woods where each footstep proved challenging due to the terrain, which was covered with the protruding roots of giant trees. By the time we reached the destined glacier, all of us were able to identify the difference between the dried and sometimes not so dried feces of wolves and bears by identifying the size of the scat and what the animal had digested.

On several evenings, we visited and enjoyed Alaska's famous Red Dog Saloon. One thing about this group: we prayed hard, but we also partied hard. Most of us liked to drink until we were woozy, sing saloon songs, and dance on the chairs…and sometimes even the tabletops. On the nights we stayed home, there were poker games late into the night.

My friend Joe and I whimsically risked our lives by stepping gingerly into a crystal-looking crevasse inside a behemoth block of ice. We joined arms carefully while the tour guide, who warned us that the particular spot on which we were standing could collapse at any second, took our photo. Standing inside the opening of beautiful, light-blue ice for five seconds transported us to another universe.

The chapel at the shrine was ruggedly built with love. The builders knew the chapel would be there for a long time to come and made certain that visitors felt the care they had taken among the many cobblestones. To be here, in Juneau, at this chapel, with this faculty who had become like family, attending Mass with our pastor who was more like a father, was a moment in time that none of us wanted to end.

But end, it had to. On our last night, we decided to stay back at the shrine and simply enjoy our final night together. A bonfire was built outside the lodge where all of us stood around in the cold and constant drizzle. We shared memories of past retreats and memories from the week we'd just spent together. After a while, we all had gotten pretty damp from the slight, but continuous, rain. None of us, however, wanted to be the first to break up this circle. Though soon we were soaking from the rain, we were trying to let every minute soak into our souls. We all seemed to be waiting for someone else to give the signal that it was time to go indoors. As the group grew quiet enough to hear the wood crackling, Joe broke the silence, pointing to the northern sky. "Hey, look you guys," he said.

I didn't know what the shimmering light in the sky was; it moved fast and seemed surreal. "It's the northern lights," said Joe.

We all joined in, simultaneously marveling at the amazing beauty before us. Our murmurs of wonder died down as we continued to stand together, staring at the northern sky. Then, as though someone had turned a switch, the lights went out. There was our signal. It was time to go to in and time to go home.

We did not know it when we'd all agreed to go to Alaska, but that school year would be Father Dennis' last one at St. Thomas the Apostle. He'd found out just weeks earlier that he would be transferred. It made this journey all the more meaningful. Dennis was the man who had helped bring us all together. My guess is that without him, none of us would ever have experienced this holy ground. Father Dennis would be the head of our family for only a few more weeks. Come July, he would travel back to Alaska for his summer vacation. Upon his return to Los Angeles, he would become pastor at another parish.

With Dennis gone from the St. Thomas landscape, for many of us it felt like there was one less bright star lighting our Los Angeles sky.

Here is a photo of my friend Joe Neeb and me standing in a cave in the Mendenhall Glacier in Juneau.

Chapter 11. The Engagement

She was late. "C'mon already," I thought. "It's a job interview on a Saturday afternoon. Traffic can't be that bad. Where in the heck is she? That's it; she's lost any opportunity to work here."

I wasn't even on payroll yet as principal at St. Thomas School. It was May, 1990. I would not get my first paycheck until July. But since seven of the nine teachers needed to be hired for my first year as principal, interviewing potential candidates seemed to be a great investment of my time, paid or not; I somehow knew instinctively that hiring the right teachers would be the single most important thing I would do as principal.

Since I was still working fulltime as a teacher at John C. Fremont High School at 76th and San Pedro in South-Central Los Angeles, it actually was pretty inconvenient for me to then spend most evenings and weekends in Pico-Union getting prepared for the oncoming school year at St. Thomas. For the teacher applicants, however, it could not have been more convenient. They did not have to take time away from current jobs to interview because I would meet them on the evening of their choice, or anytime on Saturday, or even Sunday if that was most convenient for them. I had dozens of people to interview for the seven positions. So, the fact that someone would be late? It was annoying, to say the least. This, of course, was years before we all had cell phones and could call with an explanation.

Finally, Helen Villarreal walked through the door.

"I am so sorry, I mean so, so sorry that I made you wait," she said after our introductions. The first thing I noticed about Helen was her height, most likely 5'11", a tad taller than I. The silk blouse she wore had pronounced stains of perspiration under the arms. She was young, about 25, and pretty, with large glasses that were the style at the time. As she stood awkwardly in the parish office reception area where we met, she held her large purse with both hands and shifted herself from side to side somewhat nervously.

"What happened? You couldn't have hit much traffic on a Saturday," I inquired nonchalantly. Even though she was late, I instantly liked her and didn't want to add to her frayed nerves. Although young and pretty, Helen reminded me of the schoolmarm type. My gut was telling me she could be a good fit, someone who loved teaching, I thought.

"I got lost," she said, embarrassed, even taking one hand from her purse and covering her eyes as the words came from her mouth.

"Lost? Where did you come from?" I laughed, both to set her at ease and because I genuinely thought it was funny.

Dropping her head and covering her eyes while beginning to laugh herself, she said, "Glendale. I know it's only ten miles from here, and to make matters worse, I even drove by here last night so I would know exactly where I was going, but I still got lost." Now, we were both laughing.

"Okay, so you have no sense of direction, I won't hold that against you," I said. "C'mon in and let's chat about things you're good at."

My instincts were right on; Helen was currently a fifth-grade teacher and she loved teaching. I hired her to teach the eighth grade. She turned out to be a loving person and teacher. I've said on numerous occasions that while I was principal of St. Thomas I had the opportunity to work with some of the best people I've ever met in my life. I certainly put Helen in that category. Helen was the type to show her appreciation for every kind gesture anyone showed her. I came to suspect that perhaps people had not always been kind to her over the years, and that when people *were* kind, she was genuinely moved. I was always genuinely moved by her frequent expressions of gratitude.

Over the months and years we worked together, Helen came to confide in me that her health was delicate. She was a severe diabetic and gave herself daily insulin shots. She grew weaker over the years and her routine for maintaining her health became more complicated. There were mornings when Helen simply could not make it to school on time because her routine of measuring her glucose level, injecting insulin, and measuring again caused her to run late. Her tardiness became somewhat irritating to some of the other teachers. We began each day with an outdoor morning assembly for the entire school. Many of the parents would often join us for our morning prayer, flag salute, and morning announcements. It was obvious if a teacher was not standing near his or her class during the assembly. On the mornings that Helen was running late, I assigned a teacher's aide from another class to escort Helen's students to their classroom, or I would do it myself. Some teachers felt as if I had a different set of standards for Helen; they were right, but I could not tell them why.

One day Helen came to see me in my office. "Dan," Helen's eyes immediately filled with tears when she said my name. It appeared to me to be one of those moments that she'd promised herself to be strong, but when the reality of having to say the words out loud hit her, her strength was shattered. "I have to begin dialysis treatments," she managed to say.

She'd kept me out of this part of the loop until now. "What exactly is that?" I asked with some hesitation, not sure I wanted to know.

She squeezed her eyes tightly as she explained that her kidneys were now imperfect and not able to clean the waste from her system. Dialysis is a time-consuming process that she would have to undergo several times each week in order to keep her alive. She went on to explain how she would have to visit a local hospital and sit in a chair for four hours at a time while the dialysis machine removed excess waste and fluid from her blood.

By now, she was crying hard and the words came in bunches between heavy sobs. "I'll still be able to come to work every day, but I may be more tired than usual."

"How long will you have to have these treatments?" I asked, naively.

"Until my surgery." She began to cry harder and louder, holding both hands with tissues over her eyes. I wasn't sure I should ask anything more, but I was in the dark. After a few minutes and after she calmed herself, I asked hesitantly, "Why do you need surgery?"

She seemed to pull herself together. She tossed the damp tissues in the trash, took a deep breath while reaching for more tissues, and explained, "I'm on a list to have a kidney and pancreas transplant."

"Holy smokes, Helen, that's major," I blurted, as if she didn't know.

She smiled and actually giggled, "Yeah, I know."

She talked for the next hour about her health and her feelings; I just listened. Being able to talk about it seemed to help her. By the end of our hour together, she had regained all of her composure and was in a place of apparent acceptance.

From time to time during this period, I had to call in a few other teachers to speak to them about their lack of punctuality. I had a double standard and they knew it. I didn't care. Helen was suffering and I was not about to add a heaping dose of stress to what had to be an already stressed young life.

One afternoon Helen and I were in the tiny faculty lounge together after school. I was taking a few minutes to relax away from my office and she was getting some butcher paper for an upcoming art project. Rather abruptly, Helen looked up and down the hallway as if to see if anyone was coming, then closed the door to the faculty lounge. With a coy smile she announced, "Dan, I'm dating somebody."

With delight in my eyes I leaned toward her and said, "R E A L L Y?" drawing out the pronunciation to sound more like five syllables instead of two. I truly was delighted. I had never known Helen to date anyone and she certainly seemed happy.

"His name is Chris and he's a really sweet man I met about a month ago," she explained as she slid into the chair across from me.

"Where did you meet this Mr. Chris character?" I teased.

Hesitation. She was embarrassed, casting her eyes down at the table and making me wish I hadn't asked.

"It's none of my business; you don't have to tell me a thing," I quickly volunteered.

"No, it's okay," she said shyly. "I met him through a dating service."

"Helen, that's great, why do you seem embarrassed?"

"It's just that a lot of people think you're desperate to have to go to a dating service."

"Who cares what other people think? You met someone you like and he likes you and that's all that matters."

I knew Chris had to be a special guy because Helen was so special. Plus, knowing that she was in delicate health made him even more special in my book. I liked him before I ever met him. When I did meet him I found him to be shy. He was tall, like Helen, and a very nice-looking fellow. He had been raised by immigrant parents, who, Helen informed me, were rather controlling. I don't think they liked the idea of their son dating anyone; they were quite happy having him living with them on the west side of Los Angeles. However, it was obvious from our first meeting that he paid a lot of attention to Helen. He appeared smitten.

During that school year, our annual retreat was to Juneau Alaska. We were a long way from home and I was hoping Helen would find some respite from thinking about her health problems. Instead, the trip caused her to become emotional. For one thing, she wasn't able to participate in several of the activities, like the day-long hike to a glacier, which served to remind her of her failing health. Then there was the spiritual aspect of the retreat, which we all experienced as emotional, but was particularly so for Helen. The conversations we shared with one another on that retreat seemed to go deeper and were more personal than they'd been on any prior retreat. One evening, when all of us had gathered around the fire, Helen decided to reveal to the group the details about her health. Most of the people in the room were stunned. Although by then we all knew she was a diabetic, most people had no idea of the extent to which the disease had ravaged Helen's body. There was a group outpouring of understanding, empathy, and support. I myself was the recipient of more than one understanding glance now that it made sense to the rest of the staff as to why I had allowed Helen to be late to school on so many occasions. So not only was it a moment that provided Helen with relief, it also provided understanding among all our colleagues…and, most important, it was a moment that actually contributed to later helping to save Helen's life.

Months after the retreat, Joe Neeb, our development director, and I were attending a workshop in Long Beach. Normally, I would be aware of when Helen was going to be late and would watch for her arrival. On this morning, however, our vice principal, Vince O'Donoghue, who was also a fulltime teacher, was teaching his class, so was not looking out for Helen. But Joe Walsh, the kindergarten teacher, who had a bird's eye view of the parking lot from his classroom, noticed that not only did Helen not make it in for morning announcements, she still hadn't arrived as the school day was beginning. Joe sent word up to the vice principal's classroom. Vince found someone to cover his class and called Helen's apartment. When there was no answer, Vince drove over to her apartment. Because we were a close-knit staff, we all knew where one another lived. When no one answered her apartment door, Vince called school to check whether she had arrived. She hadn't. Vince then tracked down the apartment manager and together they entered Helen's apartment only to find her in bed, unconscious.

Immediately they called 911. As the emergency personnel were making their way through early morning Los Angeles traffic, the 911 operator instructed Vince on how to keep Helen alive. It had been determined that she was in a hypoglycemic coma. She was gurgling and had a clenched jaw, and the 911 operator told Vince how to unlock her jaw and make certain her airway was clear. Still following instructions, Vince then checked Helen's pulse and propped her up in a sitting position to help her from choking on her own saliva.

The paramedics confirmed that had Vince not arrived when he did and followed the 911 operator's instructions, Helen would very likely have died. Helen was swiftly transported to a hospital just a few miles away from her apartment.

Within minutes of receiving a call from Vince, Joe and I were on the road from Long Beach to be with Helen at her bedside in the hospital. It took us almost an hour to get there. These days, it is hard to imagine life before cell phones, with information and people so accessible. Back then, while we couldn't get instant updates on Helen's condition, at least Joe and I had each other to talk to as we made our way to the hospital. What we mainly discussed was how dangerous it was for Helen to be living alone. We calculated that she and Chris had been dating steadily for almost two years. By now, both of them were in their 30s and Chris was still living with his parents. It made sense that they should get married.

Once at the hospital and seeing Helen alive, looking well, and smiling, I decided to take what so far had been a horrible day for her and turn it into the day she got engaged.

When one of the nurses finished taking Helen's blood pressure, I asked in front of Helen if the nurse could do me a favor. I explained my belief that Helen's beau needed a little push to pop the question. After such a worrisome morning perhaps the nurse could talk one of the doctors into writing a prescription for a proposal of marriage. Joe laughed, and Helen giggled as she unconvincingly said, "No, don't ask that." The nurse immediately said she would see what she could do.

Minutes later the nurse, accompanied by a doctor and another nurse, walked over to our corner of the emergency room, all with big smiles. The doctor, handing a prescription sheet to Helen, said, "I think you should give this prescription to your boyfriend to have it filled for you." The prescription read, "One proposal of marriage."

Helen was released from the hospital and we took her back to her apartment. We told her that we'd stay until Chris arrived, and urged her to give him the prescription, which would give him the nudge he clearly needed to finally propose.

"No, I can't do that to him," Helen said numerous times, with a broad smile. She liked the idea of the proposal, but I think she was hoping she would not have to prod him into making one.

"Helen, Chris is a nice guy, but if you wait for him to ask, you might be waiting a very long time. You can tell him I made you do it…but please, just do it!" I pleaded.

Once Chris arrived, Joe and I excused ourselves to return to work, anxiously awaiting the next round of results in Helen's already memorable day. Helen and I exchanged knowing glances as I closed the apartment door behind me.

The next morning at work, Helen told us that after we'd left, she hadn't been certain whether or not she should even deal with the ridiculous prescription. Finally, she did ask Chris if he would get her prescription filled, and he immediately agreed. After handing him the unfolded prescription, Chris, ever the gentleman, honored her privacy by not even glancing at the piece of paper. Out the door he went, saying he would return shortly from the neighborhood pharmacy. Helen expected that he would eventually look at the paper to discover our little "joke."

Stunned, with a "now what?" feeling overtaking her, she simply waited, hoping he would get to his car and look at the prescription without making an unnecessary trip. That was not to be.

At the pharmacy, Chris handed over the paper to the pharmacist, who quickly looked down at the prescription to determine whether they had the drug in stock. The pharmacist wryly smiled as he handed the paper back and said, "Young man, I think this is for *you* to fill, not me."

Confused, Chris finally read the prescription. When he returned to Helen's apartment, he handed her flowers, saying, "I guess we're getting married, right?"

He was most definitely right. Months later, on January 16, 1999, Helen walked down the aisle of a quaint mission-style church in Santa Barbara. On that January day, Helen and Chris were surrounded by their families, which included all of the teachers and staff from St. Thomas School. I've never seen a happier or more beautiful bride.

Postscript: On November 3, 1999, Helen had a successful kidney and pancreas transplant. On January 16, 2014, Helen and Chris celebrated their 15th wedding anniversary!

Helen and Chris on their wedding day

Chapter 12. A Friend's a Friend Forever

"...For I know the plans I have for you," declares the Lord,
"Plans to prosper you and not to harm you,
Plans to give you hope and a future..."
— Jeremiah 29:11

I'll admit it was silly. Adults in their 20s and 30s performing the teenage roles as the cast of *Grease* before an elementary school audience of parents and students, but that's how we, the faculty and staff of St. Thomas, brought to a close the 1998-1999 school year. Since by now the faculty had more males than females, the roles of Patty Simcox and Jan were interpreted by two very masculine Latino males, the P.E. teacher, Manny, and our third-grade teacher, Raymond, respectively. Both heterosexual, they liked women enough to become one, at least for that weekend in June 1999. The part of Frenchie was played by a most reluctant first-grade teacher; the part of Sonny, the horniest of all the Burger Palace Boys, as portrayed by a future priest, was over-the-top comedy just in the imagining of it.

However sublimely silly it began, it became even more ridiculous by the time the curtain went up for the final performance on Saturday evening, June 12, 1999. It was the final show in our series of three; instead of a traditional farewell celebration for me, I had requested that the faculty and staff join me in this most unlikely way of saying goodbye. After nine years as principal of St. Thomas School, nine of the best years of my life, it was time for a new challenge. Little did I realize that this silly endeavor would end up being an experience that would make our tight little faculty and staff, which already shared a lot of love for one another, even tighter than before.

I had made up my mind during the summer of 1998 that I would be principal of St. Thomas the Apostle for one more year. I have a bit of a gypsy spirit inside me. For instance, during my first year in L.A., I lived at three different addresses and worked at five different jobs. Even when I moved into an apartment where I'd live for years at a time, I never put nails in the wall and often didn't completely unpack. The fact that I'd stayed at St. Thomas for nine years was hard for me to believe. There even was a part of me that could have stayed for many more years. However, there was Vince, my trusted friend and eighth-grade teacher at St. Thomas, who also served as vice principal there. He was itching to become a principal and, in my mind, he was the perfect person to take over when I left. I had spent a lot of time mentoring Vince and was nervous that he might leave if I didn't. I felt that it would be good for the school to have new leadership, and good for me to find a new challenge. I decided to resign. Father Dennis had already left and there was a new sheriff in town. His name was Jarlath Cunnane. Jarlath trusted my judgment about Vince and we announced early in the school term that this would my last year and that Vince would be taking over as principal. We did this to give people plenty of time to adjust and for the two of us to openly make a smooth transition. At the time of the announcement, I felt quite confident in my decision and just as confident that I would find a new challenge that would be stimulating for me.

Shortly after moving to Los Angeles, I was in Santa Monica one day and passed a beautiful and ornate Catholic church that on first glance reminded me of my home church, Sacred Heart, in Jeannette, Pennsylvania. Although I had not been to Catholic Mass on a regular basis, I was a bit homesick for Jeannette so I parked and went inside to light a candle and have a quick prayer. I liked the feel of the church and was back there the following Sunday for Mass. At the time, I was still living in Venice Beach with my friend Jim, so the trek to St. Monica's was an easy one. The Mass was so different from what I had been used to in Jeannette. It was lively and joyful. The feeling reminded me much more of my experiences at Grace Church in Jeannette; it appeared to me that people really wanted to be there. There was no race to the parking lot before the Mass ended. I felt welcome and at home.

Over the years as I moved from Venice to Beverly Hills, Beverly Hills to Miracle Mile, Miracle Mile to Hollywood, Hollywood to Glendale, Glendale to Sylmar, I continued to go back to St. Monica. With each move, as I literally moved further and further from St. Monica, I attended Mass at dozens of other parishes, but only one other provided me with the same sense of welcome and inspiration: St. Agatha in midtown Los Angeles. Once I became a leader in the church by being a Catholic school principal, I felt it was important for me to maintain my attendance at church. However, those were the only two that I considered "my" church. In fact, I would rather not attend Mass than go to a church where I left feeling unfed spiritually.

Monsignor Lloyd Torgerson became the pastor of St. Monica in the late 1980s. His associate pastor was Father Ken Deasy. The experience of attending Mass at St. Monica during this period was what I considered to be a master class in spirituality. Lloyd and Ken remain two of the best teachers I have ever had the privilege of experiencing. Lloyd was the elder statesman, with a way of pulling you in to his oratory. I've often sat and analyzed what it is about the monsignor that captivates me. What makes me now, 25 years later, drive the 35 mile one way to St. Monica Church? It's his delivery. His delivery is always passionate. His voice and his presence are simultaneously commanding and inviting.

Ken was Lloyd's opposite in terms of personality. He was the motorcycle-riding priest with some hippie-like tendencies — sandals, long hair — and he took delight in making fun of the trappings of the church. It was Ken who, for the first time in my life, made Christ human to me. Ken's sermons were a bit more laid back and often involved props, ranging from a puppet to a straight jacket. I remember being so struck by a homily Ken gave on the gospel of Jesus multiplying the bread and fish for the massive crowd when they grew hungry. He gently nudged the congregation to think in terms of the miracle that day as having come from the people in the crowd.

"Imagine that perhaps, just perhaps, the miracle that day was not that Jesus made magic happen and the fish multiplied, but instead, could it have been that the people were so moved by Christ's message that what little food they had, they decided to share with strangers? Perhaps the miracle was that what little food was on hand that day fed everyone because they shared," Ken prodded.

I had never thought of Christ or biblical miracles in that light. In fact, the rather strict Catholic upbringing I had never allowed us to think in directions like that.

Lloyd and Ken were among the wonderful spiritual teachers I was discovering in Los Angeles. I came to admire them both. Eventually, they would come to know me and I formed friendships with both of them. Shortly after I became principal of St. Thomas, Ken was named pastor at St. Agatha, which is how I discovered that diamond of a community.

In the late spring of 1998, Lloyd approached me before Mass one Sunday. He wanted me to come and be principal of St. Monica High School. Not only was I honored, I had actually thought from time to time that a logical next step for me would be to become principal of a high school. In fact, since St. Monica was my parish and only ten blocks from the beach, it seemed to be a wonderful choice for me. I was excited that he was actually approaching me to consider going there. It did concern me that it was so late in the school year, but opportunity knocks when it knocks; it seems we rarely have a choice in the timing.

Father Dennis was presiding at a funeral when I walked into the church. I sat toward the front of the church but off to the side as I joined this little gathering in prayer.

Dennis had announced around Easter, just before our retreat to Alaska, that he was being transferred to another parish. I sat wondering what life would be like for our community, our school — and for me — without him. I had never been at any job longer than a year prior to coming to St. Thomas. By this time, I had been there for eight, all with Dennis as my boss and mentor. I watched him conducting this funeral and found myself starting to miss him already.

There was a homeless couple sitting in the front row of the church, crying. They were regulars at weekday Masses at St. Thomas and had obvious signs of mental illness. Dennis was standing in front of the coffin, close to the family, delivering a eulogy in Spanish. The middle-aged homeless woman, still crying, abruptly stood up, went to the coffin, and placed her head upon it. Dennis kept talking with an eye to where the woman stood. When she pushed aside the cloth that covered the coffin and attempted to lift the lid, Dennis jumped into action. First he asked the family, "*La conoces*?" which means, "Do you know her?" and in unison they quickly shook their heads no. Dennis then grabbed the woman by both of her elbows and took her back to sit beside her husband. He pointed a finger and firmly told her, "Now don't you move from there." She continued her quiet tears for a stranger's death and Dennis went back to his eulogy. These were the moments when I admired him most. Something about him made people obey, but then he could snap right back to where he was before, delivering a heartfelt message to a grieving family.

Not too long after that, I stood in the sacristy with Dennis as he was preparing to go to the gravesite service. I thought about sugar-coating my question, and then decided to just ask for his opinion. "Monsignor Torgerson has invited me to go to St. Monica High School next year to be their principal," I said.

"Uh huh," he responded as if expecting me to say more.

"Well, I'm wondering what you think of the idea."

"I think it's a bad idea, Dan. With me leaving, and then to have the school principal leave...I think it would be bad for the parish and the school to have us both go at the same time. It's your choice, but I hope you stay one more year to help make it a smooth transition," he said rather matter-of-factly.

He used the word "hope" because he knew he could not make me stay. I'd signed a contract my first two years, and from then on, we were on the honor system. For the final seven years we worked together, we never signed a contract. We trusted each other at our word. "Well, then, I guess I'll stay for another year, " I said. I immediately called Lloyd and told him that if he could wait one more year I would be ready, but that it just wasn't good for our parish to lose both the pastor and principal at the same time. I really didn't expect that he would or could wait, and fortunately he found a principal who was a good fit for St. Monica High School.

Loyalty. It was about loyalty for me. Although Dennis had not expected me to last after year one at St. Thomas, he was the one who had given me the shot at being principal. I had knocked on several doors prior to knocking on the door at the St. Thomas rectory. Those earlier experiences weren't pleasant. I would be loyal to the school I loved and to the man I so admired.

When June 1998 arrived and it was time for the parish and school to say goodbye to Father Dennis, the planning leading up to the farewell event had been going on for many weeks. The event itself was an all-day Saturday celebration on the school grounds. Dennis was not only being honored by the school community that loved him, but also by approximately 20 parish organizations and the parishioners themselves. The event was attended by thousands of people coming and going throughout the day. A schedule had been issued announcing the time that each group would make its presentation to Dennis, ranging from original songs penned especially for the occasion to native dances from the various countries represented in the parish.

There was a stage built especially for the occasion as well as a makeshift throne of sorts for our beloved Padre Dennis to sit in while he was being honored. It was a mini-fiesta with various foods representing the largely Central American community. I stopped by in the middle of the day and stayed for several hours. I was there for the presentation made by the school's students and the PTA. I admired Dennis's fortitude in taking in all of the performances while sitting in the sun for hours and being so gracious to so many people. It felt overwhelming to me, but it appeared that he loved every second of it.

I did not expect that my own leaving would arouse such an enormous outpouring of affection or result in such elaborate presentations. Most of the parish did not know me. However, the school's community and I did share a great and mutual affection. I worried that people would plan something formal to express their gratitude and fond wishes. I worried because the type of event where I am at the center makes me very uncomfortable.

The faculty for that final year was the best I had ever worked with. It may sound implausible, but I was so close to the staff that they felt like my brothers and sisters. The new pastor was announced and our first conversation was an overseas call; he was in Ireland, I in Pico-Union. Before the conversation was over we decided that the final faculty retreat I would participate in would be in the old sod of my Nana — we would be off for a week in Ireland. It certainly looked like the new pastor, Father Jarlath, and I were going to get along just fine.

Weeks prior to beginning my final year at St. Thomas, a friend and I were in the air returning from a visit to several European destinations, including the homeland of two of my grandparents, Slovenia. About an hour before landing I turned to my friend and said, "I'm going to talk Helen Reddy into doing a benefit concert for St. Thomas this year."

"And how do you think you're going to pull that off?"

"I'm not sure, but I'm determined."

Ever since I was a kid, I had been a devoted fan of Helen's. One of my first jobs upon arriving in Los Angeles was being a gofer of sorts for Helen's production company. I had met her on numerous occasions and throughout my St. Thomas years I would drop her a note from time to time or even stop by her house to see if I could persuade her into coming to the school to talk to the kids about her native Australia. I never had any luck.

But two months after returning from Europe, on Friday, October 2, 1998, I was onstage introducing Helen Reddy, who headlined a benefit concert for St. Thomas School. It was Father Dennis' first time back at Pico-Union since he'd left. We had full enrollment and the usual waiting list. The level of leadership among the junior high students was better than ever thanks to a program in leadership that the teachers and I had developed and had been named by the students, For Young Improvers (FYI). My final year at St. Thomas was going extremely well.

My personal transition was a bit more challenging. Although I knew I was leaving, what I did not know was where I was going. By February, I became worried, even a bit frightened. Perhaps I should have listened to the people who told me that you don't quit one job before you have another. Approximately four years earlier I had purchased a condominium; I now had a mortgage to pay. On July 1st, I would officially be out of paychecks. I began to actively spread the word that I wanted to be principal of a Catholic high school. Then I would add that I hoped for a school that had some challenges.

In April, I signed the contract to be principal of St. Genevieve High School in Panorama City. It was actually happening. I was leaving St. Thomas. I would have to pull up roots that had become rather firmly planted. I would be going to new soil where all of the other crops were new to me. It was only twenty miles away, but it may as well have been in another world; I didn't know the area and I knew no one there.

But I still had time to savor my last few months at St. Thomas. Our spring musical in 1999 was *Hello, Dolly!* By now, musical theater had become a staple at our school. Each year when the play ended I would say to the faculty, "Why do the kids get to have all the fun? One of these days *we're* going to do the musical instead."

Of course I would never have had us perform instead of the students. However, this was my last year and there would be no other opportunities for us to perform together. *Hello, Dolly!* was staged in mid-April. When I returned home after the final performance, I began making calls to all of the staff members. "Hey, I've got a great idea. Instead of any kind of farewell celebration" — I was already hearing rumors of a planned party — "why don't we all put on a show? Let's do *Grease!*"

We appointed one of the seasoned eighth graders to direct the show and another to choreograph us. We also invited students from various grades to be part of our chorus as well as background players. All but one said yes. None of us realized what we were getting into; learning lines, lyrics, dance steps, and trying to find the time for all of us to rehearse was a bigger chore than any of us had imagined. There was always someone who wasn't able to make a rehearsal. In fact, the first time that the entire cast was on stage together was opening night.

Because many of my fellow cast mates had never been in a play before, some of them began to lament the fact that they had signed on for this extravaganza. Over the years, we had done a couple of short plays for the students as part of the Global Studies geography curriculum we had developed. Each semester the entire school would study a region of the world, which allowed for a great deal of creativity. Usually, we would pair up the grades so that at the end of the trimester the 8th grade and 3rd grade would make a presentation about the region to the school. Some of the older students might write a play or skit depicting aspects of the culture. Twice, I wrote plays that the faculty starred in. They were usually silly pieces for which we could quickly and easily learn our lines. A few rehearsals at lunchtime or before school would suffice. I think some of the teachers were now expecting something more along those lines for *Grease*. Once they received scripts and were expected to arrive at rehearsals prepared, it began to sink in that this was no easy commitment. At one point, there was almost a mutiny. I later found out that the staff had asked Vince, their principal-in-waiting, to hold a secret staff meeting so people could express their displeasure. Vince not only talked the group out of their mutiny, he talked them into making the sacrifice for me, as a gift. My theory is that since Vince had the starring role as Danny Zuko and was possibly as much of a wannabe actor as I was, his talking to the group was just as much a gift to himself as it was to me. The truth is, the show ended up being a gift to us all.

My definition of a leader is having a vision and getting people to follow you to a place they are not sure they ever wanted to go in the first place but are glad to be once they arrive. Even though this visionary production almost came apart, both Vince and I saw something the others did not. In the end, every person expressed gratitude that they had been part of it. In fact, more than 15 years later, it remains an experience that each one of us reminisces about fondly whenever we happen upon one another. Although we were the "teachers," we learned more about each other through this experience, and in the process, we allowed ourselves to discover new aspects of our own selves.

Our friends next door at Loyola High School allowed us to use their theater for our three performances. We performed three sold-out shows for our students, their parents, our personal friends, and our relatives. By the final performance, we had had so much fun that our nerves had disappeared and we accepted the show for what it had become, a fun caricature of *Grease*. When each of us joined the St. Thomas staff throughout the prior nine years, we started out as strangers to one another. By now, we had become much closer to being loving brothers and sisters. We loved one another enough not to insist on the traditional goodbye event, but to actually spend hours upon hours with one another singing and dancing and at times making fools of ourselves. Imagine that — what could have been a sad time was literally spent joyfully...singing, dancing, and joking.

With the nerves of opening night gone, we took a few risks to make the event even more fun. Coach Manny seemed to get a bit carried away while preparing the balloons to simulate the boobs of his portrayal of Patty Simcox; they seemed ready to pop at any moment. His platinum blonde beehive wig seemed even poofier. Jan, played by third-grade teacher Raymond Saborio, actually got up the nerve to plant a big kiss on the cheek of Roger, played by 6'3" Joe Neeb, now the school's development director. Joe was one of the few in the cast who actually had real musical talent. After his rendition of "Mooning," good enough to make any girl — or guy playing a girl — swoon, Raymond, resembling more of an Indian squaw than a 1950's teenager, wearing blood-red lipstick, planted a kiss on Joe's cheek before the final syllable of his song was sung. Joe was pretty uptight at the time; it was asking a lot for a guy like him to be part of this production. Just the look on Joe's face made it "worth the price of admission," as the saying goes. In fact, Joe's reaction made us all break character and laugh right along with our audience. Throughout the night, we made up new lines and attempted to make each other laugh.

The school year had ended the day before. I was too emotional to go outside to see the kids leaving for the final time. When I heard the final bell I began to sob. I watched from the window as the students happily departed for their summer away from schoolwork. I took solace from the fact that that evening, I would be onstage with my colleagues and would see many of these students and their families then. My final bow would literally be my final bow on stage… how cool was that!

Now the final show was over and the cast and crew stood on stage singing "We Go Together." As we sang, I looked up and down the lineup of my castmates. I held so much admiration for these people. Alongside us were many of our students, who had joined us as our director, choreographer, chorus, and crew members. I was grateful to all of them for allowing me to have this much fun while saying goodbye.

As soon as the finale ended, Vince stepped forward symbolically as the new leader and led a brief and moving tribute. After presenting me with a new briefcase from the staff, Helen V, the teacher who came late to her interview in 1990 and who had been there all nine years, sang a duet with Mary Ekler. Mary, who was Helen Reddy's piano player and composer, had become a fixture at St. Thomas ever since I met her following one of Helen's concerts in 1992; we'd immediately clicked. The opening chords were immediately moving and the lyrics so appropriate yet incredibly emotional for me:

> *Packing up the dreams God planted*
> *In the fertile soil of you*
> *Can't believe the hopes He's granted*
> *Means a chapter in your life is through*
> *But we'll keep you close as always*
> *It won't even seem you've gone*
> *'Cause our hearts in big and small ways*

Will keep the love that keeps us
strong.

The one thing I had banked on about *Grease* was that it would be a joyful and happy way to end my stint at St. Thomas. Joy and happiness were the only emotions I wanted to experience because that was how I largely felt during the nine years I'd spent there.

I had never heard the song "Friends Are Friends Forever" before that moment. All it took was for those lines to be sung by these two women and I had an emotional breakdown the likes of which I had not experienced since 1986 on the night before my long cross-country journey alone to California. I was leaving somewhere I knew and was comfortable to go somewhere new and where I knew no one. On my way to California, when I said goodbye to my sister on my final night in northern Virginia, I was overcome without warning by a waterworks that I had not experienced since childhood. It was the kind of crying that becomes uncontrollable and inconsolable. Leaving St. Thomas was similar; it was like saying goodbye to family. As fortune would have it, my sister was in the audience this night, too. Her job had her attending a convention in Los Angeles and she and several friends came to see the show. She knows me better than anyone; how profound it was for me to have her there on this night, as emotional as the one we had shared more than fourteen years earlier.

And friends are friends forever
If the Lord's the Lord of them,
And a friend will not say never
'Cause the welcome will not end.
Though it's hard to let you go
In the Father's hands we know
That a lifetime's not too long
To live as friends.

Why be embarrassed, I thought. These feelings are real, and the letting go actually felt good. I realized that it was so difficult to leave because of the love that I experienced in that school and the community. I realized that the young man who arrived in California in 1986 was gone. I was now a better man made more loving and more lovable by a community into which I had arrived as a selfish stranger. I was parting as a more confident, more giving, and more loving friend, to others as well as myself.

And with the faith and love God's given
Springing from the hope we know
We will pray the joy you live in
Is the strength that now you show.

Lyrics by: Michael W. Smith

Chapter 13. A Stranger Once More

"What have I done?" I wondered as I backed my car out of the short driveway of St. Genevieve High School. It was July 1, 1999, my first day on the new job. The driveway could easily accommodate one car in while another one exited. However, the large Chevy Suburban coming toward me down the center had no intention of moving to the side. I would later come to know the driver as one of the high school students, who, at the time, had no idea the stranger he was bullying into backing his car back out onto the street was the new principal.

"This is a fine welcome," I thought. "Well, Dan, you asked for a challenge, what did you expect, a parade?" I questioned myself as I put my car back into drive to now move forward into the lot to find a parking place.

I was feeling a bit intimidated by my first encounter with a student. I found some solace in the fact that I had my dog Blue with me. Blue was a large, jet-black greyhound-lab mix. He was a bit intimidating at first sight, but it didn't take anyone long to figure out that behind that large body and somewhat menacing stare beat the heart of a puppy.

Blue had been found one day under a car at St. Thomas School. He became my dog and the school's dog on the same day. He came to school with me every day. When I interviewed for the position at St. Genevieve High School, I let the pastor know that it was a two-for-one deal. Now, Blue was eager to check out the new digs. I let him off his leash and he wandered happily beside me in and out of classrooms. Of course since it was summer, regular classes were not in session.

St. Genevieve High School is a parish high school, which is rare. While most Catholic parishes in Los Angeles have elementary schools, only five parishes in the archdiocese currently have both an elementary and a high school. Therefore, when I interviewed for the position at the parish office, I knew how important it would be to have a good relationship with the pastor. As it turned out, St. Genevieve Parish would be getting a new pastor on July 1st as well as a new principal. When I interviewed in April, Monsignor Christian Van Liefde had just been named the new pastor. At the April interview, Monsignor Van Liefde was still serving as pastor at another parish, but he was present for the interview along with numerous others representing the parish and high school. At the interview, the panel members went around the table one by one so that each person had a chance to ask at least one question. Then they asked if I had any questions. I had many, but was given the opportunity to ask just one. "What is the greatest challenge facing St. Genevieve High School?" I asked. Every person had the same response: morale.

"Thank you very much, Mr. Horn," said the archdiocesan representative as he stood to walk me to the door. "We expect to make our decision within the week." I stopped cold in my tracks and turned back to the group. As politely as possible I said, "I have no idea whether or not you folks are seriously considering me for this position. However, if you are, you need to know that I would never accept based upon this interview." I then looked down the table for Monsignor Van Liefde and said specifically to him, "You and I need to talk more. If you think I'm the man for this job, please call me so we can get to know about each other's style to make sure we're a good fit. If I'm not your candidate, I wish you all the best in finding the right person."

The monsignor was a burly man of about 50 at the time, with a thick head of white hair. He wore a smile that seemed to come easily, which indicated to me that he was an easy-going type of person. Two days later I got a call from the monsignor, who said he was just a few blocks away at the archdiocese. Could he stop by St. Thomas to have a brief visit with me? I hesitated for a moment. I was dressed in shorts and a t-shirt, the dog was under my desk chewing on a rawhide, and in a little more than an hour it would be time for us to have a rehearsal for *Grease*. "Why hesitate, "I thought. "This is probably the perfect time for him to come; after all, I did say we needed to get to know each other. This is par for how I operate on a daily basis," I thought. "Sure, come on by," I said.

I was right: easy-going he was. I immediately enjoyed his company and he didn't seem to even notice the way I was dressed, although it was hard to ignore Blue, who always fussed over company and insisted on a few pats on the head before attending to the remainder of his rawhide. Monsignor Chris, as he instructed me to call him, appeared to like dogs.

A few days later on Saturday morning, I visited him in Pico-Rivera at St. Hilary Parish and we went out to breakfast for more conversation. I learned that he had been a high school principal at one point in his career, and although he enjoyed it, he was not interested in running a high school again. He wanted someone who could do the job with little supervision from him. His main love seemed to be his ministry as a fire chaplain. He loved ministering to those who served our fire departments, and he planned to continue that ministry as pastor of St. Genevieve. He had done some research on my work at St. Thomas and was impressed. He was well aware that St. Genevieve High School had some very specific problems, like morale, which also had been causing the enrollment to drop significantly each year. An enrollment that at its peak was more than 1,000 had now plunged to 300, only a few more students than there were at St. Thomas. He made it clear on that Saturday that I was his first choice to be the new principal and offered me the position. I accepted.

I'm a creative problem solver. However, the challenge of dealing with student and staff morale in order to increase enrollment would be new for me. Our enrollment problem at St. Thomas was that there were too many children we had to turn away. Also, because I had the opportunity to hire 90 percent of the staff when I arrived at St. Thomas, those people were largely loyal to me, so staff morale had really not been a problem. As for the students, they accepted me immediately upon my arrival at St. Thomas.

Once I'd accepted the job at St. Genevieve, I quickly began to consider ways to boost morale. I knew we could not stop the bleeding enrollment issue until morale started to improve. If the current students and staff didn't feel good about the school, we would have a difficult time convincing others that they should sign on.

About two weeks later, on April 20, 1999, time stood still for me as I was watching TV and saw the students from Columbine High School, hands over their heads, running in terror away from their school and into the protection of the local sheriff's department. Less than two weeks after that, I stood frozen again in front of my TV one morning, watching a story about the students from Columbine going back to school for the first time since the infamous massacre. Because Columbine High School would need serious repairs and would be under investigation for weeks, the students had to finish the year at their rival school across town, Chatfield High School. And because the two student bodies could not fit into one school at the same time, they did a split shift. Columbine students would come for an afternoon shift after Chatfield students had completed a morning shift.

I was glued to the TV as the camera followed a group of Columbine students from the parking lot through the doors of the school. As you might imagine, many of the students, about to enter a school building for the first time since the day of the shootings, had looks of fear and trepidation on their faces. As they entered the building, however, their countenances seemed to become calm and some of the students even smiled. As the camera panned within the building, viewers could see that the students at Chatfield had prepared their corridors and lockers with expressions of welcome. There were balloons and banners welcoming the Columbine students. Some Chatfield students had written notes on their lockers welcoming their Columbine counterparts to their new school.

I got goose bumps watching the effect that the simple gestures of the Chatfield students had on the Columbine students. "Why do we wait?" I asked myself. It seems as though we save our best selves until a crisis occurs or a part of our world crumbles. It was at that precise moment that the idea was born that would become a cornerstone for a new foundation for St. Genevieve High School. Then and there I set as my goal to transform my new school into becoming a place where everyone inspires and challenges one another to become our very best every single day. Why wait? The media was reporting that Dylan Klebold and Eric Harris, the Columbine killers, had been bullied and had become isolated at their school. We were led to believe that their guns and bombs were the result of feeling alone and isolated. So St. Genevieve would become a school where no student was alone. Every student would have a place at the proverbial table of brotherhood. We would learn the lessons that schools like Columbine were providing for us. In fact, for that first year, we would have a theme to guide us in our journey together: Lessons Learned from Columbine."

For the two months before I assumed the reins of leadership, I pondered the lessons myself. By July 1st, I walked into St. Genevieve High School armed — armed with ideas about how to rejuvenate a school with low enrollment and low morale so successfully that it could become a model for other schools suffering from similar challenges.

For the first several days, I had to concentrate on some emergency issues at hand. There were staff members who had resigned and immediately needed to be replaced, including the school's business manager. There were also several faculty positions that had not yet been filled. Although I had visited the school once and was very briefly introduced to the faculty, I had not grasped the magnitude of just how ugly and needy the school was: dimly lit corridors, mismatched paint, desks too small for many of the students, some teachers' desks falling apart, and many chalkboards so worn it was impossible to read anything written on them. When I sat at my new desk for the first time and opened one of the drawers, it immediately fell apart, dumping the contents onto the floor.

The elementary school principal dropped by to welcome me. I knew her from some graduate courses we had taken together. "Sister Francina, it's good to see you, and it will be good to have you right next door," I said to my smiling acquaintance, who was young and wearing a traditional nun's habit. Hugging me, she said, "It will be nice to have you next door, too." I indicated for her to take a seat on the dingy white couch along the dark paneled wall.

"Dan, I hope you know what you've gotten yourself into," she said seriously, her broad smile having disappeared.

"What do you mean, Sister?"

"This place is in such a mess. Don't get me wrong; I'm glad you're here. But this place has really been let go. In fact, we encourage the eighth graders at our elementary school to go anywhere *but* here for high school. Our kids refer to this place as the 'gang school' or the 'ghetto school.'" She twisted uncomfortably in her seat as I just sat staring, hoping for a punch line. "I think you can change it, Dan," she continued. "I've heard of your work at St. Thomas, and I think you're the right person. But it won't be easy. Just look at this place," she said, pointing toward bookshelves that were leaning to the left and appeared that, without the support of the side wall, would likely collapse.

Sister Francina's was the most positive of the visits and phone calls I received. A cohort of teachers lined up at the door shortly after my arrival to ask questions I was largely unprepared to answer. Which classes would they be teaching? Would the budget allow for certain necessary items they had previously been denied? A creditor dropped by on my second day to yell at me for a long overdue bill, and threatened a lawsuit as he left. Then there was the local columnist who, during the previous year, had written two front-page stories in the *Los Angeles Daily News*, both of which had painted the school in a rather negative light. He was preparing a third installment and grew angry over my unwillingness to comment. The third column appeared a few weeks later; he seemed to have some sort of vendetta against the school. Finally, I found time to meet some of the students. Gangs? Sure, some of the students were a bit rough looking. But, I'd come from a neighborhood with a heavy gang presence and I wasn't seeing any evidence of that here. However, in the months to come, I would hear people outside the school make the same negative references about St. Gen's.

I suppose the pervasive negativity about the school's image was part of the reason I received so much opposition from teachers when I began to make suggestions for easing the school's dress code. The fact is, in reviewing the school's handbook, I'd been disappointed to see such a strict dress code. For instance, boys' hair length had to fall within so many inches. Dyed hair for both genders was strictly forbidden, as were earrings for boys. And that was just the beginning. "Who wants to spend the time monitoring all that nonsense?" I thought. Apparently, there were a number of people who were not only prepared to monitor it; they insisted I leave the dress code as is. "We don't want our boys being mistaken for gang members," argued one who believed a shaved head — also forbidden — could easily be a case for mistaken identity. The vice principal challenged me with, "Dan, can you imagine what the class reaction would be if one of the students walked in one day after dying her hair blue or green, or having symbols designed into his haircut?"

"Sure I can imagine," I said. "The kids aren't used to seeing that, so they'd probably laugh."

"That's right, and it would cause chaos for a teacher," he rebutted."

151

"Right," I agreed. "But that would last about one minute until the novelty wore off and then they could continue with their lesson."

My vice principal remained unconvinced.

For weeks prior to school starting I had numerous arguments with staff members who were convinced that my easing the dress code would be a cause for chaos. Finally, I was tired of the discussions and said that my bottom line was that I was not willing to suspend a student, or worse, for violating some silly aspect of the dress code, like not wearing a shoe that was ALL BLACK. I revised the code myself and ordered it to be put into the handbook.

"We may loosen the dress code for students, but we are going to set the standard for their daily behavior higher than it has ever been," I told frustrated groups of staff members. "My concern is how we treat each other and respect this campus. I could care less if a kid wants to have pink hair."

My conversations about the opening week of school caused an even bigger furor than those about the dress code. As was tradition, the calendar called for the first day of school to be only for freshmen, to conduct their orientation. The following day, the entire school would report and boom, off to the races…business as usual.

Instead, I proposed that on the first day, only the senior class would come. We would spend a half-day talking about the lessons to be learned from Columbine. On the second day, only the juniors would come, on the third day, only the sophomores, and then, on the fourth day, the freshmen, who would be welcomed to their new school by the other students

My goal was to enable quality, small-group discussions. If we used the entire teaching staff and only dealt with one class at a time, we could have one teacher leading a discussion of fewer than ten students. I would write a lesson plan that would have teachers asking open-ended questions, such as, "What do you think caused the Columbine massacre?" We, of course, needed to ask ourselves the obvious question, "Could something like that happen here?" With every school shooting that was happening around the country — from Edinboro, Pennsylvania to Jonesboro, Arkansas to Littleton, Colorado — the faces on our television screens were all teaching us the most important lesson of all: "WE NEVER THOUGHT IT WOULD HAPPEN HERE." Translation: It can happen anywhere.

In my early days at St. Genevieve, I spent a great deal of time just listening to kids tells me about their school. So many had been hurt in one form or another. Some told tales of coaches who had put them down, while others talked about teachers who had made fun of them, or about fellow students who had been bullied by upperclassmen. It was interesting — and disconcerting — for me to witness the same students who talked of being bullied resist my suggestion that they could "do things differently" as upperclassmen themselves. It seems that they had been waiting "their turn" to do to the incoming freshmen exactly what had been done to them...the same things they had hated when *they* were freshman.

The Saturday before school started, I enlisted the assistance of a group of 20 seniors to help me paint. I purchased large pieces of white foam-board, and in pencil I outlined the first name of every freshman in very large letters, one name per board. The seniors' job was to paint the names and decorate the posters. When the freshmen walked through the doors of our school on their first day, I wanted them to see their names in large, colorful print and know that we had been preparing for them. As the seniors began this somewhat arduous task, they instantly started complaining, not knowing I could hear them. "This shit's stupid," said one, to which someone replied, "Yeah, nobody did this for us!" The paint job took about six hours, and as the day progressed, some of the students questioned me as to why we were doing this. It gave me an opportunity to hear more of their stories about how their school had let them down, while giving me the opportunity to talk to them about legacy and leadership. I explained to them that often the legacy one leaves a particular place — a school, for example — is not necessarily something that individual personally benefited from when he or she was part of that place. Toward the end of the day, I heard some of those same complaining seniors saying things like, "I wish someone had done this for us!" That told me that they were recognizing that this would mean something to the freshmen.

In the coming days some of the seniors began approaching me: "You know Mr. Horn, I'm in a band. If you want, my band can play for the freshmen on their first day."

"That's a great idea, let's do it," I would say.

Another suggested, "Mr. Horn, what would you think about the idea of the seniors cooking breakfast for the freshmen?"

"That's such a good idea I wish I'd thought of it! But I'm glad you did...let's do it!"

Before long, the "first day of freshmen" was shaping up to be a grand celebration of welcome. The senior class, the St. Gen's class of 2000, was getting it. In fact, they were getting it far faster than their teachers.

"We know you mean well," said the self-appointed spokesperson for the group of four teachers who were now conferencing with me. "Perhaps you should think about going back to elementary school," she said, laughing, following up quickly with, "I'm just joking."

I wasn't laughing; I knew that she and her group were not joking. They were experienced high school teachers. I had spent the last nine years leading an elementary school.

"You have to understand, all the touchy-feely stuff you're proposing for the first week of school is too much for a high school. We can't have a full week of school without classes, without books," the spokesperson said, her fervor beginning to grow. "Your idea may be nice, but it will put us too far behind in our classes," she said as the other three, who now resembled the toy dogs that used to be in the backs of cars, simply bobbed their heads up and down.

"Well, I'm sorry you don't agree with my plans, but that's the way it's going to be," I responded.

"We are speaking for a large majority of the staff."

"Good, then you can communicate to them that their new principal has plans for the first week of school and I'm not going to change them. Tell them that they'll enjoy this 'new' first week."

Another voice from the crowd of four suggested, "What if we simply held five-minute classes that first week, just long enough for students to meet their teachers and pick up the class syllabus for the year?" The others happily conveyed their agreement with his suggestion, realizing that they were losing this battle.

"It makes no difference whether the students receive the syllabus that first day or not; you'll have the entire year with them. Allow me to have this first week."

"But..."

"Meeting adjourned," I announced.

Unfortunately for me, that was not the last meeting like that I had prior to the beginning of school. I marveled at the idea that everyone thought that to get the school back on a new and positive track of growth we should continue to do everything the "way we've always done it."

Fortunately for me, I had the final word. The first week of school was sure to shake things up. One thing I found to be very empowering was that there had been dire predictions about St. Genevieve and its future, and most people who knew about the school expected it to close. But instead of feeling pressured about that, I felt freed up to try new ideas.

The first day arrived and in came our senior class. I began the day by talking about legacy and eventually led into the discussion of Columbine. Then we broke into the small groups, and students and teachers went into classrooms to have their discussions. The morning ended with students being asked to write letters to several incoming freshman. Their assignment: "Write what you wish a senior would have written to you on your first day." We were teaching empathy. The letters would be written all week long from all of the upperclassmen as well as the teaching staff.

Several days later, when the freshmen finally entered St. Gen's, they received the welcome posters the group of seniors had painted, along with letters from several of the upperclassmen. I still hear from students who were part of that freshmen class, who have kept their posters and letters all these years. We continue the tradition to this day. Each year, we begin school with the seniors and we discuss our school's theme for the year. We end our week with a grand celebration in the tradition of the very first Welcome Freshmen Day held in August 1999.

But back to that very first week…

So many people had mentioned the negative columns that had been written in the *Daily News* and I had a distinct feeling that many students and teachers were somewhat embarrassed by the current state of St. Genevieve High School. I, however, was confident in what we were doing for our first week. It was a way of making the deaths and injuries that had happened at Columbine and other schools to have not been in vain. We were a Catholic school, after all. And being in a position where most people expected us to fail regardless of what we did gave us a sense of freedom and allowed us the opportunity to educate differently. At the same time we were educating for character, we were able to pay homage to those who had died while simply attending school.

So, as the "day of freshmen" approached, the anticipation and excitement was building. I sent out a press release to the local newspapers and television channels:

"Explosion expected at St. Genevieve High School on Friday"

Remember, this was before 9/11. I chose the headline to get the attention of media, which usually like to report on the negative. Now it would be up to them as to whether to cover the day's activities at St. Gen. The idea for the headline came during the first day with seniors. In one classroom, they were discussing the fact that at the shooting in Jonesboro, Arkansas, the young gunmen had someone inside the school pull the fire alarm so that as the students exited for the fire drill, they would become targets for the gunmen, who were hiding in the woods, waiting.

"Wow, that's gnarly," announced one of our seniors after hearing that. Another senior responded, "We should do that on Friday. We should make the freshmen think it's going to be a typical first day of school, and then pull the fire alarm. When they go outside for the drill, we can lead them over to Madonna Hall and when they walk inside we'll have an explosion of welcome."

I couldn't have put it any better myself.

We did just that.

Confused freshmen, wondering why they were having a fire drill on their first day of school, were led by a group of seniors across the campus to Madonna Hall, our parish hall. Once the first freshmen walked through the doors, a live band struck up the music and upperclassman were on their feet all around the hall cheering as the shy and bewildered freshmen were ushered to their seats. Around the room were the creatively decorated posters with the names of each freshman written large enough to be seen from a distance. Imagine the freshmen's surprise upon walking into the room and being greeted by music, art, cheers…and television cameras! Yes, three local TV stations had come to cover this unique event. So did reporters from the *Los Angeles Times* and the *Daily News*. But this time, when the story was on the front page of the *Daily News*, it was *good* news for the community about a school that was on its way back.

After that week, even some of the more negative teachers had to admit that it was a week to remember, a week when a major shift could be felt in the culture at St. Genevieve. Some admitted that the feedback they received from their students was overwhelmingly positive. One commented, "Most of my students today could not believe I was asking them for their opinions on what happened at Columbine. They said at the end, 'we have to do more days like this,' and I agree."

I agreed also. That week was the birth of our school-wide program in character education; we just didn't know it at the time.

After the seniors served breakfast to the freshman, and the atmosphere calmed down a bit, I took the microphone to explain to everyone gathered what the impetus for this day had been. I recalled the Columbine shooting only four months earlier, and challenged students to live the lessons learned from that horrific event. "No one should feel like a stranger in their own school," I said. "We all have a place at the table of St. Genevieve. And by making a place for all at our table, we have an opportunity to leave a legacy of welcome and acceptance at this school. If that is what we are about, we won't have to worry about a shooting happening here. If that is what we are about, people will stop looking down at our school and begin looking up to us because we will have chosen to be our best selves every single day. That is the best way I know how to honor those who died at Columbine."

Each year, as we welcome a new freshmen class to St. Genevieve, the numbers grow bigger, as do the celebrations. Now we are faced with the dilemma of having to turn students away because we simply don't have the room for all who want to come here. Every year, the seniors serve breakfast, and every year we paint the names of the freshmen on foam-board. The freshmen class assembles on the front steps of St. Genevieve Church and proudly holds their names high in the air for their first class picture.

Something we did not do that first year, but has since become a tradition, is the overnight freshman retreat in the gym — the girls' retreat led primarily by the senior girls and, the following weekend, the boys' retreat led primarily by the senior boys. The seniors pass along the lessons of manhood and womanhood from a senior students' point of view, giving talks that we hope will help our freshmen avoid some mistakes along their high-school journey. By now, our seniors have had this experience as freshmen, and they look forward to the opportunity to help lead and guide the incoming freshmen along their way.

Our freshmen come to us from more than 40 different elementary schools. So while many are strangers to one another initially, one of the goals of the retreats is that no one feels like a stranger for very long. The students sleep — or try to sleep! — on the gym floor on those weekend nights of the retreat. There is usually a great amount of fun as well as friend-making. On both weekends, I drop by about midnight to say hello. It is now another tradition that I gather the group before I leave and tell them a chapter from our school family history book. On those nights, I recollect about the days when few people wanted to come to St. Genevieve High School. I tell them about the school's reputation and some of the reality from 1999. Of course, I always tell them about the lessons we learned back then. I want them to know that the St. Genevieve High School they are excited about attending today is largely the result of two key things:

1. The tragedy of Columbine High School and the lessons we learned from it.

2. The legacy left by the St. Genevieve class of 2000, who decided that instead of bullying the incoming strangers, they would make them feel welcome in their new home.

Chapter 14. Playoffs

Although…
1. I grew up in western Pennsylvania when the
    Pittsburgh Steelers were the supreme team of the
    NFL, and…
2. Dan Marino and I both graduated from the University
    of Pittsburgh in 1983, and…
3. Terrell Pryor is from my hometown of Jeannette,
    Pennsylvania…
I am not a football fan.

Truthfully, I've never been able to understand the
game; it's got too many rules. I don't like rules, never have.
In fact, I'm not much of an athlete. I've played some
backyard sports, a little volleyball and a lot of Wiffle ball. The
only organized sport I ever played was Catholic league
basketball when I was in the fourth grade. The policy of the
Catholic league was that any boy who wanted to play, could.
No one was cut, no matter how poorly they played or
inexperienced they were. Most of my friends were going to
play for the league so I foolishly went along. For some
reason, I thought it might be fun to learn to play; I was under
the assumption that some coach would actually teach me.
Little did I realize that all the volunteer coaches expected
that those boys coming to the Jeannette Junior High School
gym every Saturday night would pretty much already know
how to play the game. After all, it was the early '70s in a
small industrial town and most of the boys had been playing
sports from a young age. However, to the best of my
memory, prior to reporting to the first practice that year, I
don't ever remember picking up a basketball, let alone
running and dribbling at the same time. After a couple of
weeks of practicing in front of the volunteer coaches, I was
one of the last to be chosen for the St. Francis team. I could

tell by the look on the coach's face that he wished he could have made cuts. Even then I remember thinking, "Why does he have to be so obvious about his disappointment in picking me?" With both of our heads hanging down as I walked toward his bench, I think we both had the same thought, "Sure wish the league allowed boys to be cut." I certainly would have preferred it.

Not knowing the rules and with little instruction, I was a disaster on the court. Every Saturday night I would get knots in my stomach, hoping Coach would not put me in; he had to…policy. To make matters worse, because all eight teams would play on the same night each week and because it was a small town, the bleachers would get rather full for these games. The only real coaching I ever remember getting was from my sister Mary, who would come to the games with her high-school friends and stand high above the court on a balcony next to but above the bleachers. Each and every time someone would pass me the ball, I could hear her voice yelling louder than any of the others in the packed gym. "Shoot it! S h o o o ot, shoot," she and her friends would bellow. The pressure seemed unbearable at times. However, I lasted the entire season, and thanks to Mary, I scored a total of four points… all for opposing teams.

After that, I never played another organized sport again. Sad thing is, I think I could have become a good athlete. Even as a youngster, I was built like an athlete. But no one ever tried to teach me or coach me or even encourage me. Eventually, as I grew older, I only grew more embarrassed by my lack of knowledge and ability, and so I'd avoid organized sports like a plague.

Prior to becoming principal of St. Genevieve High School, I had taught in Catholic elementary schools, and I had taught in public high schools. However, I had never taught, let alone been an administrator, in a Catholic high school. Therefore, I was not aware of the dynamics that athletics, and in particular, football, play in the life of a Catholic high school. Catholic schools depend on enrollment, and of course tuition, to stay alive. In most Catholic schools, tuition is the largest source of income, providing for teachers' salaries as well as most other operating expenses.

In 1999, St. Genevieve High School was on the verge of shutting down due to declining enrollment. In little more than a decade the enrollment had plunged from more than 1,000 students to around 300. The school was showing the signs of a sinking ship. The plant itself had been neglected and numerous course offerings were no longer available. With the decline in enrollment came a decline in income; therefore, it was only natural that most everything — from academics to athletics to the arts — would suffer.

At the time that I assumed the principalship of this famously failing school, I honestly thought that the simple formula for success that I'd used at St. Thomas the Apostle School would be the same formula for turning around St. Gen's. I would make the school Catholic, *truly* Catholic. My goal would be that every person who entered the St. Genevieve doors would feel something special, a spirit of welcome and of kindness. One definition of Catholic is "universal," yet too often in my own life's experiences, I'd discovered that many people felt shut out or pushed aside by their Catholic school or church experiences. I witnessed a trend among numerous friends who had moved away from the church that had been part of their lives since birth. I had seen many a school where crucifixes hung on the walls of each classroom and religion was taught daily, but, in my opinion, were far from *Catholic*. In many of these schools, you not only felt as if you didn't belong, you felt as if you didn't even exist.

To provide a truly Catholic experience at St. Gen's, I hoped to create an environment in which every person felt a sense of belonging. I wanted to build a Catholic community within the walls of the school building that provided a conducive setting for students to discover their dreams and realize their potential. Looking back at my experience with the Catholic basketball league in fourth grade, I remembered feeling that I wasn't wanted. I never sensed that any adult there cared enough about me personally to take me aside and actually coach me. By the end of that season I didn't know anything more about the game than I knew at the beginning, and I thought far less of myself.

Because of the negative experience I'd had attempting to play organized basketball when I was nine, it would take me decades before I realized that athletics was possibly the most fertile ground on which to sow my own philosophy of Catholic education and community. It was not until I began my career at St. Gen's — my tenth year working as a principal — that it became obvious that with the right people in the right places, young athletes could have the exact opposite experience from the one I had endured. For years, I would not even think about, let alone talk about, my season of humiliation and fear on the court. Now, I was finally realizing that those dads and grandpas who had volunteered to coach on Saturday nights meant no harm; they simply were doing their best. From them I learned that sometimes a coach's best is simply not good enough. Because of that group of dedicated but clueless coaches, St. Genevieve High School almost thirty years later would benefit. I would use the sad experience of a nine-year old boy who suffered a season of Saturday night anxiety attacks, and turn it into an opportunity to hire an athletic director who would find coaches who loved their sport enough to actually coach. I was determined that our coaches would provide our students the experience of being able to proudly represent their school and discover hidden talents within themselves.

St. Genevieve was not attracting the top athletes who would arrive already accomplished in their sport. There were boys trying out for our football team who had never played the game before. Sound familiar? Although I knew very little about the game, I knew instinctively what was needed: the right coaches. We needed coaches who were not about recruiting players, but were, instead, up for the challenge of actually teaching and coaching.

In retrospect, I had never imagined that athletics, the environment in which I felt the most uncomfortable, would play such a pivotal role in saving St. Genevieve High School. Genevieve is a saint known for saving a city from an attack by Attila the Hun and his army. She had saved Paris in the fifth century. The school that bore her name in Panorama City, California at the start of the third millennium was not about to go down without a fight. We would use an army of athletes and coaches to help put us back in contention for enrollment, an improved reputation, and victory.

Although we'd had sports teams at St. Thomas, athletics was not the reason most families chose an elementary school. However, athletics was often a significant consideration in selecting a high school. Not only were athletics important, but football — as I should have known, but didn't — is the marquee sport. The football scores are what make the newspapers. The football games are what have people talking on Monday mornings. It is the record of the football team that both boys and girls often ask about first when we visit eighth-grade classrooms to tell prospective students about our school. Alumni involvement — and their contributions — can be significantly affected by the performance of the football team. As the marquee sport, a good (or bad) football team can bring free publicity, and sometimes not the kind a school wants.

Since there is only a small practice field on our campus, our home games had to be played at a neighboring campus willing to rent us space. Nearby Birmingham High School had a large stadium, which is where our team, the Valiants, would play their home games for the 1999 season.

Although the field lights were on and there were maybe 10 to 20 people meandering about when I walked into the stadium for the first game of the season, I realized that I had made a mistake and instantly felt foolish. I had shown up on the wrong night. I thought for sure I was told that our home games were to be played on Saturdays, since Birmingham High played on Friday nights. Since my arrival in July, I had been so overwhelmed with learning new information and attempting to solve problems that I could not possibly fault myself for screwing up the date of the first football game. I assumed it had either been played the previous evening or perhaps it was not a home game. I began to beat myself up wondering how I could have missed the first football game of the season. I didn't want to have to explain my mistake.

My embarrassment was magnified when I noticed our school's athletic director walking toward me from the direction of the concession stands. How would I explain my mess-up, I wondered.

Wait a minute. Why was *our* school's athletic director at Birmingham High that night? I was so rapidly attempting to make sense of my mishap that at first it had not seemed odd that he too had the wrong place, wrong time.

Happily, I had not missed the first game of the season. Sadly, however, the crowd for our team would not grow much larger than those few already in the stands. I quickly learned that Valiant football games were not the place to be on a Saturday night. This was an image that my brain had a difficult time computing. Although I certainly was not much of a football fan, in my hometown of Jeannette, Pennsylvania, Jayhawk football games were definitely the place to be on Friday nights. Thousands would overflow from the stands. Most merchants on our main street closed their stores early on Friday nights during football season. Not only would they not have much business, most of them wanted to attend the games, too. In fact, we used to have much bigger crowds at my old Catholic league basketball games than this sparse group. I only wish that so few people had attended those Saturday night games when I'd attempted to play basketball. Needless to say, this poor showing for the Valiant opening game was very surprising to me. Soon a bus arrived with fans for our opposing team; we were well outnumbered.

When our team emerged from the locker room, they seemed hopeful and spirited; there had been high energy in their warm-ups. Within the first few minutes of the game, the opposing team scored and the Valiant's energy instantly disappeared. The collective Valiant body language cried, "Here we go again," and we were off to another losing season.

The following Monday I started asking questions about the low attendance at the game. I came to discover that our Valiants held the record for the longest losing streak in our division's history — 0 wins and 37 losses! Much of the school and community had simply stopped supporting the team. The small number of committed boys who played obviously loved the game, regardless of who came to support them. They loved the game enough to press on even though it appeared there were few — very few — who seemed to care about this team. However, when the time came to order letterman jackets, there were several who indicated that they did not necessarily want to advertise which school they played for. But when we won one game that season and our losing streak was broken, it highlighted the fact that a re-birth of sorts was underway at St. Gen's.

By the fall of 2000, with the losing streak behind us, I felt it was time to make some changes in our athletic department. I hired a new athletic director, Marlon Archey, whom I had met during my first summer, and who had now been on staff for a year. Marlon was a fit, affable, African-American man slightly younger than I was at 39, and we'd immediately hit it off. Marlon had played college ball for North Carolina State University and was a sports fanatic. He had previously coached for the school part-time and had stopped by my office after a summer soccer practice. For the first year, he was our admissions director. At the end of our first year at St. Gen's, it became obvious to both of us that he would be an excellent fit for the role of athletic director.

My first year was difficult because the staff was three times as large as the one I'd had at St. Thomas, and I had never been a high-school principal before. I had to spend time learning what everyone did and begin to make assessments as to how well they performed. One of the most difficult things about that first year was not having anyone I knew well enough to trust to go to for opinions or to bounce ideas around with. Over the months, Marlon became one of the people I grew to admire and trust. Since I felt so inept at dealing with athletics, I felt that Marlon would be the perfect choice to assume those duties.

The head football coach announced his resignation for the following year. He was a full-time physical-education teacher and I had decided to revamp the phys-ed program in order to allow every student to have P.E. four days a week during all four years. That first year I discovered that P.E. was only required at St. Gen's freshman year. Many scientific studies at the time were publishing statistics about childhood obesity in our country and about the growing numbers of young people with diabetes. P.E. and the arts were often the first to disappear in schools that were struggling with budgets. It would be unconscionable, I thought, to have our students graduate from high school without a profound sense that fitness = success. People often equate success with wealth and luxury. I believed it was necessary for students to understand that without good health, none of the money and none of the gadgets will matter. Therefore, our cutting-edge approach was to have every teacher conduct a fitness class of their choice during the last 45 minutes of the school day. By seeing their teachers also participating in fitness classes, the students would get the message that fitness is for everyone, and it is for life. By taking this approach, we also eliminated the need for a full-time P.E. teacher. Marlon and I then set out to hire a new head football coach.

From the beginning of our relationship, Marlon and I agreed on the importance of implementing character education into our athletic program. At the first league meeting that I attended with my fellow principals, one angry principal approached me and said, "The teams at your school are made up of thugs." Another one piled on with, "Your athletes make this league look bad." My initial response was to defend the athletes, but I kept my mouth shut and listened; at this point, they knew more about St. Genevieve athletics than I did. A couple of months later, I listened to the details of the bench-clearing brawl that happened at one of our girls basketball games played at home. Seemed our girls started the fight. There was definitely room for some character development.

Once we hired a new head football coach, we worked with him to make some additional new hires we thought would benefit our program. Our interviews with potential coaches always stressed the aspects of positive reinforcement and character-building that we felt were essential to the job.

In addition to strengthening our P.E. and athletic programs, I was simultaneously concerned with building up the arts, and couldn't resist an opportunity to blend the two. To this end, I convinced the seniors on the football team to sing and dance for the Welcome Freshman Day coming up in August 2000. I predicted that the time they spent rehearsing would not only be a bonding experience for them, but it also would encourage the freshman to attend football games and would help bring some additional positive publicity to the school. The team's amazing interpretation of the Four Tops' "Sugar Pie Honey Bunch" accomplished all of the above and garnered an article — with an accompanying color photo of them singing in their football uniforms — in the *Los Angeles Times*. The school was ready for a new football season!

For the new season, there was a definite improvement in team morale. The Valiants garnered enough wins that...guess what? In winning the final game of the season, we became league champions and were eligible for the playoffs! Unbelievable. With some wins under our belt, more people were coming out to support our team. That final night of the regular season had those of us in the stands as well as the players on the field in celebration mode. It was a joyous moment.

However, with the last hot dog eaten, the alma mater sung, and most of the fans well on their way home, the moment of euphoria for the team, the coaches, and Marlon and me became all too fleeting. The league representative was attending our game and was monitoring the scores of the other schools in our league. Not only were we the Santa Fe league champions that night, but so were two other schools. Not only were we going to the playoffs, but so were the two other teams from the league…and we were all tied for first place. Our joy was turning quickly to confusion. Which team would actually receive first-place entry into the playoffs? The first-place entry would assure our team a home game; otherwise, we could possibly be traveling over four hours to some remote region of California. Also, a first-place entry would assure us of facing a lower-ranked opponent, giving us better odds of winning and advancing to the second round of the playoffs, something completely unimaginable only a year earlier. Smiles were replaced by furled brows and the brightly lit stadium suddenly became as dark as the metaphorical cloud now hanging over our win. Our rental permit only allowed the lights to be on until 10:00 p.m.; good thing we hadn't gone into overtime that night.

I was still attempting to wrap my brain around what was happening as we walked from the blackened field out to a dimly lit parking lot. You mean it was actually possible to be the league champion and have a third-place entry into the playoffs? Of course it was possible, and it was just our luck. When our huddled group of players, coaches, athletic director, and principal finally got to a spot in the parking lot where we could at least see each other's faces, the league representative explained that to determine first, second, and third-place entries into the playoffs, there would then and there have to be a coin toss. The league representative further explained that he would be the representative for one school, our bus driver was assigned to be the representative for another school, and, with our coach too nervous to make the call, one of our players would be the representative for our school.

As the coin was tossed into the air, each of the three representatives shouted their choice. The league representative called "tails" on behalf of the Cardinals. Les, our bus driver, called "heads" on behalf of our cross-town rival, the Bell-Jeff Guards. Our running back also called "heads." The coin landed with heads winning. Now another coin toss would make the determination between St. Genevieve and the Bell-Jeff Guards. What!? Are you kidding? Another coin toss? I couldn't believe the scene playing out in front of me, and I was deflated. Had this Valiant team not earned a break? No other school in this league had suffered through the ridicule and bad reputation that St. Gen's had in recent years. With all the muck that we had been wading through for the last year, hadn't we earned a little good luck? What were the chances that the winds of good fortune would breeze in our direction for a change? Why couldn't that feeling of happiness following the game have lasted longer than the few minutes it did? I was pessimistic. Good luck never seemed to come our way.

The fact is, anything positive we'd experienced was never from luck; it was always due to grit, determination, and hard work. And on this occasion, the positive effects we'd earned disappeared the instant we learned that our fate about the playoffs would depend on the outcome of a series of coin tosses. The winner in this contest would be determined by a force that was a stranger to us: lady luck. Somehow, the fact that we were standing largely in darkness seemed to be a sign of what was to come. I silently cursed and was aggravated. I found myself wishing that we had not had those brief moments of celebration back in the stadium; it was only going to make the impending disappointment more profound.

As the league representative searched his pockets for another quarter to toss, it was eerily quiet. There were some clicking sounds made from the cleats on the shoes of some players who were nervously moving about. We had formed a half circle several people deep underneath a dimly lit street light in this now barren parking lot. The league's coordinator stood facing us as he formally conducted league business by way of a quarter. There was the faint hum of conversation from neighbors on the third floor of a nearby apartment building playing a card game on their balcony.

"Ready gentleman?" the league coordinator asked as he held out the quarter for everyone to see. The boys on the team resignedly nodded approval.

I stood still and stiffened my spine. I braced myself for disappointment, but stood unprepared for what was to follow. Instead of hearing the coin hit the ground, I heard the voice of one of the players.

"Wait!" commanded the strong baritone voice of one of the team's captains. "Let's pray to St. Genevieve...take a knee," he continued. Instantly, my disappointment turned to wonder. What was happening? Following his command, the team, coaches, and I went down on one knee, and as this inspiring young man held out his hands to his teammates beside him, every man on the ground became connected by hearts as well as hands. This moment turned into something that nobody there had expected we'd experience when we arrived earlier for a football game. The rough patch of asphalt became our holy ground. The dim glow from the overhead streetlight became a candle. The men kneeling and holding hands were the church, and the baritone voice praying confidently, "Sweet Genevieve, help us," became our inspiration.

We listened to his prayer with our heads bowed, but for a few seconds I raised my head and looked around. I was determined to remember this moment. Something had changed; I felt it in my bones. These were the boys who some thought made our league look bad, yet now they brought a tear to the eye of the coordinator sent by the league to conduct the coin toss. These were the same boys who some had referred to as "thugs," there on one knee praying to our patron saint to intercede. I wanted to remember the moment when our school's athletic program had turned in a new direction. I studied the faces, some muddied, some with tears, all sincere.

"We've worked so hard this season, and we want this opportunity more than anyone knows," the young man's prayer continued. "Look down upon us…be with us…we're counting on you."

For me, the coin toss no longer mattered. I didn't care who won the toss. We became victorious that night in a manner none of us could have expected. We were experiencing something phenomenal. Wherever heaven is, it seemed closer to that parking lot in North Hollywood than anywhere I had ever been. For a second, I allowed that humiliated nine-year old boy to have the experience of being part of a proud and cohesive team, together, down on one knee in prayer. Then I allowed the man I had become to bask in the overwhelming pride in having helped restore a sense of believing and an atmosphere of caring amongst this extraordinary group of athletes. Imagine that. We all arrived for a football game that night and upon our departure we knelt down, we bowed our heads, and we were in a truly Catholic league of our own.

Andrew, our league representative, said that since St. Genevieve had won our game with Bell-Jeff during the season, our team would make the call during the coin toss. We remained kneeling while the coin was tossed. As the coin was in the air, our player once again called, "Heads." The coin hit the asphalt, spinning for only a second before it fell flat. It was too dark to see. The bus driver had a pen with a tiny flashlight at one end. He pointed the pen at the coin, pressed on the end to make the light flash onto the coin, and his voice called out, "Heads!"

Lady luck had smiled upon the Valiants that night, and her name was Genevieve!

Postscript: From 1990-1999, St. Genevieve High School had various teams make the playoffs 11 times. From 1999 to this writing in February 2014, we have had various teams make playoffs 101 times.

Chapter 15. All Souls' Day

The Community of St. Genevieve High School
Cordially invites you to a
Celebration of Character
Sunday, November 2, 2003 at 4:00 p.m.
In the high-school gymnasium

It was billed as the largest celebration in the history of the high school, with all parishioners, alumni, and current students and their families invited to attend on a Sunday afternoon in November. By fall of 2003, the school had changed dramatically, though the reputation from the 1990s still persisted throughout much of the community. However, all of our students, as well as the entire faculty and staff, and some wonderful guests were there. It was not a packed gymnasium as we'd planned for, but everyone who was there had, in one way or another, been part of the four-year renaissance that had changed St. Genevieve High School from a failing school on a crash course careening toward closure to that of a model for the nation.

Only two weeks earlier, on October 14, 2003, our faculty had spent our weeklong retreat in Washington D.C. Typically, we would not have gone to Washington on retreat, but months earlier, when we completed what was a rather challenging and at times frustrating site visit from representatives of the Washington D.C.-based Character Education Partnership, I vowed that if we were to actually win the award, the entire staff would visit D.C. to accept the award on behalf of our school. In late spring, when word arrived that we were one of 10 schools in the nation to receive the prestigious title National School of Character, I began to plan our trip.

What I had not planned was the coming months becoming some of the most challenging times of my life. Throughout my adult life I had heard about and met many people who had suffered from their own personal demons and the proverbial "dark night of the soul." Come that fall, I was about to fall myself, far and deep into my own dark night, which would last months. I was not only depressed, but also consumed by my feelings of sadness; eventually, a fear set in. After a few weeks of nothing but dark days, I began to wonder if I would ever be able to snap out of this dire mindset. I withdrew into a personal cocoon, losing trust in almost everyone I knew outside my own family. It was as if a spiritual atom bomb had dropped on my soul and decimated my spirit. Although I was surrounded by hundreds of people every day, I had never felt so alone. There were moments when I even contemplated suicide. Little did I realize at the time, but I was about to embark upon the spiritual journey of my life.

While I usually loved visiting Washington, D.C. and normally would have been elated to be arranging this excursion for our staff, I now had lost all enthusiasm for planning this retreat. I had even less interest in planning a celebration of character. Character? How could I plan a celebration of character when I was feeling so alone? It took great strength on my part — strength that I wasn't certain I had — to not turn the entire fall of 2003 into my own personal pity party. In fact, I had to summon my inner strength on a daily, sometimes hourly, sometimes minute-by-minute basis, to avoid simply curling up into a ball…and staying that way.

I'm not usually a committee person. I find committees often get in my way. Fortunately, I recognized that without other people helping to organize our celebration of character, it simply might not happen. Yet even with the help of the committee members and their countless hours of work and service, there were still so many moments that I wanted to chuck it all and say to hell with it. Those were the moments when I most needed to call upon that inner fortitude, which now, sadly, seemed so elusive. Instead of strength, the sense of being alone permeated my existence.

In the end, our trip to Washington turned out to be among the best retreats we'd had to that point in my St. Gen's history. We made memories among those D.C. memorials that will last a lifetime. For much of the trip, I was able to make myself be present and divorce myself from the pall I was experiencing.

Being on a retreat obviously reminded me of my years at St. Thomas, for it was that little school and its parish priest, Father Dennis O'Neil, that had inspired these very retreats, which had since helped to transform two different school communities. I kept feeling the need to talk with my friend and mentor. Dennis had been plagued for several years by what I perceived to be a bogus, but nonetheless very real, lawsuit. Someone from a former parish had accused him of assault. I desperately wanted to hear first-hand from Dennis how he had been coping with the stress. I decided that I'd call him as soon as I got home.

When St. Gen teachers John Van Grinsven and Maxine Bush took the stage at the Crystal City Marriott across the Potomac River from D.C. to accept the National School of Character Award, I was completely present. As a montage of school photos played in the background, four years of the hardest work of my life was paying off right before my eyes. I was so happy at that moment, and so proud to stand alongside my fine colleagues — offering up a proud, and very loud, ovation — on that Friday, October 17th, 2003.

We arrived back from Washington late the next evening, Saturday, October 18th. Still groggy and jet-lagged, not just from the trip, but from life, I wearily answered my telephone when it rang Sunday morning. It was my friend

Vince. He had just heard a rumor that our mutual friend and mentor Father Dennis had died.

Ridiculous, I thought, and asked, "Who told you that?" As Vince and I conversed about the rumor, we both experienced the exact same thing. Denial. The first stage of grief. I suggested to Vince that he talk to some of the parish leaders or the current pastor of St. Thomas the Apostle, where Vince was currently the principal. If this rumor was spreading, we would need to quash it, and fast.

Within minutes my phone rang again. It was Vince.

"It's true, Dan," he stated matter-of-factly. He had talked with the office at the parish and the rumor had been confirmed. "They're not sure, but they think it was a massive heart attack."

"I'll bet you that Dennis' court date had been set. He was overcome with worry. I'll bet that's what gave him the heart attack," I said. Vince was one of my closest friends. We had been roommates on several occasions. In fact, Vince had been living at my house when my depression first struck. He and his wife, Marisa, had been going through a trial separation. We were a sorry pair during those days, but he definitely provided good company for me and helped lighten those first darkened days. Since Dennis had left St. Thomas, Vince, Manny Abaunza (who'd played Patty Simcox in our production of *Grease*), Joe Neeb and Raymond Saborio (who'd played, respectively, Roger and Jan in *Grease*), and Dennis had remained friends, and had a pretty regular poker game. We were all last together in August of 2003 at Raymond's wedding.

The last time I'd had an opportunity for a serious conversation with Dennis was at his home in May of 2003. All of us were supposed to play poker, but at the last minute, the rest of the group flaked. I suggested to Dennis that I would still come and we could have dinner together. By now, Dennis had become Bishop Dennis, the auxiliary bishop of the diocese of San Bernardino, California. It turned out to be a great evening and, unknowingly to me, a great goodbye.

Dennis toured me around his new neck of the woods. We visited his office at the archdiocese of San Bernardino and he took me through a couple of the quaint, smaller towns that I had never visited before, including a visit to the historic Mission Inn Hotel in Riverside, and a drive through Redlands.

When we returned to his house, we realized that my dog Blue was missing from my car, and following a quick search, we found him visiting Dennis' neighbors. We then sat down for a meal of barbequed steak and had a rather serious conversation. Dennis was worried; it was a state in which I had never seen him, and he and I had dealt with some serious situations working together in the inner-city of Los Angeles for eight years. But I had never seen him like this — ever. I reminded him that years earlier, when the charge against him had been made, he'd laughed it off and said it was nothing to worry about. The fact that someone had filed charges against him for physical assault had become public, broadcast on the Spanish-speaking news channels, and several families from St. Thomas had called to alert me that our former pastor and friend was in trouble. None of my callers believed the news story, but wanted me to know just the same. I'd called Dennis late, after the broadcast, and he literally laughed into the phone. That was the Dennis I knew. "Dan, it's nothing to worry about; it's a lie. Get some sleep," he advised.

The Dennis who now sat across from me with a worried countenance was a stranger. When I reminded him of that phone call more than two years earlier, his response was, "Dan, look at all that has happened since then," referring to the sex abuse scandal that had been rocking the entire Catholic world. "Where will you find a jury these days that will believe a word a priest has to say?" He went on to say that if he were to lose at trial, one that had been scheduled and delayed several times by that point, he would no longer be able to get insurance and would not be able to practice as a priest. In other words, he would no longer be able to continue to live the life he loved, the life to which he was called by God.

A few days after Dennis' death, I learned that the trial was not just coming up, but on the Friday evening that Dennis died, he had already been through the first week of what promised to be a two-week trial. He died on Friday, October 17, 2003, the same day our school was honored with an award for teaching character.

I also learned that his body had not been discovered until Sunday morning. The nun who'd entered his house because he could not be reached on the phone, found him kneeling beside his bed, his hands folded in prayer. My psychic energy leaves no doubt that Dennis was not only in prayer, but that he was having a moment, a truly personal and moving moment with our Creator. He prayed for justice and he received it instantaneously.

Dennis Patrick O'Neil was one of the best people I've ever known. He served God by serving people. He has been described as a "spiritual consul-general to the immigrant community of Los Angeles." During the time we ministered together, I always thought of him as the pope of Pico-Union. When he walked the streets of our Pico-Union neighborhood, he received a hero's welcome; it was like walking with a celebrity.

I believe that the evening he died was one of those rare moments when the bounds between the heavens and San Bernardino became so thin that they became one. It was a holy night for Dennis as he prayed to his Creator and came face to face, nose to nose with the Grand Ordered Designer of the Universe, GOD, and it was determined that in the case of this inner-city pope, a courtroom would not decide his fate. His fate was decided *there* at *that very moment*. The Verdict: a life well lived, Dennis O'Neil...a life well lived and so well done. Time to come home...let it all go...leave it all behind...time to come home. Whose heart would not beat fast enough to spin beyond control at such an unexpected but long anticipated divine moment? Don't bother to rise from your knees, Dennis O'Neil...just come home, my son...come home. It was what Dennis had waited for all of his life...when he answered God's call...one more time.

Exactly a week after standing in the Marriott Hotel's ballroom in Virginia, pleased that I'd allowed myself a few minutes to be joyful, away from the months of funk, fear, and self-pity I had been enduring, I now stood in a church in California, the same church in which Dennis had been ordained as bishop, watching as his casket was brought forth as the Litany of the Saints was sung. When Dennis' name was sung as part of the litany, I cried uncontrollably, realizing that the man I called Father so many times had truly been a father figure in my life. I loved Dennis as if he really were a father to me. I longed for his quick, don't-dwell-on-the-negative, to-the-point advice. It would be no more.

Nine days later was the Sunday we had set aside months earlier for a celebration at St. Gen's. It was November 2, 2003, our Celebration of Character. Celebrate? When we first received the news that the school was being nationally recognized, the school's leadership team and I knew that we'd want to have a celebration once we returned from Washington. It had been a very long fall term. I've learned to be grateful when time seems to fly; it usually means that life is good. But those autumn days seemed to drag on forever.

In planning our celebration, members of the committee brainstormed for days about who should be the keynote speaker. The person had to fit the occasion. We reminisced about how our character program had started by accident in 1999 with the theme, Lessons Learned from Columbine. All of a sudden someone had the idea that we should invite one of the parents whose child had been murdered at Columbine.

November 2nd is known as All Souls' Day in the Catholic faith — a day to commemorate all those who have died. When we originally set the date for our Celebration of Character, it was not because of its being All Souls Day, but because of its proximity to the date we received the award in Washington. So on All Souls' Day, 2003, as the California sun was beginning to fade into the Pacific at about five o'clock that afternoon, I had the difficult task, yet the distinct honor, to introduce our keynote speaker for the event: Mrs. Beth Nimmo. Beth is the mother of Rachel Scott, the first student murdered at Columbine High School.

A gracious, soft-spoken Colorado woman, Beth was not like most of the other speakers we had hosted over the years. She was a mom. Dressed in fall colors and petite in stature, Beth began taking us on a journey that was unforgettable. Her words transported us to her world in Littleton, Colorado, and introduced us to her family, especially to her son Craig and daughter Rachel, both Columbine students on that tragic day. Appearing with Katie Couric days after the shooting, Craig recalled his moments in the library, and how he'd led a prayer with fellow students and watched two friends die on either side of him. Katie Couric would later describe that interview as one of the most memorable of her career. Beth described the relationship that Rachel had had with both Dylan Klebold and Eric Harris prior to that day. They knew that Rachel possessed a Christian heart and was proud of her faith.

Beth also told us about Rachel's final moments as they had been described to her by her daughter's friends. She told us that as Rachel walked outside, taking a shortcut from one part of the building to another, the assailants shot her once from behind. As Rachel bled on the ground, they approached, taunting her and putting a gun to her forehead, asking her if she still loved Jesus. Did she still believe in her God? When Rachel answered, "You guys know I do," one of them shot her at point-blank range, ending her life and thus beginning the infamous Columbine High School massacre.

I've always heard the expression, *you could have heard a pin drop.* Now I understood exactly what that meant. As Beth spoke, I literally heard each time someone shifted in the bleachers or moved a foot. I could hear the breathing of the people sitting near me, and the faint sobs of others throughout the gym.

When Beth came to the point in her talk when she spoke of her forgiveness for the two young men who murdered her daughter and explained that it was only in forgiving that she was able to triumph over her tragedy, it was a transforming moment in my life. It was as if at that moment, my life had been blessed by Beth Nimmo. It was if at that moment, our gym had been blessed by Beth Nimmo. Although we had used it on numerous occasions for Mass, the St. Genevieve High School gym was now holy ground and was blessed. It wasn't so much her *story,* but her *example* that turned our gym into a church that day.

During the weeks of planning for this celebration, the big question had been what would we put on the agenda following Beth's talk? What or who should follow Beth's story? Our decision had obviously been divinely inspired. We'd agreed that the entire student body and staff would learn and sing the song "God Is," by the Reverend James Cleveland. It turned out to be the perfect complement to Beth's message.

> *God is my protection, God is my all in all,*
> *God is my guide and direction, God is my all in all*
> *God is my joy in time of sorrow, God is my all in all,*
> *God is my today and tomorrow, God is my all in all,*

God is the joy and the strength of my life,
Removes all pain, misery, and strife,
He promised to keep me, never to leave me,
He's never ever come short of His word.
I've got to fast and pray, stay in His narrow way,
I've got to keep my life clean everyday,
I want to go with Him when He comes back,
I've come too far and I'll never turn back
God is, God is, God is, God is, God is,
God is, God is, God is,
God is my all in all.

The next day, Michael Josephson, the founder of Character Counts — the highly effective and popular character education program — told the listeners of his daily radio broadcast about our celebration, describing it as the most extraordinary school event of his life.

As I drove up Highway 101 to Pismo Beach for a few days' rest, I received numerous phone calls from people who had attended Sunday's event. I chose not to take the calls; I felt like my heart was in my throat and I knew I would become too emotional if I attempted to talk about what had transpired yesterday. Instead, as I drove, I listened to the phone messages; several people cried as they conveyed their gratitude for having been invited to the celebration. Listening to those voices, I too shed some tears as I attempted to keep my eyes on the road while still being refreshed by the sight of the blue Pacific to my left.

After I checked into my hotel, I immediately wanted to go walk on the beach. To get there, I had to walk down 102 wooden steps, which I descended slowly. With each step, I counted a blessing in my life. I knew that I would still have some shaky days ahead of me, but I now allowed myself to be lifted out of the darkness that had been months in the making. I realized that I still had some control over my own feelings and emotions. I could choose to stay in a darkened emotional corner dwelling on my negative feelings or I could focus on the positive messages surrounding me from people who loved me. That choice was mine. I landed purposefully on each step, allowing each moment to permeate my existence, telling myself that in that moment I had a choice to make…to think negatively or to think positively. I could descend those stairs in such a manner that would take the beautiful sunset, the crisp fall air, the call of the seagulls, and the roar of the ocean for granted. I could allow my sadness to overpower anything beautiful before me. Or I could do my very best to summon strength and power and love. That was the essence of Beth Nimmo's message. That was what Father Dennis would want me to do.

It was a long walk down, and I allowed myself to close my eyes from time to time, taking in the sounds and the smells of the beach below. As people passed me on the stairs, I listened to the lightness and laughter in their relaxed conversations and willed myself to feel the light even as the evening temperatures grew cooler by the second. When I reached the bottom of those stairs the sun was an orange sliver about to disappear into someone else's morning.

There at the bottom of the stairs, standing in the shade of the gathering dusk, with the cool November breeze hitting my face, I met a man who was strong and confident, and I liked him instantly. It was me. I was changed. All Souls' Day had renewed my own spirit and soul.

As I looked at the footprints in the sand, I was reminded of the famous poem in which Jesus tells the lonely soul, "Those were the times I carried you." I realized that since Sunday afternoon, I had been feeling God's presence strongly surrounding my weakened spirit. I wasn't feeling alone anymore.

I've always believed that there are saints among us, and I always try to recognize the saints in my life. I don't believe we need a decree from the Vatican to know that someone is a saint. They are living amongst us if we care to see them.

The reason why we did not have the character celebration event on All Saints' Day, November 1st, was because our homecoming football game had long been scheduled for that day. But who says that you can only celebrate the saints on November 1st? Without even realizing it, we celebrated the saints among us on November 2nd. And through those saints, we definitely touched the souls of so many people in attendance that special day.

At the beginning of our celebration, I paid my own personal homage to my recently deceased friend Dennis O'Neil, telling the audience some of the many amazing things about him. And then we all experienced — live, up-close, and personal — a still-living saint from Colorado, Beth Nimmo.

Our Celebration of Character was the first of some of the most memorable and transforming moments that many people have experienced in their lives, right there in the St. Gen gym. I believe that all of those moments that have followed have occurred due to the grace and the goodness of the two saints — Dennis and Beth — who each had a hand in transforming the St. Genevieve High School gym into holy ground on November 2, 2003, All Souls' Day!

Bishop Dennis O'Neil

Beth Nimmo and Craig Scott being blessed by the Valiants in January 2013; this was Craig's first visit to our school, Beth's third.

Chapter 16. Memories Among the Memorials

My sister Mary moved to the Washington D.C. area in the fall of 1973. Over the years, I visited her dozens of times, and each time I'd become a tourist, always enjoying the enduring beauty of our nation's capital. In fact, one year I taught at JEB Stuart High School in Falls Church, Virginia and resided in Arlington only blocks from Arlington National Cemetery. During the year I lived there, I still behaved more like a tourist than a resident. Several times each week I'd take the short drive over Memorial Bridge and park near the Lincoln Memorial. My stomach had butterflies each time I prepared to jog the distance to the U.S. Capitol. I loved running through the Mall, always beginning on the Constitution Avenue side with the marvelous sight of the back of the Capitol building as my halfway mark. Once at the Capitol, I would circle around to the front and jog back on the Independence Avenue side with the huge columns surrounding the statue of Lincoln sitting in his massive granite chair as my final destination. I always gained energy as I passed the obelisk of the Washington Monument and the other beautiful sights, which I never tired of seeing. On Constitution Avenue, I'd always stare left, where the White House seemed so close and accessible. On the homebound side of my jog, upon reaching the Washington Monument, my head always tilted left for a view of what was my favorite monument at the time, the circular Monticello-like design of the Jefferson Memorial sitting across the Potomac Bay.

One lazy day I decided to walk the route, and discovered a hidden treasure. Along the reflecting pool on the Constitution Avenue side of the Capitol, dwarfed by the massive memorials surrounding it, is the memorial to the signers of the Declaration of Independence. It is a tiny island that jets across a short span out onto the reflecting pool. There are chunks of granite resembling tombstones that bear the engraved signature of each man who signed the July 4th document. On nice days after a jog I often returned to that seemingly rarely visited tiny island, where I would listen to some music or meditate.

A visit to our nation's capital should be on every American's bucket list. It is as inspiring as it is beautiful. I always looked forward to my visits to the various monuments, and I still do today. However, none of my journeys among the memorials has been quite as memorable nor as moving as the one I took precisely 30 years after my sister's bold move from small-town PA to big-town DC.

It was the fall of 2003. St. Genevieve High School had been designated that year as a National School of Character. When I discovered the previous spring that the awards ceremony would be held in our nation's capital, I vowed that were we to be among the winners, I would find a way to finance our annual retreat there. I so badly wanted our entire staff to experience the grandeur of Washington. As soon as we received word that the award was ours, I began to plan the journey and search out funding.

What I had not planned for was the torrential rain that greeted us shortly after our arrival. We flew into Dulles and had a bus waiting to take us to the Embassy Suites Hotel near the Foggy Bottom Metro stop. Since we had already rented a bus to take us from the airport to the hotel, I extended the service into the evening to take us to Gatsby's Tavern, a uniquely Washington dining experience located in Alexandria, Virginia.

Our school staff of 39 was a rather eclectic bunch, with ages ranging from 24 to 68. We had teachers from eight different states as well as from Russia, Colombia, Mexico, and the Philippines. We were all shapes and sizes, including those who were always impeccably dressed as well as those who were mostly casual. We were rather evenly divided between genders, marrieds and singles, and temperaments. I loved the fact that we were a diverse body — we always had things to learn from one another.

I had planned to make the most of our four days in Washington by beginning our tour right after dinner with visits to the Lincoln Memorial, Korean War Memorial, and Vietnam War Memorial — three incredible sights located within walking distance of one another. Although it was well into the evening in Washington, we were still on L.A. time. A few of the group, however, had already adjusted quite well to the time difference and requested to be taken back to the hotel. My calculations told me that by the time the bus drove the short distance to the hotel, the rest of us could have a leisurely walk to all three monuments and the bus would be back waiting for us when we were done.

Approximately 30 of us decided to disembark and see some of the sights at night. On our approach to the Lincoln Memorial, there was a clap of thunder and the skies let loose with a torrential rain, a rare experience for us Californians. By now, the bus was blocks away, taking the others to the hotel. We all ran for cover, laughing and splashing along the way. When we reached the top of the impressive stairs leading to Lincoln looking out into the city and surrounded by his Gettysburg Address carved into the granite walls, our laughter subsided; we stood at the feet of the likeness of one of our country's greatest and bravest leaders. We quietly took it all in.

This was the first visit to Washington for many of the staff. There were few visitors other than our group on this rainy night, and a quietness filled the air broken only by the percussive sounds of the rain. We did what most visitors seem to do: we stood in awe. We stared at the figure of the man who had transformed our country by staring hard into the eyes of racism and abolishing slavery. After a while, some group members started to wander around on their own, reading the words on the walls and taking in the various views of the city that this monument offers.

Then we began to gather behind the columns looking out into the sheets of rain that were blocking the bright lights that illuminate the Washington Memorial and the Capitol. With the storm showing no signs of weakening, I wondered what we were going to do; as the leader of the group, I'll admit feeling an uncomfortable pressure to make a decision in situations like this — I know that some of the group are not going to like the decision, whatever it is. I also start to think like a principal and worry about liability issues…what if someone slips and falls, what if someone gets sick…when internally, I'm really eager for everyone to get to see what I know they'll be missing if we don't have time to come back. Soon, however, several other staff members asked aloud what we should do. "Where is the Korean War Memorial from here?" asked our dean, a hearty Boston native.

"It's right over there, near where the bus dropped us off," I responded.

"Well that's not far; we're already wet, let's go!" he said and didn't wait for an answer. He was off and the group followed. I was relieved that someone else had made the decision for us.

Those who had umbrellas shared with some who didn't and the rest of us just got wet. By the time we reached the street below, I could hear the groans as people stepped into the flooded gutters, their shoes and socks getting drenched. It was difficult to see who was who, with umbrellas, hoods, hats, and various other items covering faces and heads. One positive was that by now, we were the only people braving the rain, so I knew that everyone in sight was part of our group. As we made our way toward the Korean War Memorial, the complaints increased as some wanted to make known their discomfort and disapproval. I started to regret that we simply had not waited for the bus. I was beginning to think that this tour was not going to stir our patriotic feelings and help us bond as I'd originally planned. We were all soaking wet; even those with umbrellas could not avoid the drenching since the rain was now coming down hard at an angle.

But as we approached the Korean War Memorial, magic happened. The Korean War Memorial is unlike any other. Rather than a building or a single structure, it is an open field with 19 stainless steel statues of soldiers, each larger than life-size — between 7-feet by 3-inches and 7-feet by 6-inches tall. Representing all branches of the armed forces, they are dressed in full combat gear, and dispersed among strips of granite and juniper bushes, which represent the rugged terrain of Korea. On one of the nearby walls is the inscription: FREEDOM IS NOT FREE.

"What in the world are we complaining about?" one member of the group said aloud. The sight of the statues, accompanied by those spoken words, transformed our evening from that of a foul-weathered complaint-fest into an unforgettable evening of tribute to bravery, strength, and patriotism. Silence quickly prevailed and the mood became reverent. We stopped rushing, taking our time to be thankful for our freedom and for the people who came before us who fought to make it possible. Our mad dash was replaced with a thoughtful and thankful stroll among the statues. I actually became somewhat grateful for the rain; it provided a perspective of appreciation I'd never before experienced at that memorial.

The downpour continued as we approached the massive black granite slabs that comprise the Vietnam War Memorial. The Memorial Wall is made up of two black gabbro walls that are 246 feet long and sunk into the ground, with the earth behind them. The memorial is designed so that the wall begins at your feet and is only 8 inches tall with just a few names at that point. As you walk along, you gradually descend as the wall grows taller and the number of names grows longer. When you reach the halfway point, the 10-foot wall is towering overhead. At night, subtle lighting from the ground up illuminates the names of more than 58,000 soldiers who either died or were missing in action. The design also allows visitors to see their own reflections in the wall, providing a continual reminder of past and present.

It is a heart-wrenching experience at any point in the day to visit this incredible memorial, but I believe that the quiet of the night is a particularly compelling time to be there. In fact, if you visit Washington, I suggest that you visit all three of these memorials after dark for optimum viewing.

By the time our meandering group had reached the center of the memorial's adjoining walls, our computer teacher, Kelley Endreola, instructed everyone to move in closer so we could form a tent of umbrellas and bring every one of us out from the rain. Yes, it was still coming down pretty hard. Kelley was a 30-something single mother whose son was enrolled in our school. Kelley's half-brother Jerry, who had served in Vietnam and who now lived in California, had a cousin who was killed in the war. He had never had the opportunity to visit D.C. himself to pay his respects at the monument. Kelley told him that we were going there for our retreat and said we would look for his cousin's name on the wall and offer a prayer there together. Jerry was so touched by this that he wrote the staff a letter and asked Kelley to read it to us during our visit.

There we stood on this cold and rainy night. We were in one of the most visited cities in the world with a population of more than a half-million people and yet we stood alone, as one. It was a humbling moment to have our little group of thirty standing together by ourselves. Then I realized that we actually stood with the memory of the 58,267 soldiers who were honored here. As we listened to Kelley read the words of her brother thanking us for making this pilgrimage for him, I came out from underneath my umbrella and closed my eyes, turning my face up to the heavens. I allowed myself to enjoy the cold, invigorating splashes of rain hitting my face. I thanked God for this moment in time. There I stood with so many members of my staff, most of whom I admired and found inspiring. I was so grateful to God for this particular moment of my life. I was feeling fortunate, fortunate to be one of the 58,297 souls being baptized under the waters of that October night's Washington sky.

Chapter 17. Lucy's Revival

A most delicate seven-year-old face just inches from mine. She was oh so vulnerable-looking, due largely to an absence of hair and eyebrows caused by ongoing chemotherapy treatments. Standing in the center of the gymnasium floor flanked by her hopeful and desperate parents, the tiny girl waited, unknowingly, with wonder in her eyes. Her parents had told her that the high school students — who were now overflowing the bleachers — wanted to pray for her, but certainly she could not have imagined what this prayer would be like. Actually, none of us imagined what it would be like.

Upon discovering that Lucy, a second-grader at St. Genevieve elementary school, was suffering from leukemia, I invited her parents to bring her to our upcoming night school, where our community and our guest speaker that evening could, hopefully, provide inspiration and say a prayer over her.

Shortly after becoming principal at St. Genevieve High School, I decided that a great way to turn around the low student and staff morale and to distinguish ourselves again in the community, would be to begin a program in Character Education. None of us knew what the program would look like, but we began to consider our needs and design a program to address the issues. For instance, when cheating became rampant on the campus, we looked for resources we could use to effectively deal with that. We discovered the HBO-produced movie, *Cheaters*, a fascinating and true account of a high school academic decathlon team that gets hold of the test and is forced into a moral dilemma. We showed the movie to our entire school and developed a lesson plan of our own. When some racist language was being used on campus, we consulted the

Museum of Tolerance for some possible ways of dealing with the issue. Weeks later, we hosted T.J. Leyden, a reformed white supremacist, who came to lecture. Because T.J. became a target after leaving the brotherhood, he arrived with an armed guard for protection. Our students immediately responded to T.J.'s talk with positive feedback and actions. From that point on, we began hosting a Character Education Speaker's Series.

We learned about an organization called the Character Education Partnership based in Washington D.C. This group provided resources for schools who wanted to implement and build effective programs in Character Education. They held a convention each fall, and we started sending representatives to attend. The first convention some of us attended was in Atlanta. During one of the forums there was a panel discussion, and the participants were asked to introduce themselves. By the time the Reverend Dr. Gerald Durley finished his two-minute introduction, the two other St. Gen staff members and I exchanged looks that said "are you thinking what I'm thinking?" Turns out, we were. "We've got to get him to come to St. Genevieve," said our Dean of Character, Patrick Palmeter. We had never hosted a speaker from outside California. We didn't know how it was done or if the reverend would even accept our invitation. Then, of course, we had to consider the budget. Now we were talking about airfare and hotel expenses. It didn't matter. I would figure out a way to bring this man to our school if he accepted. If he could be so inspiring in a matter of two minutes, imagine what he could do in thirty.

The pastor of the Providence Missionary Baptist Church of Atlanta, Georgia, Dr. Durley, as we came to refer to him, was charming, and graciously said he would be delighted to visit our school. After his first visit to St. Gen's a few months later, we knew we would have to make him a regular part of our speaker's series. He accepted our invitation to come back.

The parents of the little girl suffering from leukemia had also graciously accepted an invitation from us, an invitation for our community to say a prayer over their daughter. However, Lucy's doctor advised against her attending our event because the hundreds of people in attendance would expose her to a smorgasbord of germs. When I heard this, I called Lucy's mother and told her I would have to take back our invitation. "Oh no, we were so looking forward to having Lucy be there," she said.

"It's better to be safe and follow the doctor's instructions," I advised.

"But this would mean so much to her father and me," Lucy's mother continued in a pleading tone.

Although I had never met Lucy or her parents, nor had they ever attended an event at the high school, the offer of community prayer provided a sense of hopefulness that the family found difficult to resist. Who could blame them? When a child is suffering from a disease that could bring death, why wouldn't a parent want to receive prayer from as many people as possible?

"I have an idea," I offered, not wanting to cause any further anguish to Lucy's mom. "We will still pray for Lucy. Why don't you or your husband attend the event and you can accept the prayer on Lucy's behalf?"

"I suppose we could do that," she said, a twinge of disappointment in her voice.

"Why don't you talk it over with your husband and decide which one of you will be present."

Lucy's mother called back two days before the event. She'd had a second conversation with the doctor, who said that if Lucy only attended the assembly for the duration of the prayer, he would consent. The child's health sounded so delicate to me that I again offered the option of one of the parents accepting the prayer on Lucy's behalf. Their decision had been made; they would attend the event with Lucy if we would allow them to. Of course we would; this obviously meant more to these parents than I could have ever imagined.

The night of the event I instructed one of our staff members to escort Lucy and her mother into an office and wait until someone came for them. Lucy's father would sit next to me at the assembly and hear Dr. Durley's message. I instructed a second staff member to wait until Dr. Durley had finished his talk and while the audience was applauding, escort Lucy and her mother to the entrance of the gym and wait for my signal to come to the Valiant crest painted at the center of the gymnasium floor. The school mascot is the Valiant; we are proud to be one of the few schools in the country with this unique and, for us, extremely appropriate mascot.

Dr. Gerald Durley had been one of Martin Luther King's foot soldiers during the civil rights movement. Although he had only visited St. Gen's once before, he instantly became a favorite speaker among our students. At 6-foot 5-inches, Dr. Durley towered over most people he met. With a booming voice and a preaching style reminiscent of Dr. King's, Dr. Durley stands out in pretty much every crowd.

He was first a guest of ours back when the school was struggling and still on its way to national recognition. Those were the days when so many other schools, and so many in our very own community, looked down on St. Gen's, and most didn't hesitate to let us know it. We found Dr. Durley to be one of the most motivating speakers we had ever hosted. And, it seemed, Dr. Durley returned our admiration. From the beginning of our friendship, it was clear that he saw potential in our little school. He encouraged us to reach higher and to challenge ourselves to become more than we were. Our night school events were designed to help us along this path. When we held these special night school events, we changed the hours of the school day from a morning start time to an afternoon start. Students would go to classes and then, after the dinner break, would join their parents in the gym to hear the guest speaker or for some other special event such as Mass.

On the night of this, his now second talk at St. Gen's, Dr. Durley was fired up. His fierce and fiery energy was beginning to ignite the hundreds of students and family members in the audience. He had a way of delivering a message that reached into your soul and tugged at your core. And while the stories he shared with us were different each time he spoke, the core of his message was always consistent: to love ourselves more, to love humanity more, to never give up, and to always find the best in ourselves in order to find the best in others. One of his most memorable phrases, always delivered in his impassioned style, was: "The only time you ever have a right to look down on another human being is when you're offering them help in getting back up."

Just when it seemed he had reached a pinnacle of emotion, the audience would respond with approving screams, cheers, and applause, indicating that they didn't want him to stop; they wanted more. Their approval seemed to fuel this holy man into even more of a teaching, preaching frenzy.

"I used to get in trouble as a kid. People made fun of me because I used to stutter as a child. I wou-wou-would st-stu-stutter when I spoke to people, and a lot of the kids would ma-ma-make f-f-fun of me," he said, giving a painful example of how difficult it had been for him to complete a sentence. I would become so angry and that anger caused me to make bad choices. People would see me coming and they would say to one another, 'Here comes that Mrs. Durley's boy, she sure has her hands full with that one. Poor ole' Mrs. Durley,' they would say."

It was on the night that his own son was born and put immediately on a respirator as he barely clung to life, that the young Gerald Durley made an agreement with God.

"If you allow my son to live, I will turn my life around and devote the rest of my life to serving You," he bargained. His son received a miracle, and Gerald Durley kept his promise. Once he began studying and praying, he became happier with his life and became more confident. He found that when he preached, his stuttering disappeared.

With commanding bravado, he demanded, "SO WHAT DO YOU THINK OF MRS. DURLEY'S BOY NOW?!"

Thunderous applause from his audience!

Piercing the applause, he continued, "ALL THINGS ARE POSSIBLE WITH GOD, ALL THINGS..."

The microphone he was using seemed unnecessary since his voice had a natural amplification that reverberated off the gym's cinder-block walls. He was breathing hard as sweat poured down his forehead, and his traditional African garb began to darken from perspiration.

"ANYTHING AND ALL THINGS ARE POSSIBLE WITH GOD. DON'T EVER LET ANYONE TELL YOU WHO YOU ARE. YOU DECIDE YOUR FUTURE. ALLOW GOD TO BE WITH YOU ON YOUR JOURNEY AND YOU CAN ACCOMPLISH ANYTHING...ALL THINGS ARE POSSIBLE WITH GOD!"

Darkened spots appeared on the shirts and blouses of many in the audience as their tears streamed down their faces from being so moved by Dr. Durley's message of perseverance, self-love, and hope. There was a palpable connection between our speaker and his audience.

"YOU ARE CAPABLE OF ANYTHING. DON'T LISTEN TO THE NAYSAYERS. LISTEN TO YOUR HEART. BECOME WHO YOU ARE MEANT TO BE AND DON'T EVER... DON'T EVER... DO YOU HEAR ME VALIANTS, DON'T EVER LET ANYONE PUT YOU IN A BOX AND DEFINE YOU!

"YOU, STUDENTS OF ST. GENEVIEVE, ARE CAPABLE OF ANYTHING...YOU DEFINE YOUR FUTURE...KEEP GOD IN YOUR LIFE AND ANYTHING... ANYTHING...ANYTHING IS POSSIBLE."

As he belted the final words, "THANK YOU, ST. GENEVIEVE HIGH SCHOOL," the standing crowd with roof-raising cheers sent up a message of gratitude and love. The scene resembled a hot summer night's tent revival meeting. We were indeed revived.

As he approached me, he leaned down and whispered humbly, "I hope that's what you had in mind."

"Are you kidding?" I said, "That's more than I could have ever imagined. You're incredible."

I had become so caught up in the power of Dr. Durley's emotional message that for a moment I had forgotten our other special guest for that evening. I was quickly reminded by turning to Lucy's father, who was seated right next to me. I wondered what he was thinking after hearing such a powerful message of hope. Then I spotted the tiny young girl with her mother waiting in the doorway of the gym. It was not easy to see their faces. During the event, the gym's bright fluorescent lights were turned off in favor of soft purple and pink lights to provide an atmosphere in which the audience would feel more comfortable letting their tears flow.

"Remember that we are going to pray for the child who has leukemia," I quietly reminded Dr. Durley.

Wiping the sweat from his brow with a handkerchief, he replied, "Oh yes, where is she?"

I drew his attention to the gym's doorway. His eyes changed from exuberant excitement to rapt focus. It seemed as though he would no longer allow himself to hear the cheers continuing to come from the students, who were oblivious to the child waiting her turn to stand at the center of their attention.

It was now time for our two guests to meet. I raised my right arm into the air, giving a signal to the staff member to walk the mother and child to where Lucy's father, Dr. Durley, and I were standing. For these events we usually hired a band led by our musical director, Allan Shatkin, who was also the college counselor for our school as well as a keyboard player for special events.

When Allan saw my signal, he began to play "Anointing Fall on Me," by Ron Kenoly, on his keyboard. If you've never heard it, I encourage you to listen to it on YouTube, preferably while you continue to read the rest of this chapter. It is a simple yet powerful song, which up to that time, we sang prior to the start of our Masses. For this occasion, we simply changed the lyrics from "fall on me," to "fall on you." The lullaby-like melody first had the student body swaying in unison, keeping time to the music. Students in the bleachers and the seniors, who sit in chairs on the floor — a senior privilege during assemblies — soon began to put their arms around the shoulders of the students next to them. Once Lucy was standing at the gym's center, the senior class formed a caring arch facing the students in the bleachers. Lucy and her family were surrounded by a caring community.

Now meeting Lucy for the first time, I knelt on one knee so I could look directly at her. Her trusting eyes looked right into mine. She looked delicate enough to melt. "Hi, sweetie, welcome to St. Genevieve High School," I said. "I'm Mr. Horn, the principal. Our students heard you were sick and wanted to give you a blessing to help you. The blessing is a pretty song, and I know you will like it. That tall man is a good friend of ours," I pointed to Dr. Durley, "and he is going to pray for you, too. You know Father Marcial, don't you?" She nodded to show that she recognized our pastor and friend, Fr. Marcial Juan. "This is for you, to make you feel better, so enjoy it, okay?" She gently nodded her approval as the music continued to play in the background. Our students already knew that Lucy was coming and why. But for those parents and guests who didn't know, I stood up and said, "This is Lucy and these are her parents. Lucy has leukemia and I'm going to invite us all to pray for God to bless Lucy and her parents."

"Ladies, are you ready to lead us?" I asked.

"Yes," came the resounding response from the female members of our student body. With their soprano *la la la la la la laaaaaa*, they joined the music already playing to begin our version of "Anointing Fall on Me," and were soon followed by our young men with their collective baritone *ah, ahhhhhhhh*. Then I signaled the band that Lucy, her parents, and our community were ready to bless and be blessed; the band transitioned from playing softly to full volume. On cue, all the young women of St. Genevieve filled the air with the sweetness of their collective female voices, *la la la la la la...* followed by the collective male baritone, *ah, ah*. This was repeated until on cue, all sang together the words:

> *Anointing...fall on you,*
> *Anointing...fall on you,*
> *May the POWER of the Holy Ghost...fall on you,*
> *Anointing fall on you.*

These were the words. Beautiful words being sung to a beautiful melody by hundreds of teenagers with caring hearts all praying for a miracle.

The underclassmen, singing from the bleachers to Lucy's right, along with the seniors arched to her left, all with arms tightly wrapped around each other's shoulders while swaying in time to the music, created a rocking-cradle image.

We repeated the words several times, and then the singing stopped. Several students had volunteered to offer personal words of hope and prayer, and they took their turns at the microphone. Some spoke to God, others spoke directly to Lucy. Then Father Marcial, our pastor, an older man and also in somewhat frail health, offered his anointing prayer. He was a familiar and comforting face for Lucy and her family.

Finally, it was time for our guest from Atlanta to meet our ailing young guest. The visual alone was enough to bring tears to anyone's eyes. There stood the reverend Gerald Durley, a giant of a man, proudly African-American, in his mid-sixties, with life experiences that included the peace marches of our civil rights movement in a deeply divided south, as well as several decades of a life dedicated to serving God. He reached down with his massive hand lightly touching Lucy's head, looking down on this trusting soul to offer a hand of help and healing. Accepting the blessing, wide-eyed with wonder and looking incredibly fragile, was a very small and very ill Filipina whose threatened life had barely begun.

That night, we all prayed for a miracle. It was prayer in its purest form. So many of us were strangers to one another, but at that moment of prayer, we became one in our belief that God holds the power that can work through us. We became bonded in our care for this child and in our good wishes for her distraught parents. We were united in our hope and in our prayer that Lucy become well again and that she live long, live well, and live happily. Once all the words were spoken, the grand sound of all the gathered loving voices concluded the song of anointing. As soon as the blessing was finished, Lucy's parents quickly offered handshakes and words of gratitude, and then whisked their precious one from the gym to the sound of thunderous applause, which left many of us filled with hope.

Does prayer work? Recent reports claim that a growing number of scientists and doctors are proponents of the power of prayer. One thing is certain: it can't hurt.

One of the most important lessons I think our school has taught students over the years is that we all have the power to bless and to be a blessing to our world. We all know from a young age that we have the ability to tear others down; many of us have been torn down during our young lives. At St. Genevieve we stress to our students that we all have the ability to lift other people through our words and our actions.

As Catholics, we believe that it is the priest, the bishop, the cardinal and the Pope — holy men — who are able to bless and anoint others. At St. Genevieve, we make sure to teach our students that you don't have to wear the robes or have been ordained to bless others.

Our blessing of Lucy that night happened somewhat by accident. Upon hearing of this ailing youngster from our elementary school next door, it seemed only natural to offer comfort to her family, especially knowing that our minister friend was about to visit. However, on that night, the inspiration drawn from the sincere and caring faces of students taught me about blessing, and I have continued to pass along that teaching time and again. We all have the power to bless and to curse. Why not choose the positive? We all have the power to lift others or to crush others. Why not choose the positive? Living positively equals living happily. Is there any more important lesson a school can impress upon students?

When Rev. Durley returned to our campus in the fall of 2010, it was during our homecoming week of celebration. Sitting in the audience to welcome him back home to St. Genevieve was the not-so-little girl named Lucy. She was now in the fifth grade, had long, beautiful brown hair and full eyebrows. Best of all, she was healthy. She and her parents were there to say a personal thank you. Unfortunately, they were not able to stay for Dr. Durley's homecoming speech that night; Lucy had school the next morning and had homework to do, even though the doctor had said he'd be more than happy to excuse her absence.

Lucy waiting for her blessing with her hopeful parents

Lucy and Dr. Durley together again in February 2014

Chapter 18. Blessing of the Cardinal

We were celebrating Mardi Gras. Actually, we were calling it a Mardi Gras Mass, but since it was the Friday before Ash Wednesday, technically it should have been Vendredi Gras, right? Those of us involved in the planning were experiencing some moments of high anxiety because we had invited Cardinal Roger Mahony to preside at this Mass, and he had accepted. A cardinal in the Catholic world is very high ranking, as there are only about 180 cardinals total. In the archdiocese of Los Angeles, where there are five million Catholics, St. Genevieve parish is only one of approximately 300 parishes that make up the Corporation Sole of which the cardinal is the CEO. This would be Cardinal Mahony's first visit to our school since I'd become principal. While we were somewhat nervous about his upcoming visit, we also were excited about being able to show off for the boss.

One of my priorities upon becoming principal was to make our school Masses into events that our students and community would look forward to attending. I had largely stopped going to Mass as a youth because I found it boring. Now, as principal of a Catholic school, I felt it was my duty to do whatever I could to make going to Mass meaningful for students. However, several of the priests at St. Genevieve indicated a lack of interest in helping me on this quest. When the subject of Mass came up at staff meetings, one of the parish priests typically said, "Why don't you just have the students come to the regularly scheduled 8:00 a.m. parish Mass?" In my mind I would answer, "Because it's too early and it's boring." However, I usually came up with a more polite response.

My Sundays at St. Monica and St. Agatha parishes had given me plenty of ideas about how to make Mass more joyful. Now I jumped at the chance to invite priests from other parishes to preside at our Masses, including Monsignor Torgerson from St. Monica and Father Ken Deasy from St. Agatha. Our students also found them to be inspiring. I also had the Masses moved from the enormous parish church, which was built for more than 1,000 congregants, to our school gymnasium, where we could arrange the seating so that our small school of 300 students could have the experience of feeling close knit and be near the altar. I replaced the traditional organ and the traditional music with professional musicians and music that was contemporary, upbeat, and fun. I invited students to act out the gospel readings, read prayers during the Mass, and dance during the offertory. I also scheduled many of the Masses in the evening, when parents could easily join us in our celebrations. With each new Mass, students increasingly participated in the music and prayer, and pretty soon they actually began looking forward to going to Mass — a phenomenon that is quite unusual in many Catholic high schools. I looked forward to our cardinal being able to experience the joy our students exuded while attending Mass. I felt that the sight of several hundred teenagers joyfully celebrating Mass on a Friday night would have to be an uplifting experience for the cardinal.

Although this would be his first visit to our high school, Cardinal Mahony was no stranger to me. I did not know him personally, but over the years I had been in his company at dozens of events. I don't think he'd mind if I described him as being a bit stiff, and I'm sure I wouldn't be the first to have done so. I soon grew concerned that he might not relate to the joyful expressions of our students during our Mass. I became concerned, too, that the students might not relate to him or his message because his delivery was so different from what they had grown accustomed to. However, he was the head of our archdiocese and for many of our faculty, students, and their families, it would be an honor to have him preside at our Mass.

This cardinal at this particular time in our church's history was under siege with attacks from various groups, and especially from the media. There had been years of criticism over his decision to spend more than one hundred million dollars to build a new cathedral that the *Los Angeles Times* had dubbed the "Rog Mahal," as in The Roger Mahony Mahal. Plus, we were at the height of the priest sexual abuse scandal in Los Angeles. There had already been large settlements made in some dioceses around the country. The entire nation was waiting to see the result of the record number — 550 — of lawsuits against the archdiocese of Los Angeles. Day in and day out, there were stories in the *L.A. Times* as well as on talk radio and TV about the scandal and pending trials. Often, there were very pointed and personal attacks against Cardinal Mahony. Whenever I visited the cathedral, there were protesters on the sidewalk entrance. Most of the signs they carried had personal insults directed at the cardinal.

Although I have my own feelings about how matters might have been handled better, I do not believe it is acceptable to invite someone to be your guest and then criticize or denigrate that person. Instead, I found myself attempting to practice the very lesson I often criticized others for not attempting: to find the living Christ within others and ourselves.

The preparations for our Masses were typically handled by a small committee comprised of our campus minister, music director, choir director, and me. During our planning sessions for the upcoming Mass, I found myself asking aloud, "Can you imagine what it is like to be Cardinal Roger Mahony these days? What must his life be like right now?" Discussions ensued. Our campus minister suggested that if we wanted real meaning in this Mass, we should actually mention the scandal as well as the journalistic and legal siege the cardinal was currently dealing with and then offer to have our community bless him. How incredible it would be for our students and families, regardless of where they personally stood on these controversial issues, to take time to imagine what the cardinal's daily life was like right now. We could then offer him strength through a blessing. This could be a most humbling experience for him and a most empowering experience for our community. I loved the idea.

After our community had blessed Lucy, we began to offer some other guests the same blessing using the song, "Anointing Fall on Me." However, I didn't know if by offering this blessing to the cardinal, we would be doing something that would go against church pedagogy. I certainly didn't want to do something "wrong" in the eyes of the church or of the cardinal. After more discussion with the committee, we decided to take a chance.

With so many scandals raging across the country, there were fewer and fewer priests. Not only was the church experiencing a drought of men entering the priesthood nationwide, but many of those practicing had been removed due to the accusations. The church was largely unprepared for the lack of seminarians and was stunned when the bench began to be cleared by the scandal. Many were asking about the future of the church. At St. Genevieve High School, our answer was: we are not only the future of the church, we *are* the church *today.* By providing our students with the tools and the experience to bless and lift the leader who had been "shackled by a heavy burden," we would emphatically be telling them that you don't have to wear the robes or the collars or be ordained to be or give a blessing in this world.

Within the first five minutes of Cardinal Mahony walking onto the campus, I was regretting the decision we had made to bless him. Wow! Was he ever in a foul mood. Whatever made me think that it would be a good idea to offer a blessing to this cranky cardinal?

We had asked him to arrive early to take some pictures with our honor roll students and then to have dinner with our faculty and guests. He strolled in just as the honor assembly was concluding, and approached me at the podium.

"Welcome, Cardinal Mahony, I'm Dan Horn," I said, smiling, as I offered a welcoming handshake. While shaking my hand and looking over my head, he said sternly, "I know who you are. Can you tell me what all these parents are doing here? I did not come prepared to talk to the parents."

Before I could answer, he continued, "Is this going to be the seating arrangement for the Mass? I don't understand why you have parents in the center of the group of students."

I felt like I was a child again and the principal had just walked into the room to chastise me. Even as a child, however, I did not take kindly to people talking down to me or using agitated tones. The smile left my face and my warm feelings toward him cooled. I became matter-of-fact. "Cardinal Mahony, I can change the seating arrangement, but I can't un-invite the parents. We informed your secretary that this Mass would include parents."

"Leave the arrangement as it is," he said, sounding frustrated.

As some teachers came to escort him to the site where dinner would be served, his very pleasant secretary confided that he had indeed told the cardinal that there were going to be parents at the event. He explained that it had been a "long and very trying week" for the cardinal.

My mind was racing. Should we or shouldn't we? On the one hand, it made sense that after such a hard week, receiving a blessing could really do what it is intended to do. On the other hand, the man I had been interacting with for the prior three minutes definitely did not seem to be in possession of any sort of receiving spirit.

We had set aside almost 90 minutes for dinner. Our pre-event dinners tend to be lively and fun. I usually have to push people out of the room so the event can start on time.

With almost 100 people attending this dinner, I'd hoped that 90 minutes would not seem too rushed.

When the cardinal walked into the banquet, his face looked grim and he immediately sat in the proffered chair. The jovial conversation became hushed and the soft music playing in the background could now be clearly heard throughout the quiet room. Whatever conversation followed took place in whispered voices. One hundred people went through a sumptuous Polish buffet, prayed, made toasts, engaged in conversation, and ate dessert, all in just 50 minutes. I had asked several teachers to act as hosts to the cardinal and sit with him during the dinner. After about an hour, one of the hosts came to me to say that the cardinal was ready to begin the Mass. Around the corner from our banquet, the students were eating their dinner and not all of them had even been served at that point. The cardinal's request was ridiculous.

I went to his secretary and explained that all the students had not yet eaten, and besides that, we knew more parents would be arriving at 7:00 p.m.; it simply would not be fair to them to begin early. Another teacher's quick thinking sent some students into the room to invite the cardinal to take a tour of the school. Although I was relieved, I felt as if we were sending our student lambs into the lion's den.

By now I was worried that the cardinal was obviously in a rush to leave, which certainly did not align with what our somewhat overzealous planning committee had designed for the evening. As the Irish sometimes say, the planning was a bit OTT...Over the Top. For instance, since we had rather vehemently argued about which hymn should be the opening for the processional, we finally decided that we would have a processional medley, combining three or four upbeat hymns that the student body loved singing. Our philosophy was "more is more," but now it became quickly and painfully clear that the cardinal subscribed to the "less — and fast — is best" philosophy.

With the student-led tour of the school completed — without a smile or any sign of appreciation or approval from the cardinal — it was finally time to get the Mass underway. The band began to play a Mardi Gras-style rendition of "Just a Closer Walk with Thee," and on cue hundreds of enthusiastic teenage voices welcomed their cardinal to a Friday night Mass in uptown Panorama City. From the volume of the students' enthusiasm, it truly seemed as if there was no place else they would have rather been.

Although the Mass was in our gym, we put effort into making the ambience a warm and welcoming one. The bright fluorescent lights were turned off and beautiful colored lighting lit the walls, providing more of a theatrical environment. It was not light enough for me to see the expression on the cardinal's face as he processed in past the hundreds of students standing in the bleachers. His head was tilted in their direction and it seemed as though he was looking for something or someone in particular.

Our underclassmen sat on the home side of the bleachers. The altar was centrally located in front of the opposing bleachers, and the choir was in back. Hundreds of chairs formed a semi-circle around the altar, with our seniors in the front rows and students' families behind them. I sat in the front row with the seniors. By the time the cardinal reached his chair beside the altar, I could clearly see what looked to be an authentic smile cross his lips as he joined in the singing. It occurred to me that after a hard week, the thought of celebrating a lifeless Mass with uninterested teens was probably something he had not been looking forward to. Within the first few seconds of entering our gym, he must have realized this was not going to be a typical high-school Mass experience. It really is hard for many adults to comprehend the infectious enthusiasm our students have for singing together and celebrating Mass.

"Well that was really something!" he said to the students as "Awesome God," the final song of the medley, concluded. "I only wish that every high school sang like this at Mass." Thank you cardinal, I thought. Now watch what happens. With that little compliment, the students' participation would likely go through the roof…and so it did.

When it was time for them to respond "amen" it came back as a resounding "AMEN!!!" The cardinal was showing his joy, and his prior lethargy had been transformed into positive energy. Seems this was just what the doctor ordered.

During his homily he asked questions and hands flew into the air with each question. "Well, I'm not used to seeing so many students eager to answer questions at Mass; this is good."

Next question, more hands. "My, this is contagious, seems you all want to be heard from tonight." I don't think he realized that his now positive spirit and comments were encouraging the infectious spirit.

"Well, let me see, have we heard from a freshman yet?"

A resounding chorus of "NO!" came from the freshman section of the bleachers.

"We can't let that happen, can we? Only the freshmen put up their hands for the next question," he instructed. Seems the seating arrangement wasn't a problem after all.

At the start, we'd provided the cardinal with a Mass planner that had instructions as to which songs we were singing and which of the Mass parts would be sung or spoken. On the planner he used as his guide, we had indicated that following communion and prior to the final blessing there would be "Announcements." It is typical at a Catholic Mass that any special announcements to the congregation are made at that point in the Mass. Therefore, following communion, he sat and waited for someone to make announcements. I stood and nervously walked to the lectern, took the cordless microphone, and walked to the gym's center. Turning toward him, I said, "Cardinal Mahony, our gospel this evening was that of the Good Shepherd. It is the perfect gospel for this particular moment. I'm sure I speak for everyone in this room when I say to you, our Shepherd, you're under attack." I studied him for a response and I could see that he was listening intently.

"Day in and day out, the wolves in the legal profession attempt to bring our shepherd down. Every day, the wolves in the media are looking for blood. I'm sure most everyone here wonders, how do you get out of bed each day *knowing* what you may face? How do you get out of bed each morning *not knowing* what you might face? It takes strength."

As I tried to read him it appeared that he had actually let his guard down a bit. I could feel him thinking that here was a community that understood. Here is a community that is voicing compassion. I think he realized that we understood that this was a difficult time in his life and a blessing is exactly what he needed. I don't think he ever expected that the announcement we were about to make was: "Cardinal Mahony, before your final blessing this evening, this Valiant community would like to offer you *our* blessing. If you accept, please join me here on our Valiant crest."

Immediately he stood, and as he approached, he seemed to be a totally different person from the man who had arrived several hours earlier in almost the exact same spot, inquiring about the seating arrangement and guest list.

The senior class took their places surrounding him. Maybe just a tad too intimidated to put their arms around his shoulders, those right next to him placed their hands on his shoulders. The music played, and then our community began to sing our blessing with the words:

> *Anointing, fall on you,*
> *Anointing, fall on you,*
> *May the power of the Holy Ghost,*
> *fall on you,*
> *Anointing fall on you.*

He looked out into the audience of parents standing on the gym's floor facing him, the senior class members standing beside and in back of him, and the underclassmen standing and looking down from the bleachers. When he'd entered the gym for the first time that evening, it was as our cardinal, the boss, asking questions of me in a take-charge sort of way. Now he stood in the gym's center, a wounded shepherd, accepting a healing message from members of his teenage flock. Now it was he who gave the impression that there was no place he would rather be. Several students, one from each grade, had volunteered for the spoken part of the prayer along with one of the teachers. As the music played softly, the spoken prayer began and he immediately bowed his head, and genuinely seemed to be receiving the words with an open mind and open heart.

It was 8:30 on a Friday night. He'd had a long week. This moment seemed to be reinvigorating him. I was close enough in the circle surrounding him that I could see a tear form in the corner of his eye. I'll admit, I watched somewhat intently waiting for that tear to stream down his face. It never did. However, there was no doubt in my mind that we had accomplished what we had set out to do: to provide a blessing for a man we knew had to feel broken. We attempted to lift his spirit, and that is exactly what we did that night.

Following the blessing, he announced, "Usually when I visit a high school I give the student body the next day off from school. In your case, I wish I could give you a month off!" Obviously he was wishing he could provide students with a gift equal in magnitude to the one he had just received. "Of course, I can't do that. But I want you all to know that I appreciate your blessing very much. And I'm going to make your principal promise that he will find a day on your calendar to reward you with a day off from school." During the recessional song his secretary found me and told me that the cardinal was standing in the lobby of the gym and he wanted to shake the hand of every student in the school. I was stunned, but I made the announcement. After the last hand was shaken, two of our teachers escorted the cardinal to a room where he could take off his vestments. I waited for him in the corridor so I could walk him to his car.

"Wonderful, that was absolutely wonderful," he said as he joined me in the corridor. The smile was of a nature I had never seen on his face before; it was a wide grin.

We began walking toward his car and as he stopped to watch the students and families departing, he was happy to shake hands with parents and pose for pictures. He kept reflecting on the Mass and how joyous it had been. He wished that other principals would see our students at Mass to know what was possible.

It was now after 9:30 p.m. and he seemed in no hurry to leave. His was among the last of the cars to leave the lot that evening.

The following Monday I received a voicemail from our superintendent saying that she heard that we'd had an incredible Mass at St. Gen's on Friday night. "In case you're wondering how I know, I received a phone call from the cardinal telling me so. It was the first personal call I've received from him in the five years I've been superintendent. He wanted me to know how wonderful the Mass was and how blessed he was by the event."

Mission accomplished.

| Archdiocese of Los Angeles | Office of the Archbishop (213) 637-7288 | 3424 Wilshire Boulevard | Los Angeles California 90010-2202 |

August 4, 2006

Mr. Daniel Horn
St. Genevieve High School
13967 Roscoe Blvd.
Panorama City, CA 91402

Dear Mr. Horn:

It is with gratitude that I send this letter of congratulations to all who have worked to make St. Genevieve High School such a fine example of Catholic education.

The recent improvements to the school plant make it a model for secondary education, but it is the wonderful Spirit evident in the welcoming attitude of the St. Genevieve students that is most impressive.

The celebration of your annual Mardi Gras Mass this past year is one which I will long remember. The liturgy was beautifully planned and celebrated, and the students obviously have an understanding and ownership of their faith.

St. Genevieve High School is truly a place where students will be accepted, challenged, and formed as young Catholic men and women, and I am grateful to all of you for your dedication and commitment.

May God continue to bless and guide the Staff and Student Body of St. Genevieve High School.

Assuring you of my prayers, and with every best wish, I am

Sincerely yours in Christ,

+ Roger Card. Mahony

His Eminence
Cardinal Roger Mahony
Archbishop of Los Angeles

eb

Pastoral Regions: Our Lady of the Angels   San Fernando   San Gabriel   San Pedro   Santa Barbara

Letter from the Cardinal

Chapter 19. Dark Night in Nigeria

The first and only time I ever spent the night in a rectory, a residence for priests, was the day I met Father Scott Santarosa. Sam Robles, principal at St. Malachy School, was a mutual friend of both Scott's and mine. Sam had arranged for the three of us to drive to San Francisco for a conference on fundraising and development. At the time, Scott was serving as vice president of Verbum Dei High School. All of us were interested in adding some tools to our fundraising tool belts. Raising money is a necessary and constant chore in most Catholic schools.

Although I'd been looking forward to driving the 300 miles from L.A. to San Francisco with Sam, I had become less enthused when he'd told me we would have a third person on our journey. I discovered that our new passenger was a priest; now I would have to be on my best behavior!

By the time they arrived to pick me up, I had lost most of my enthusiasm for this trip, certain that this stranger would impede my enjoyment of it. However, Scott and I immediately hit it off. He was thirty-something, about 6-feet tall, slender, and very easy to be with thanks to his great sense of humor. He seemed somehow familiar to me. I felt as if I'd known him for a long time, and surmised that perhaps I had known him in another lifetime. We formed an instant friendship and I was very glad he was along for the journey.

I had assumed that we'd stay in a motel in San Francisco, but when we were on the outskirts of the city, Scott announced that he had made arrangements with a fellow Jesuit priest, who was the pastor at St. Agnes Church, for the three of us to spend the night at the rectory.

The accommodations were not only very comfortable, they were right on the edge of the Haight-Ashbury district. I had been to San Francisco several times, but had never visited the famed Haight-Ashbury. After settling in, Sam, Scott, and I walked around the area and then chose a place for a leisurely and highly enjoyable dinner.

After a long ride followed by a long dinner, the three of us got a bit of a late start the following morning. We then got somewhat lost looking for the conference venue, and had difficulty finding a parking space in the crowded city. By the time we walked several blocks to the site, we had lost all enthusiasm for the day-long event. Just as we reached the door to the room where the conference was being held, Sam jokingly said, "Now that we're here, let's call it a day."

"I'm for that," said Scott, enthusiastically.

"I'll third that," I agreed.

We studied one another's faces to see if one of us was kidding. As we looked from one to the other, we began to laugh and rushed toward the exit door. Like high school kids ditching class, we ran to the car as though someone might actually be chasing us. We were three otherwise responsible men running from the very responsibility that had brought us to the City by the Bay in the first place. Once back inside the car, we discussed our options for the day. Although all three of us had been to San Francisco before, we decided to become tourists. Since we were near the wharf, we began with a ferry ride over to Alcatraz. The last time I'd been in the city and tried to visit the island prison, it was during the government shutdown in 1997 and Alcatraz, which is a federal park, had been closed. This was a far more perfect way to spend the morning than sitting in a stuffy conference room. Following our tour of Alcatraz, we rode down Lombard Street, the crookedest street in the world, rode the cable car, and most of all, enjoyed the thrill of being utterly irresponsible.

Once back in L.A., Scott, Sam, and I agreed that our next adventure should be a weekend in Las Vegas. As the date for our trip drew near, neither Scott nor I could reach Sam, who was still the connection between Scott and me.

Eventually, it was the day we'd planned to drive to Las Vegas, and we still had not heard back from Sam.

"What should we do about the trip?" Scott asked.

"I'm willing to go if you are."

"Yeah, why not, I've reserved this time off."

Once I picked Scott up for the trip, all awkwardness disappeared and once again we found it very easy and even fun to be in each other's company. We spent two days enjoying some gambling, good food, and had plenty of time to learn about each other's lives. We became confidants. Upon our return, Sam had some poor excuse as to why he hadn't returned either of our calls.

"I've just been so unbelievably busy," he lamely offered.

However, Scott and I now had a friendship that no longer needed Sam as the bridge to bring us together. Our jobs in Catholic schools often required us to attend the same events. We also made it a point to get together for dinner from time to time. Shortly after our friendship began, Verbum Dei High School found itself without a principal in the middle of the school year and Scott was appointed interim principal. It happened rather suddenly, and Scott didn't always feel up to the challenges he was presented with as principal. I was happy to be able to offer advice whenever he asked for it. The Verbum Dei community had hired a new principal for the next school year, and Scott was relieved to return to his former responsibilities.

Although he was happy to be back in his former position at the high school, I was saddened to learn that it would be his last year there. In fact, it would be his last year in Los Angeles for a period of time. Scott explained to me that prior to taking his final vows as a Jesuit priest, he still needed to complete the final formal period of his formation called the Tertianship. Once the school year ended, Scott was going to travel to New England where he would spend 30 days on a silent retreat, after which he would be sent for almost a year to a third-world country to serve, but he did not yet know where. Sitting with him in a restaurant months before his departure, Scott seemed excited about his forthcoming mysterious adventure. However, when I saw him only days prior to his departure, Scott's excitement had turned into apprehension.

I'd invited him to come by for lunch at St. Gen's, which was already back in session as our academic year begins the last week of July. As we sat in our school's conference room having lunch, I could sense Scott's nervousness. Although he still smiled, he lacked the easy and laid-back spirit I had come to know him by. At one point I simply asked him, "Are you nervous, Scott?"

Without hesitation, he responded, "Yes, Dan, yes I am. In fact, I don't know if I'm more nervous about staying silent for 30 days or about the unknown assignment that is going to follow." At that moment, I searched my brain for words of comfort. I had none.

A few seconds later, I remembered that our student body was gathered in the gym having a singing practice for an upcoming event. "Scott, I'll be right back," I said excusing myself. I walked the short distance from the main building to the gym. All 500 students were in the south bleachers, and the stands were packed. Our music director had a microphone set up next to his keyboard. When the student body finished the song they had been working on I took the microphone in hand. I explained to the students and faculty that I had a good friend visiting the school who was there to say goodbye. I let them know that Father Scott had been ministering for the last several years at Verbum Dei High School; our students knew it well. I provided the details of Father Scott's upcoming year abroad and explained that he was nervous, "just as any of us would be." I then asked, "If I brought him in to the gym right now, would you sing 'The Anointing?'"

A resounding and collective "YES!" came from the bleachers.

"Would any of you like to volunteer to come down to the floor to offer a prayer for Father Scott?" Dozens of hands flew in the air. I quickly pointed to six individuals to come down from the bleachers to join me on the floor. I then asked the entire senior class to come out of the bleachers to stand with me on the floor. "When Father Scott comes into the gym, we're going to stand next to him and behind him. Those closest to him can place your arms around him, or put your hands on his shoulders. The seniors and Father Scott will face the rest of us so we can surround him with our love, prayers and fond wishes. Everybody ready?" I asked.

"READY!" came the response.

I then went back to the conference room where Scott was sitting contemplatively.

"Scott, can we take a break from lunch for a few minutes? There's something I'd like to show you in our gym."

"Sure," he responded, immediately standing up as if he were glad for a break from his thoughts.

Applause filled the gym when the students saw Scott enter. Wherever his thoughts had just been, he was now smiling and fully focused on our students. "What's going on?" he asked me as I led him to the center of the student gathering. I took the microphone and answered him so everyone could hear.

"Well, Scott, what's going on is that when you told me a few minutes ago that you are nervous about your upcoming travels, I remembered that our students were here practicing some music."

By now our music director was softly playing the notes of "The Anointing." As soon as our students hear that music they instinctively place their arms around the shoulders of the students standing next to them. Then they begin to sway. Scott's attention was drawn to the bleachers, watching the extraordinary sight of students holding one another. There is always a calm that fills the air once the hundreds of students begin to sway. I always liken this sight to that of a giant human cradle. Scott's eyes were then diverted to the senior class standing behind him, arm-in-arm, also swaying. He appeared mesmerized.

I continued, "I came to the gym and interrupted the students' music rehearsal and told them a little bit about you and your upcoming experiences. I told them that you are a friend, and asked them to bless you before you go. Scott, these are the Valiants of St. Genevieve High School. We'd like to offer you our blessing. Will you accept?"

With a broad grin he said, "I would love it." The seniors stepped forward and two of the students in the front center section separated from the group to invite Scott to stand next to them as they placed their arms around his shoulders and he put his arms around theirs.

"Are you ready to lead us, ladies?" I asked. Another resounding "YES!" from the female members of our student body.

The song was led by our girls, followed by our boys, and eventually we all joined together singing the words:

Anointing, fall on you,
Anointing, fall on you,
May the power of the Holy Ghost,
fall on you.
Anointing, fall on you,
Anointing, fall on you,
May the power of the Holy Ghost,
May the power of the Holy Ghost,
May the power of the Holy Ghost,
fall on you,
Anointing fall on you.

The piano played softly as the six students who'd volunteered to pray passed the microphone from one to another. Each one offered sincere and heartfelt words to Scott. They prayed for his safety, for God to take care of him, for him to be inspiring and inspired. Like so many other people whom we have blessed this way, Scott looked up into the stands and it appeared to me that he was attempting to record this image in his memory. It was a beautiful image. These students, who were strangers to him, offering loving and hopeful words of prayer. He looked from one side of the bleachers to the other. Every few seconds, he would look at the senior students on both sides of him and turn to catch a glimpse of those behind him. It appeared to me that at that very moment, there was nowhere else in the world that Scott would have preferred to be than right there in our gym.

When the blessing was finished Scott asked to say a few words to the students. He thanked them for their blessing. He told them it was a special moment that he would always remember. They applauded as we exited the gym. A few minutes later, I bid my own personal farewell as Scott drove away.

I received a post card a month later as Scott was completing his retreat. He reported that he was fine and the retreat had been a beautiful experience. It would be almost another year before I heard from him again. He was back in the States. We chatted a few times, promising to get together soon. It was almost Christmas before we finally were able to make time on our schedules to meet for dinner. We sat outside at one of the restaurants at The Grove, one of L.A.'s popular shopping and dining areas. It was beautifully decorated for the holidays and there were crowds of people. The restaurant had plenty of outdoor heat lamps to make it feel toasty as we sat out in the cool air. We were happy to see each other. It had been more than a year, but we still had that familiar feeling between us. I felt like I was welcoming a long-time friend back home. The conversation flowed fast and easy throughout dinner. Scott's overseas assignment had been in Nigeria and he shared stories and impressions from his time there. I filled him in on the highlights of my life since I had seen him last.

Once our dinner plates were taken away, Scott became serious. "Dan, I'd like to share with you something else that happened to me while I was in Nigeria."

"By all means, tell me," I said, leaning forward.

Earlier in our conversation he had described the extreme poverty in the nation of Nigeria, and about the high rates of crime due to the poverty.

"Nigeria, especially after dark, can be a very dangerous place," he continued. "There are not a lot of street lights, and in many places, they are non-existent, including on the streets surrounding the rectory where I was living. One evening, five of us priests went out together. When any of us went out at night, we did not get out of the car until we reached our destination. Upon our return to the compound where we lived, we would honk the horn so the caretaker would come and open the gate from the inside. This particular night was no exception. The driver pulled up to the gate and honked the horn. As we were waiting for the gate to be opened, two cars, lights out, pulled up on either side of our car. They appeared from out of the darkness. Eight young men with guns got out of the cars and surrounded us. They opened the driver's door and pulled him out of the car, had him lie face down on the ground, and then fired shots. I was sure he was dead and that the rest of us would be next. Then, they made the guy in front of me get out. I thought I would be next. I imagined that like our driver, I would be forced to lie down with my face on the Nigerian pavement and be shot. I was thinking, this is where my life will end. These kids with guns did not care who I was. They did not care that I was a Catholic priest, that I was the son of Carol and Ed Santarosa from Sacramento, California or that I had a family who loved me. I was at their mercy and I was about to die, right there on a street in Nigeria. I feared that I would die at the hands of strangers who saw no value in my life. Then, as quickly as they had come was as quickly as they left. Apparently, they had gotten enough gold chains and cell phones that they decided to drive away looking for other victims. I jumped from the car and ran to the driver, who was face down on the pavement, motionless. I shook him. No movement. I shook him again and he moved. Then he sat up. He had been playing dead.

I was relieved that he was alive, relieved we had all survived, but it was the most frightening moment of my life."

"Oh my God, Scott, thank God none of you were killed," I said, stunned. Scott sat staring across the table somewhat drained after having relived the moment for me. "Are you all right now?" I asked.

"Yeah, I'm all right," he offered slowly. The next day I was praying in my attempt to recover from the event. It was jolting for me to know that my life was so cheap to those gunmen. I was feeling incredibly alone and abandoned. At one point during my praying, I closed my eyes and you'll be interested to know that the image I saw in front of me was of the students at your high school. Remember the blessing they gave to me?" I nodded. "I remembered their concerned-looking faces and their prayers for my safety. The memory of that blessing helped to console me."

I just stared across the table at Scott, feeling sorrow that he had suffered such a harrowing event.

"Remembering that blessing was God's way of reminding me that my life is important and that I matter," he said to me, nodding his head as if in affirmation.

Chapter 20. Singing in the Rain in Plains

The rain clouds began to figuratively gather in the summer of 1985 when I read *First Lady from Plains*, Rosalynn Carter's autobiography. I found it charming. A day after I finished it, I penned a letter to the author with my positive review and expressed gratitude that she had written the book in such a folksy manner. After Rosalynn's quick trip to my hometown of Jeannette, Pennsylvania during the 1980 presidential campaign, I'd written a college term paper on the effect she'd had on the election. From my research and from her autobiography I learned that she is tenacious, compassionate, driven, and committed to making our world better. I became an admirer.

I received a response to my letter a few weeks later. It was a short, typewritten thank you. Below Mrs. Carter's signature was a handwritten note that read: "I think you should get involved in politics. I think you would enjoy it."

"She actually read my letter," I kept repeating to family and friends. I then went to my typewriter and wrote, "Dear Mrs. Carter, I can't believe you actually read my letter!" I told her that I would like to meet her and ended with, "Even if you want me to come to Plains and help you clean fish one afternoon, I'll be happy to do it." I thought that might touch a chord since I'd learned from her book that she loves to fish.

Months passed. I forgot that I wrote the second letter. It was February 1986, a rainy Friday. I was living and teaching in northern Virginia and can remember being glad that the long week was over; it felt good to be out of the cold rain. The phone was ringing as I walked through the door to my apartment.

The conversation went something like this:
Me: Hello

Caller (sweet, soft, deeply southern female voice): Hello, is this Danny Horn?

Me: Yes it is.

Caller: Hello Danny, my name is Madeline Edwards; I'm Mrs. Carter's secretary in Plains. I'm calling because of the letter that you wrote to Mrs. Carter several months ago.

Me: You're kidding…

Madeline: No, I'm not kidding. It's been so long you probably thought your letter got lost in a well somewhere down here.

Me (stunned): No, I didn't think that. I just thought Mrs. Carter wouldn't have time to answer it.

Madeline: No, not at all. As a matter of fact, Mrs. Carter wants you to come and have lunch with her.

Me: Well, Madeline, you just tell me the time, the date, and the place, and I'll be there!

Madeline: Well, now that we know you'll accept, I'll be calling you back to arrange the details.

When Madeline called back, she instructed that on a particular day in March, I was to go to the federal building in Atlanta, where the Carters had their offices. I went, as arranged.

Rosalynn was unpretentious, sweet, and accommodating. In between her meeting with a Middle East peace team and an interview with the "Today Show," she took time to have lunch with an admirer simply because she had been asked. I must admit, I was a little relieved she hadn't invited me to clean or even eat fish. Personally, I don't like the sport or the menu item. One of the topics of our conversation that day was my confiding in her that I was considering a move to Los Angeles to pursue an acting career. She was very encouraging of it.

After I arrived in L.A., I would send a note to Rosalynn every so often and always received a polite response. The last time I wrote to her was when we won the Blue Ribbon Award at St. Thomas School, and I asked if she'd come to

Los Angeles to present the award. She politely declined my invitation.

More than ten years later, after St. Genevieve High School had received the National School of Character Award, I was invited to make a presentation about our school at a forum in Atlanta sponsored by the Character Education Partnership. I made the trip to Georgia with one of our teachers and four students. I chose one student from each grade — two boys and two girls, each representing a different race. Roxanne Brush was the teacher I asked to accompany me. She had joined the staff my first year at St. Gen's. She was young, energetic, and had a wonderful personality. It turned out to be a great group to travel with; everyone got along well and we had fun together.

Knowing that former President Carter taught Sunday school when he was at home in Plains, I did some research and discovered that, lo and behold, the day after the forum concluded, President Carter was scheduled to teach. I extended our trip through Monday, and on Saturday, we rented a van and made the three-hour trek to Plains. Prior to our leaving Los Angeles, I had each student write a letter to the Carters, telling them about themselves, our school, and why we were coming to Georgia. I also wrote to Rosalynn, reminding her of our luncheon date almost two decades earlier. I hoped the letters would allow our students an opportunity to meet the Carters and perhaps have a photo taken with them.

Our students actually moaned when we pulled into Plains. There were fields, and woods, and in the downtown, only a few stores.

"What are we going to do here all day?" they wailed.

"You'll make your own fun," I responded.

That evening, at the Plains Bed and Breakfast, where we stayed, Miss Jill, the owner, made us feel right at home. Two of her friends dropped in to visit, and while the students had fun exploring the small town and surrounding neighborhood, the adults sat around the kitchen table getting to know one another. Jill and Gene Stuckey owned the

Plains Bed and Breakfast. The lived in Atlanta and, being good friends of the Carters, came down on the weekends that President Carter was in town teaching Sunday school.

"I just got off the phone with Rosalynn," Jill announced. "She said that they read your letters and they're looking forward to meeting you all tomorrow at church."

"You must know the Carters pretty well," I said somewhat stunned that she had just hung up the phone with the former first lady.

"We've all known the Carters for years," said Jan Williams, one of Jill's friends. She and her husband George owned a local peanut warehouse. Jan recounted stories of flying to the inauguration on Air Force One in 1976. As a young woman, she'd been Amy Carter's teacher. The Carters invited her to spend a few weeks with Amy at the White House until they all got settled in. Jan delighted in telling the story of when, on Inauguration Day, a reporter said to President Carter's mother, Miss Lillian, "You must be very proud of your son today." Miss Lillian responded, "Which one?"

My mind was already planning a return to Plains. Next time, I would bring a larger group of students and they would make a documentary featuring some of the citizens from Plains telling their stories.

The next morning, there were special seats roped off for us in the sanctuary of Maranatha Baptist Church. The approximately 80-member church had three sections of pews, accommodating some 300 people. We were seated on the left side about six rows from the front. Shortly after we sat down, a Secret Service agent entered through the front, with Mrs. Carter following; she came right to our pew. The rope was lifted, and she shook hands and greeted the students and Roxanne, and said to me, "It's good to see you again."

A few minutes later a smiling President Carter entered, and there was an explosion of flash bulbs. Earlier, Jan Williams had instructed the congregation that it was fine to take pictures when the former president entered but not after he began the lesson. There was to be no applause at any time. "Where's everybody from?" President Carter asked the congregation.

"Thailand," called out one man. "Argentina," said another. "Maryland." "Idaho." "Kentucky." "Scotland." There were people from across the country and from all over the world.

"Rosalynn, would you like to introduce your guests?" Mr. Carter asked.

Rosalynn stood and said, "Jimmy, I'd like to introduce you to my friends from California." She told the congregation about having met me years earlier, and about our school being a National School of Character.

Jimmy then turned to us and said, "We read your letters, or rather Rosalynn read them to me. We're delighted you're here. I hope you'll come back."

The next fall, I did go back to Plains, and brought a larger group with me. I had set aside some funds in the school's budget for this purpose and had received additional funds from one of our school's benefactors to make the trip possible. This time I took eight students, — four to conduct interviews, four with cameras to record the interviews, and two to help with behind-the-scenes tasks, like ensuring that everyone we interviewed signed releases. We spent two days scouring the town of Plains looking for people to interview who had lived there during the 1976 campaign. This was the fall of 2007 and we did not realize it until later, but director Jonathan Demme was making his own documentary of Carter at the time called *Man from Plains*. Ours was eventually titled *Project Plains*. I know I'm biased, but I do believe that ours was more interesting.

Each one of us was simply awestruck by the open arms and hospitality of this town of 650 people. Everywhere we went, people welcomed us and shared their stories. On Saturday night, Miss Jill had invited a house full of company to have dinner with us. Following dinner, the students conducted interviews around the dining room table. Among the guests were Kim Fuller, Jimmy's niece, and daughter of Billy Carter. Sitting next to Kim were her teenage son, Bud, and her young adult daughter, Mandy. Also at the dinner were Dan and Nelle Ariail; Dan was formerly the Carters' pastor. The B&B was filled with people who seemed just as glad to have us there as we were glad to be there. As the students conducted their interviews, people stood at both doors leading to the dining room.

Mayor Boze Godwin was there with wife Betty. Boze was a tall, rugged-looking man of few words. He had been mayor of Plains for several decades. His wife Betty was petite, pretty, and sassy, with a personality that charmed children and adults alike.

Before the evening ended, most of us Valiants were talked into a visit to the local haunted house followed by snipe hunting at the local cemetery where most of the deceased Carter family is buried. If you have never been snipe hunting, I recommend you visit Plains...the snipe are in season in the fall!

After several months in the making, the documentary premiered in the St. Gen gym in February of 2008. Joining us for the occasion were several of our friends from Plains, including George and Jan Williams, Betty Godwin, Jill Stuckey, and Kim Fuller. After the documentary was over, each of our guests honored us by sharing a story or expressing gratitude to the students for making them feel so welcome in Los Angeles. When our choir sang "Midnight Train to Georgia," the students and their families went wild when our guests from Plains could not contain themselves and showed off a few of their dance moves.

The next fall, Pastor Dan Ariail, his wife Nelle, and First Lady of Plains Betty Godwin came for a visit. As luck would have it, they visited the weekend of our fall musical. The show: *Singin' In the Rain*. It was the best show we had ever done. It was perfectly cast, and our students acted well and performed the many tap numbers to perfection. During rehearsals, the student leads had gotten the opportunity to meet Debbie Reynolds, who offered some tips on one of the dance numbers. Gene Kelly's widow, Patricia, visited the school and talked to the cast about her husband's love for that musical. Never before had students been so invested in a show.

We don't have a theater at St. Genevieve; we use the parish hall, which has a stage, but no other theatrical accoutrements. We have to bring in lights, blackout curtains for the windows, sound equipment, and for this production, our crew built a six-foot extension onto the stage complete with overhead sprinklers and drains. To my surprise, as well as the audience's, when it was time for our Gene Kelly character to sing in the rain, woo-la, like magic, it actually rained on the stage!

Miss Betty, wife of the mayor of Plains, was intrigued by the kids and by the show itself. "If ya'll can find a way to bring the show to Plains," she said in her warm Southern drawl, "the townspeople will put the kids up in our homes, we'll cook for ya'll, and sell tickets for the show. Ya'll just need to figure out how to bring the show to us. Will you consider that?"

In what seemed like an instant, we were loading trucks with props and saying goodbye to several of our staff members who were flying to Plains a week before the show opened there to make all the necessary arrangements. It was March 2009, and we were taking our show on the road!

The only weekend that we could possibly make this production a reality coincided with our annual faculty retreat. There was no question as to where the retreat would be this year. The 45 members of the staff would fly into Atlanta the day after the 67 members of the cast and crew arrived. Now that was a road trip! It was the very definition of "team effort." Between Miss Betty and her Plains crew and our team of Valiants, we managed to make flight arrangements, bus arrangements, overnight accommodations, and meal arrangements for 112 people for up to five days.

We also had to secure permission from the National Parks Service to use a National Historic Site, the Plains High School Museum — and not only to use their restored and preserved auditorium as the venue, but also to extend the stage to include plumbing and drainage like we had for the show in Los Angeles. To our surprise, the Parks Service agreed. In retrospect, all these hurdles seem almost insurmountable. The fact that we got everything done was a testament to the power of community and teamwork. I forgot that we were partnering with people who had the Peanut Brigade mentality; if they could get one of their own elected President of the United States, this project was a cakewalk.

On Wednesday, those of us who had gone early welcomed the students, who immediately began rehearsing. On Thursday afternoon, our faculty and staff arrived to begin our retreat. That evening, students and staff gathered for dinner in the town's quaint meeting hall for supper prepared for us by some of the locals. Coach Manny slaved over two hot grills, cooking 50 pounds of ribs assisted by my brother Bob, who had brought his family down from Pennsylvania for this special event.

Just as we were about to offer prayer, two Secret Service agents entered abruptly and brought the room to complete silence. To our surprise, in walked Jimmy and Rosalynn Carter, who immediately received a standing ovation. After warmly greeting us and telling us how much they were looking forward to the show, they joined us for prayer and shook a few hands before saying goodbye.

On Friday morning, while rehearsal got underway at 8:00 a.m. in the historic Plains High School auditorium, the faculty gathered at Maranatha Baptist Church for the official start of our retreat. Weeks earlier, I had written to Rosalynn requesting that she speak to our faculty on the topic of her personal spiritual journey, and she had agreed. The time for her talk was set for 9:00 a.m. She would be our first speaker and would be followed by Dan Ariail, the former pastor to the

Carters. As we waited for Rosalynn to arrive, the room was hushed in anticipation. Knowing that former first couples always travel with Secret Service protection provides some mystery as well as a bit of apprehension.

In introducing Rosalynn, I mentioned the letter that I'd written to her in 1986 and my offer to help her clean fish if she would agree to meet me. "I made the same offer when I asked her to give this talk to us. She agreed to talk with us this morning, but this time, we're all cleaning fish this afternoon," I joked. At least I hoped it was a joke.

Rosalynn has a deep voice and speaks quite softly. There was no microphone as she was only speaking to a group of 40 or so. Most of us leaned in to hear her stories, which took us on a journey from the small town where we were, to the White House, and finally to countries all around the world. She talked to us about her childhood, informing us how prominent a role religion played in the south, especially during her childhood. She had been raised Methodist, and the church provided a social experience as well as a religious one. She remembered the revivals that were a big part of her life growing up.

Of course the stories from her White House days and beyond were the most fascinating for me. I enjoyed hearing her recall the trip that she and Amy made to the Vatican to visit Pope John Paul II and then about his visit to the White House. Her off-the-cuff comments often belied her former role as first lady. For instance, in concluding the story of her and Amy's visit to the Vatican, she added, "It was the first time in my life I had ever worn a hat." And when describing the historic visit Pope John Paul II made to Washington, she threw in the fact after the pope's visit, Jimmy remarked, "I think he would make a good Baptist!"

Rosalynn possessed a stunning recall for events and dates. At one point when she could not remember the exact year of an event she was describing, off went her secretary to research the correct date. She quickly returned and Rosalynn corrected herself, noting that she wanted us to have accurate information. After forty-five minutes, she apologized to us for taking so much of our time! Then she sat down while her good friend Pastor Dan began his talk to us. It was obvious that the two enjoyed a close friendship. Rosalynn said she had mentioned to Jimmy the evening before that she didn't know if she should speak before or after Dan. Jimmy advised her to go first or there might be nothing left to say!

Not only did Rosalynn stay for Dan's entire 30-minute presentation, she also joined him in answering our questions. She stayed until every question was answered and not a hand was left in the air. Then she posed for photos with our group. On her way out, she graciously provided autographs, hugs, and handshakes, and then, as if we were all her good friends by now, she said, "I'm looking forward to seeing you all at the play tonight."

In the afternoon, the staff visited nearby Andersonville, a Civil War prison site. I stayed back to help with serving lunches to the students over at the high school. I was doing my best to be present with my staff for our retreat, while also being available to our student cast, and spending time with my niece and nephews, who had come to Plains at my invitation. It was organized chaos, but I loved it.

By 5:00 p.m. on Friday, the cast had finally finished their rehearsals. Everyone was exhausted; the opening night curtain would be going up in two hours. The cast and crew dispersed to the various homes in which they were staying, with the instructions to be back in one hour. It was past closing time for the High School Museum; I was the only person there. I went out to the back steps to sit and enjoy a moment of silence. I could see a Secret Service vehicle approaching. The agent stepped out of the car and placed traffic cones in the spot where I assumed the vehicle carrying President and Mrs. Carter would park in less than two hours. I watched as he surveyed the sight. He was then joined by a second agent and they began inspecting all of the props, which were lined up on the side lawn. After the inspection, he and the other agent remained on site, securing the grounds until the arrival of the Carters.

It didn't take long for the auditorium to be completely filled. More Secret Service agents entered and dispersed to various locations. Jimmy and Rosalynn entered near the stage and immediately began to greet members of the audience. Their seats had been reserved earlier in the day by the Secret Service. I was happy to see that my brother and his family were seated directly behind the Carters. Dr. Gerald Durley, one of St. Gen's favorite guest speakers, and his wife Muriel, were seated next to the Carters. They had driven down from Atlanta to see our show.

We had learned that President Carter believes in punctuality, so as the clock struck 7:00 p.m., the orchestra began the overture. I took a seat in the last row of the theater. The students performed like professionals. They remembered every line, every song lyric, and every dance step. They all sang beautifully. The tap dancing was superb.

During one scene, the Debbie Reynolds character jumps out of a birthday cake. As stage crew members dressed in black did their utmost to not be noticed carrying the huge plastic cake onto the stage, a Secret Service agent sitting a few rows in front of me sharply turned his head toward an agent posted in the lobby with a look that said, "Has that thing been searched?" The other agent calmly nodded his head. I nodded, too. After all, I had watched earlier as the cake had been inspected.

During the performance I daydreamed about St. Genevieve High School back in 1999 when there had been only a music appreciation class. In those days, there was no live music happening anywhere in our school's curriculum. Then, as I listened to the opening chords to that dance number made famous by Gene Kelly and his umbrella, I remembered some of the musically talented students in the early years who had gotten few opportunities to express themselves.

My attention was quickly brought back to the marvelous moment in our school's history that was now happening right in front of me: it was raining on the stage in the high school that Jimmy and Rosalynn Carter had attended 70 years earlier. Our very own Gene Kelly, with his masculine baritone, began singing, "*Do, do, do, do, do, do, do, do, do, do, do...*" Many members of the audience leaned forward in their seats *oohing* and *ahhing*. As our Gene Kelly character sang the line, "Come on with the rain," he stomped in what had become a puddle, sending water spraying out across the first ten rows of the theater, where the Carters were sitting. The audience cackled with delight.

When the show was over and the cast had taken their final bows, President Carter, a carpenter himself, was on the stage inspecting the new addition to the stage at his old high school. He seemed intrigued as he looked above the stage to see where the rain had come from, and then was just as intrigued as he inspected the drain.

"It was just as good as anything I've seen on Broadway," he said about the performance. "I hope y'all will come back again."

"We've never had this many people come to Plains from Americus," said Rosalynn. "This was really wonderful," she said, beaming.

On Saturday, the cast and crew had two more shows to do. Prior to the matinee, students and adults gathered at the large field in front of what was now the Plains High School National Museum. I had scheduled a softball game there for the staff. During the 1976 campaign for president, both Jimmy and his brother Billy were the captains of local softball teams, and this was the field where the two teams would settle their rivalries. We'd forgotten to bring our softball equipment along, so we settled for playing kickball on this historic field. On Saturday afternoon, between performances, we had Mass together on that field.

On Sunday morning, we all attended Sunday school taught by our new friend, Mr. Jimmy, as the students referred to him. By Sunday evening, most of us were feeling that mixture of ready-to-go-home and not-wanting-the-experience-to-end. We concluded our stay in Plains by attending the Sunday evening worship service at the

Maranatha Baptist Church. The church welcomes dozens, and often hundreds, of visitors every Sunday morning. However, on Sunday evenings, the church service is likely to be attended only by members. This Sunday evening there were approximately 30 members in attendance plus our delegation of 112.

As the service concluded, Pastor Jeff Sommers said, "And now Dan will come forward to lead us in our closing prayer." There was a laugh from everyone when both Pastor Dan Ariail and I stood and began to walk toward the front. Typically at the evening service, the other Dan, the former pastor, led the closing prayer. He had not been made aware that this evening I had been invited to lead our community of Valiants in "The Anointing."

We all stood and formed a circle and together we sang the song of anointing. As I scanned the faces in our prayer circle, seeing our students and staff with our friends from Plains, including the former first couple, I was both proud and humbled. I was reminded of our school's mission statement:

To Know God
To Live With Honor
To Change the World

The Carters exemplified this mission. They live their lives in ways that truly are changing our world for the better. Here we all stood, shoulder to shoulder with two people who have devoted their lives to these three tenets. Together we sang:

Anointing, fall on me,
Anointing, fall on me,
Let the power of the Holy
Ghost
Fall on me.

During the spoken part of the prayer, most of us became emotional. Patrick Palmeter, our Dean of Character, and a large man, seemed moved in a large way. His was not the only voice that indicated that this was an emotional moment. Many students and church members had tears in their eyes, as did President and Mrs. Carter. We had indeed become their "friends from California!"

We were getting ready to make the 3,000-mile trek back to the City of Angels. It was a weekend that had changed many of us. We were taking inspiration from a historical town that had flexed its spiritual and political muscle to catapult one of its own into the most powerful position in the world. And, we were also taking back the inspiration from a couple who have Christ as their constant model, and who continue to change the world.

We may not have changed the world that weekend, but we came home inspired…and we had made it rain in Plains. That's just how we roll!

Meeting Rosalynn Carter for the first time in Atlanta 1986

Receiving the Key to Plains, from left, Rosalynn Carter, Betty Godwin, former President Carter, Dan, Mayor Boze Godwin

Chapter 21. Prince Jimmy

Homecoming 2009 was special. It was the 50th anniversary of St. Genevieve High School. Only 10 years earlier, most people who knew of the high school would have predicted its demise long before it had the chance to turn 50. Instead, the high school was more vibrant than ever.

In 1999, enrollment was at 300 and declining fast. By fall of 2009, enrollment had climbed to 600, the school was nationally recognized for its program in character education, and had a solid, well-earned reputation in academics, athletics, and the arts. It was time to celebrate.

Since our practice field was only 50 yards long, we rented the stadium at Polytechnic High School, a local school just two miles away, for our games. It soon became a tradition for Homecoming Saturdays to be an official day of school. In my early years as principal of St. Genevieve, attendance at games was deplorably low, driven, in large part, by the fact that our teams lost more than they won. However, my hunch was that the low turnout itself was partially responsible for the losses. The way I saw it, a cheering crowd could actually help us win some games. Therefore, I decided to make the events of Homecoming mandatory. Students reported on Saturday afternoon and were not dismissed until the game ended that evening. I felt that this would provide an opportunity to teach our students about community, branding, and supporting our team. They would learn how much fun it can be to attend a time-honored tradition of a high school football game with stands packed by their peers. What else were they doing on Saturday nights? Not much, as far as I could tell.

Additionally, taking a page from my hometown of Jeannette, Pennsylvania, I implemented a Homecoming parade. The route stretched from our school to the

Polytechnic High School football stadium. Although Jeannette never actually had a Homecoming parade, it seemed like there was a parade for just about every other occasion. There were always huge Fourth of July parades lasting up to several hours. I can still remember blisters from the sunburns I endured after being in the hot July sun for so long. One year our little city of 10,000 people had a Fourth of July crowd of more than 100,000 watching our parade. For us kids in a tiny industrial town, that was something to brag about.

Anyone was welcome to register and march in Jeannette's annual Halloween parade. The Halloween parade, appropriately, took place at night. When the parade was over, people would gather in front of City Hall, where the winners in various costume categories — scariest, funniest, individual, group, etc. — were announced. I'm proud to say that several of my friends and I won first-place prizes two years in a row. Several of my friends formed a club we fondly called the Asscals, a tribute to Spanky and the Little Rascals. Our first prize was for dressing as hobos carrying instruments; we had a sign identifying us as the Asscal Marching Band. None of us played an instrument, but we had a good time pretending. The second year, I dressed in my mother's wig and a bridesmaid gown my sister had worn in a wedding, and was dubbed Ms. Woman's Lib. The other Asscals were my slaves who pulled me down the main street on a throne with wheels. We borrowed a bra from one of our better-endowed female friends and burned holes in the cups, then placed the bra on the front of our banner. That was when we were in high school and not too old to have fun and be silly.

The annual Jeannette School Parade was held during the final weeks of school. As a youngster, I spent many a sleepless night prior to parade day. The excitement was almost too much for me to bear. On the last Thursday of May, all students would report to their respective schools at the regular time. After attendance was taken, we would receive a small American flag to carry, and would then be led by our teachers to Clay Avenue, the main street of Jeannette. Our Catholic school did not require us to wear a uniform on parade day, which made it extra fun in my book. Often many of us would have brand new tennis shoes for the occasion. These were moments filled with pure joy — I loved knowing that all the schools in the city, seven at the time, were also marching their student bodies to the town center. Every school was assigned a side street on which to line up. All of us kids knew that there were hundreds of parents and townspeople along Clay Avenue waiting to cheer us on as we paraded. Jeannette Junior High and Senior High Schools both boasted large marching bands in those days. When the bands would strike up and the city police cars, lights flashing, would roll first in the parade, my heart would pound with excitement and pride knowing the parade was starting. After the parade, almost the whole town would descend on Kennywood Park, near Pittsburgh, for a day of picnicking and amusement rides. These were some of the most exciting days of my boyhood.

Many years later, I was stunned when the city of Los Angeles granted us a permit in 2002 that would allow us to close a two-mile stretch of the three eastbound lanes of Roscoe Boulevard for a St. Genevieve High School Homecoming parade. I imagined that the students would be as excited as I used to be about participating in a parade.

The students, however, could not believe that we were requiring them to *"w a l k,"* — they whined as they said it — the entire two miles to the stadium. I'll admit, our Jeannette parades were usually only about six blocks, maybe a quarter of a mile, if that. I hadn't thought about the distance. Once I did, though, I thought, "So what, it's good exercise."

Seven years later, in 2009, the student body was greatly looking forward to the annual St. Genevieve Homecoming parade. There was now an excitement about these parades similar to what I had experienced growing up in my small town. Each year between 2002 and 2009, our parades had grown larger, and for the 50th birthday of the school, we were pulling out as many stops as our budget would allow.

We hired a plane to circle several times during the parade to write in the October sky, "Happy Birthday St. Genevieve." Chuck D, from Public Enemy, had been a recent speaker at the school, and he and his lovely wife, Gaye, agreed to be our Grand Marshals for the parade.

Our cheerleaders, boys' dance team, girls' dance team, marching band, and the entire cast of our fall musical, *Footloose*, practiced for weeks, and put on a show-stopping halftime show that stretched 80 yards across the field.

For the previous two years, our local fire department had joined us with their hook-and-ladder truck, and all of our cheerleaders rode atop. This year, however, we also had the good fortune of having Santa Claus ride along with the cheerleaders. We had begged Mr. Palmeter, our jovial dean, to play the role and because it was the school's 50th anniversary, he agreed.

It was special to have Homecoming queens from every decade return to ride in convertibles along the parade route. The highlight for our students was Whanita Lonsberry Moore, the very first Homecoming queen in St. Genevieve High School history. Whanita, perched on the top of the rear seat in a convertible, rode in the parade, and was on the field at halftime to crown the Homecoming queen of 2009. Some women are just born for the role of queen; Whanita was one of those women, with just the right combination of grace, style, and humor. She had an easy smile, curly blonde hair, and had maintained a curvaceous figure.

Every year we rent or borrow convertibles to carry the candidates for Homecoming kings and queens. No one knows until halftime which one of those convertibles carries that year's king and queen. Since it was our big 50th anniversary celebration we wanted to involve as many students as possible in the week's festivities. Therefore, it was decided that for the first time in the school's history, we would allow the freshmen, sophomores, and juniors to also elect a prince and princess, who would represent their class and ride in a convertible during the parade.

The day the class princes and princesses were announced, I was genuinely surprised when I learned that the junior class had elected as their prince the shy and often isolated redheaded boy named Jimmy.

With flaming red hair, glasses, and skin as white as chalk, Jimmy easily stood out in the crowd of Valiants. Our school had a Caucasian population of approximately 2% and in that tiny population Jimmy was the only redhead. When Jimmy had applied and been accepted to St. Gen, I'll admit that I worried a little for him. Although our school is well known for its welcoming spirit and 99 percent of the time I can count on the Valiants to make both students and adults feel welcome, there are never any guarantees. Even though the vast majority of students at St. Genevieve High School understand how important it is to accept everyone, from time to time we have those rare few who hate life and want others to hate life too. Usually they are weak in spirit and look for targets, which are often those who stand alone or who stand out.

Jimmy had Asperger's Syndrome, which is a form of autism. People with Asperger's are challenged when it comes to social interaction. Not only did Jimmy stand out being the only redhead in a handful of Caucasian students, his anti-social behavior caused him to stand out even more. A gentle and kind soul, he was one of the most polite students I've ever encountered. I found myself hoping he would not suffer from any form of intimidation or bullying on our campus. Character education and moral development take constant work and attention. There is always a chance — even on the best campuses, even if all bases have been covered and all lessons taught — that bullying will take place.

One day at lunch, shortly after Jimmy's arrival at St. Gen's, a few of our cheerleaders approached Juan Jasso, the director of admissions, and a man protective of all the freshmen. He is the one man on campus who comes to know every single freshman as well as their families. "Some of our cheerleaders pointed at Jimmy during the lunch hour and wanted to know his name," Juan reported to me. "I became suspicious so I asked one of them why she wanted to know his name."

"We noticed that he is always by himself, so we brought him some cupcakes," was the girl's response, Juan told me. They wanted to try and make him feel welcome. The young woman Juan had questioned had actually baked the cupcakes herself.

Although many of our students tried reaching out to Jimmy, he simply preferred to be on his own. He maintained a positive attitude, and he would speak when spoken to, but he preferred to fly solo. His independence and his intelligence impressed his classmates. "Mr. Horn, Jimmy got the highest grade on our algebra test," a student would say, loud enough for Jimmy to overhear while students passed me in the hallway. "Congratulations, Jimmy," I would call after him. He would stop and wave with a smile to acknowledge he had heard. His classmates never grew comfortable with the thought of Jimmy simply fading into the background. Many of the students did their best to get to know him. They learned that it was simply his preference to be by himself most of the time. So they allowed him to be alone but never lonely.

By junior year, Jimmy had earned the affection of his entire class and of most of the school as well. Most of the time when I saw him he would be making his way down the hallway intent on getting to his class on time, his skinny arms holding what looked like every book from his locker. He stared straight ahead, keeping his eyes sharply focused, and seemingly unaware of the hundreds of bodies moving in every direction around him or of the hundreds of voices creating a loud, excited buzz of hurried conversations.

"Morning, Jimmy!" I usually would shout in his direction, breaking his concentration. He would pause long enough to say a polite and efficient "good morning." On the occasions when it almost seemed he might veer from his planned route and come over to shake hands, he would remember that both arms were securing books, and he would take a pass on the handshake.

Our theme for homecoming that year was: "MICHAEL JACKSON." There were contests to dance like Michael and dress like him, and the music of Michael filled our activities throughout the week. Only a few months earlier, Michael had died suddenly, just miles away at the UCLA Medical Center. Michael Jackson was the perfect theme for our 50th anniversary celebration because not only was it a way to pay homage to a great entertainer who had recently died, but Michael Jackson had had hit songs during each decade of our school's existence. Every generation of St. Gen graduates could relate to his music. The choice also brought back some special memories for me. I recollected those early days of my arrival in Los Angeles. I'd had a myriad of part-time jobs back then when I was still pursuing an acting career. One of those jobs was a two-week gig during the summer of 1987 as a band runner, a fancy name for gofer, for Michael Jackson.

Michael was about to release a new album entitled *Bad*, and was preparing for his *Bad* tour. My job included driving band members to and from their hotel, answering the phone during rehearsals, taking messages, and keeping the refrigerator stocked. The rehearsals were unlike traditional, cobbled-together run-throughs. Each of these rehearsals was a full-fledged Michael Jackson concert, complete with lights, dancers, and costumes. I watched many of these concerts while sitting in the rear of the rehearsal hall near the fridge and next to the phone. The job didn't pay much, but I was enjoying every minute of it.

Of course, what stands out in my memory most is Michael himself. For weeks, I watched him during the grueling rehearsals, and the more I watched him the more I came to admire him. He was a gentleman; literally, a gentle man. Even at times when tempers were flaring during a rehearsal, Michael was always calm. He was kind to every person I saw him interact with. Sometimes he would spot the newspaper or a magazine I was reading and he would wander over. He'd politely and shyly say, "Hello, okay if I have look?" He would glance at the headlines, then go off to rehearse. I was much too intimidated by the security and his entourage to strike up a conversation. I would just nod or say, "Sure, go right ahead." I was in the company of a legend and I felt fortunate to be there. Here was arguably the greatest entertainer ever to walk the face of the earth, and he seemed shy. As much as the public loved Michael, there were so many in the press, and some in his own inner circle, who were determined to see him crash. What is it about our society that makes us enjoy watching people rise to a certain level of fame only to equally enjoy watching them fall from grace? What is it about our society that allows us to take gentle souls like Michael and make them into targets? It happens with adults, and even more so, it happens with children.

When Jimmy heard the announcement that he had been elected junior class Homecoming prince and that he would be riding to the game with the elected princess in a convertible, he politely declined. He was worried about his little sister, who was now a member of our freshmen class. He did not want her to feel bad since he would be riding and she would have to walk.

Juan Jasso called Jimmy's mother and explained that her son had been chosen for an honor by his class, but that he had decided to turn it down. Juan suggested that she encourage Jimmy to accept this honor since his class sincerely wanted him to be their prince for the entire week, especially for the two-mile parade ride in the junior convertible behind their class float. Jimmy's mother agreed to talk with him. The next day, Jimmy agreed to ride in the parade.

The entire Homecoming week was exciting as it could be. During the class competitions, each class had a unique chant. The juniors chanted, "JIM-ME, JIM-ME, JIM-ME!" They were obviously proud of their choice. Jimmy simply sat in the stands, quiet but smiling.

This particular Homecoming was the first time in over 20 years that the St. Genevieve football team would have a Homecoming game with an undefeated record. The day before the game, *Los Angeles Times* sports columnist Eric Sondheimer wrote a column headlined, "At 7-0, a revived St. Genevieve football program merits a parade."

We hosted the largest crowd for a St. Genevieve High School football game in well over a decade. The stands were overflowing, and dozens of former Valiant football players were on the field watching from the end zone. The stakes were high; the St. Anthony Saints had come prepared to sock it to us. We won the game and were thrilled that our winning streak continued.

Even with the wonderful victory, the record crowd, and the amazing halftime performance, the main image I could not get out of my head was the incredible sight of that year's Homecoming parade.

There was the convertible carrying a smiling, waving, redhead, our "Prince Jimmy." Instead of marching in the parade, I positioned myself midway along the parade route. As the parade passed by, many of the marching students did the same thing I had done decades earlier whenever I'd recognize a familiar face. They shouted, whooped, and screamed, *"Hello Mr. Horn!"* They were having fun and they wanted to be noticed. There were hundreds of people waving hands, just having fun being part of a community. On that day we created a small-town feel within our big city. Strangers waved from their cars, honked approval, and gave the "thumbs up." Even those inconvenienced as they attempted to exit the Hollywood Freeway onto Roscoe Boulevard honked and waved. Who doesn't love a parade? Who doesn't love being part of a community? And who doesn't love winning?

With the record attendance, spectacular halftime show and grand parade, we experienced several victories that day aside from the one on the scoreboard. But the greatest victory of all was knowing that in its 50th year, our school had become an oasis for young people of every persuasion to succeed, a school where everyone had a place at the proverbial table of equality and acceptance.

Michael Jackson was a man who was widely misunderstood and thus became a target for tabloids and legal predators. Michael would have loved our school and how we were able to touch both the hearts and minds of young people. I believe it would have made him happy to know that there was a school like ours that ensured that young people who otherwise may have become targets, were instead respected. I'm certain that he would have smiled as widely as I did while watching that convertible carrying an enthusiastic redheaded boy waving happily at the crowd along two miles of Roscoe Boulevard.

For one entire week at St. Genevieve, we danced to the music of Michael Jackson and treated our prince of a man named Jimmy like royalty. It was Homecoming!

Junior representatives Angel
Candelaria and Jimmy Musser

The junior class prince and princess riding in their convertible

Chapter 22. Angels Everywhere

"Something's going on," I said to my passenger, Vince. We were suddenly stuck in Friday evening traffic on Roscoe Boulevard, a six-lane thoroughfare that usually rides like a bustling freeway. But not today. We were just a half block from our school, and traffic was at a standstill, brake lights flashing as far as we could see, drivers milling outside of their cars with the engines running. I'd never seen Roscoe Boulevard like this.

Vince, my good friend, and I were arriving back to St. Genevieve High School after chaperoning a four-day Kairos retreat in Pismo Beach. We were tired to the bones. The Kairos retreat is for high-school seniors, and is a rewarding and emotionally grueling experience for both participants and chaperones. After driving 200 miles to get home, we were eager to retrieve our things at school and begin a weekend of some well-deserved rest. But the traffic was not cooperating.

"Why is everyone stopping?" I wondered aloud. "This makes no sense."

My car inched slowly forward, until I could just squeeze onto Ranchito Street, leading to the school's driveway. As I turned in, tires squealed ahead of us, a driver sped up quickly and swerved into the oncoming lanes. Now the roadway was entirely blocked in both directions. A crowd was beginning to gather, buzzing with confusion about what they were witnessing.

I could see our athletic director, Marlon Archey, quickly exiting from his car in the school's lot. "A baby was thrown from a car," he screamed, while running toward the commotion on Roscoe.

Could this be? A baby tossed from a car? Both Vince and I joined Marlon, dashing through the gate to see how we could help. We gathered with other bystanders, who were beginning to crowd the sidewalks. We soon learned it had not been an infant that was thrown, but it was a tragedy just as horrific. What happened that afternoon, I will never forget.

The gruesome details became known in short order. A mother and her eight-year-old daughter were crossing Roscoe Boulevard, and when the light turned green, they stepped into the crosswalk. When they reached the third lane of traffic, a drunken man drove his pickup truck through the red light, hitting the girl in broad daylight.

Her third-grade backpack, strapped around her shoulders, got caught on the man's vehicle and this tiny soul was dragged along the boulevard the entire length of our school's parking lot, approximately seventy yards. Her bloodied body was hidden from view, but we all feared the worst.

At this moment, the long drive home and the exhaustion from the Kairos retreat were the last things on my mind. But little did I know how helpful the many lessons from that retreat would be as this tragedy unfolded.

Kairos is a Greek word meaning "God's Time." During our previous four days at the Kairos retreat, we'd engaged in many profound discussions. Following a long and intense day, as the group was about to adjourn on Wednesday, a student asked, "Where is God when someone suffers from a tragedy?" He looked around the quiet room. "I'm not talking about death," he said, and clarified, "everybody dies. I mean when horrible things happen to good people."

In this instant on Roscoe Boulevard, his question came flooding back to me.

Often at Kairos retreats, students share personal stories about their families and life experiences. This particular student shared memories of a horrific moment that had occurred in his own life, and asked the group's leaders, "Where was God when that happened to me?"

I'm certain none of us were prepared to answer that question once he framed it in the context of what had happened to him. I struggled to find the right words, and tried to speak from my heart.

"It boils down to faith," I said. "God is everywhere. God does not cause tragedy, but God is there during the tragic moments. At a time of suffering, if we look hard enough, we can see God. We can find the spirit of Christ in those who are there to help."

I continued, uncertain if my words would truly bring comfort to this young man. "Sometimes, it's that person who is there to pick you up after a fall, to reach out a hand to help you, or to whisper in your ear that the angels have arrived. The spirit of Christ lives in those angels on earth. You must learn to look for the angels, even in the most difficult situations, and be prepared to become one when you have the opportunity to help someone else."

I sincerely trusted my words with my heart and faith, but I felt somewhat inadequate at that moment, unsure if my beliefs would translate to this student who had personally experienced such pain. Nevertheless, I assured him and his peers that his revelation took great bravery.

"By revealing what happened to you, it allows us to get you some help and it opens the door for others in the room who have suffered silently to step forward and reach out for assistance in dealing with their own heartaches and pain," I told this young man, who was stronger of character and courage than even he yet knew. "You've become an angel tonight. Always remember to look for the angels and you will see God."

Now, as I stood on Roscoe Boulevard amidst the confusion of this real-life horrible accident, I quickly flashed back to the Kairos retreat, and realized I was confronted with putting my own advice into action. In the street, near the spot where her daughter had been hit, the mother stood wailing, "My baby, my daughter, where is my daughter?"

Her cries rang out in excruciating agony.

Gently, I stepped toward her and led her back to a bench at the nearby bus stop. She was sobbing uncontrollably, desperately calling out for her child.

I didn't know where her daughter was at this point, or what condition she was in, so I wasn't sure how to respond. Off in the distance, I heard the sound of sirens becoming louder as the paramedics were drawing closer, and instantly thought to myself, "The angels are about to arrive."

Cautiously, I said to her, "Your daughter is going to be fine," secretly hoping that I was telling the truth. "Help is on the way. Do you hear the sirens? People are coming to help her."

Her eyes raised up and looked directly into mine. "Help me find her," she pleaded. "Do you know if she is alive?"

I did not, but fortunately, a young couple behind us said they had just seen her little girl, and that she *was* alive, was able to speak, and was in need of some medical assistance. Paramedics soon arrived and we all accompanied the mom to the ambulance.

The young couple looked shaken. They whispered to me that they had seen everything, as their car had been directly behind the pickup truck that had caused the accident. They'd watched in horror as the drunk driver careered obliviously through the red light, hitting the young girl and dragging her small body under the wheel.

When they realized the driver had no intention of stopping, their instincts took control. It was this brave couple whose car I'd witnessed swerving quickly into the oncoming traffic lane, stopping all traffic going both ways. They did so intentionally, blocking the pickup and giving the intoxicated driver no choice but to stop.

I knew then that I was in the company of two angels.

With an ambulance already there, a number of fire trucks arriving, and more sirens in the distance, the scene was becoming increasingly chaotic. Crowds grew on both sides of the street, as hundreds of cars attempted to make their way through. To my amazement, many people drove directly through the emergency scene, clearly aware that something was terribly wrong but more concerned about getting to their destination than with stopping to help people in danger.

I stood next to the ambulance, trying to help the aching mother make a phone call to her husband. "It's 310, no, no the area code is something else, what is it, it's 818," she said frantically as she tried to remember and dictate her husband's cell phone number to me. She placed her hand across her eyes as if trying to block out the current reality to help her recall the number.

I could see our freshmen drama teacher, Dani Brown, arriving at a brisk pace. Without hesitation, she stepped off the curb and into the oncoming traffic. She raised both hands toward the cars, commanding them to STOP. And they did. Traffic came to a total halt, making the accident scene safer for all.

Watching Dani fearlessly raising her arms to stop the traffic in that moment of emergency, I felt as if I was watching an angel unfurl her wings.

Meanwhile, before the police arrived, the drunk driver and his passenger attempted to escape. They began to run away, weaving in and out of the crowd, and finally turned onto a side street where they were quickly out of sight. My friend Vince, and several others, sped into the neighborhood in hot pursuit, a self-styled posse, returning in just minutes with the two guys in tow. You could see a sense of satisfaction in Vince's eyes after capturing the driver. He and the others knew that they were responsible for helping justice be done that day.

More angels, indeed.

One of the paramedics told the mother that they would airlift her daughter to the UCLA Medical Center, about 30 minutes away. The mom was still on the phone to her husband, and asked me to speak to him while she and the paramedics talked. The dad's fearful voice resonated through the cell phone.

Clearly, he was in shock — crying, anxious, upset — as any father would be. Through his tears, he was trying to make plans about how to get to his little girl's side. He said he would wait for a bus to bring him to the Valley, then get his car and drive the long route back to UCLA.

Instinctively, I knew that on a Friday in Los Angeles, such a commute would take several hours, and this was a man who was probably in no state of mind for such a drive.

The noise on his end of the phone was loud, and there was pandemonium and confusion on our end, too. It was difficult enough for this shaken man to communicate, but even more so with the rattles of the cell phone connection, and the noise from the scene.

In that moment, I felt I had to be direct, even though this man was a total stranger to me.

"Listen to me," I insisted. "Can you hear me?" I wanted to be sure I got his attention, in the midst of the shock and tears of his human nightmare. "Yes, I can," he said. "I'm listening."

"Find a cab," I shouted into the phone, to be heard above the sirens nearby. "Find a cab, now!"

"A taxi?" he inquired.

"Yes," I said. "Get into the nearest taxi and tell the driver to take you to the UCLA Medical Center." He repeated the name of the hospital back to me.

"Leave right now and flag down a taxi. We'll be sure your wife gets there soon."

"Okay, thank you," he said. "I'll do that now." As he hung up, his shock and tears were replaced momentarily by a determination to get to his dear daughter as soon as he could.

The mom and the little girl were now in two separate ambulances, which were preparing to depart for a waiting helicopter.

"Your husband is going to meet you at the hospital," I told the mom, resting my hand on hers. "God bless you and your family."

The ambulance doors closed, and the vehicle sped off toward the helicopter that would bring them to the hospital.

I never saw the little girl. Honestly, I'm not sure I could have seen her without breaking down. But Marlon Archey from our school did see her. I hadn't seen Marlon since Vince and I first arrived, as he was running directly into the scene of the accident. Marlon had gone straight to where the little girl lay bleeding, to see if he could help.

Now, as the sirens of the retreating ambulances echoed in the distance, Marlon appeared, looking dazed. Her injuries were bad, he said. Skin and tissue had been torn from her chest. Pieces of asphalt were embedded in her flesh. He thought her legs had been broken; he witnessed the driver backing up over her legs before he was stopped. She was speaking, but severely injured. Thankfully, her backpack may have taken much of the blunt-force trauma and helped to save her life, but her condition was possibly dire.

As he sat by her side, Marlon thought of his own daughter, who was the same age as the injured girl. This compassionate father opened his gentle heart, to soothe and calm the little girl he didn't even know, in the midst of blaring noise and intense chaos on busy Roscoe Boulevard. She was a third grader at St. Genevieve Elementary School, she had told him, obviously in great pain but still alert. He held her hand, and promised to sit with her until help came.

Marlon discovered that she liked soccer. He introduced himself as the high school's soccer coach, and promised her that when she was a high school student she could play on his team. This seemed to bring a little smile to her bruised face, but her physical agony was obvious.

Here, just minutes after the horrible accident, surrounded by the panicked commotion of six lanes of traffic, a kind man sat with a suffering girl. She would have a long road of recovery ahead, but in those moments, she was comforted by an angel named Marlon.

These are just a few of the angels who helped a young girl on that fateful day, and there were many more who were instrumental in her healing in the months ahead. The paramedics, doctors, nurses, and her loving friends and family were by her side to ease her back to health.

On the day of the accident, life felt surreal. It was harrowing, and everything happened so fast. Confusion reigned.

There was so much noise that day — screaming sirens, anxious voices in the crowd, brakes squealing, engines revving. Policemen barked out instructions as children cried, clinging tightly to their mothers. Above this din were the heart-wrenching sobs from a desperate mom who almost lost her child, the kind of deep, anguished sobs that none of us wants ever to have to feel.

I will never forget those noises. But, as my memory takes me back to that horrific day, those are not the noises I remember most.

The noise that drowns out all of the others is the sweet sound of an orchestra of angel wings. From the young couple who blocked the drunk driver's car to Vince and his posse who nabbed the driver from escaping to Dani and Marlon, and to the many others who acted selflessly and without doubt.

Even in the midst of incredible tragedy, you can always find these guardians on earth; you can always find God's messengers. As I had said at the retreat, "At a time of suffering, if we look hard enough, we can see God. We can find the spirit of Christ in those who are there to help."

That was so true on this particular day. God had sent his angels…and they were *everywhere*!

Marlon Archey and Crystal in February 2014

Chapter 23. Getting Reddy

The lyrics of the song that was playing could have been written by me:

*Leave me alone, won't you leave
me alone
Please leave me alone now,
leave me alone
Leave me alone, please leave me
alone, yes leave me
Leave me alone won't you leave
me alone
Please leave me alone, no leave
me alone
Leave me alone, just leave me
alone, oh leave me*

It was Saturday morning, January 5, 1974. I had turned 13 the day before, and someone had given me Helen Reddy's *Long Hard Climb* album for my birthday. The album featured "Delta Dawn," which had been a number-one hit. That particular week, "Leave Me Alone" was at number 3 on *Billboard*. The D.J. on our local radio station, Jeannette's own WBCW, was sponsoring a contest and would award a free two-liter bottle of Pepsi to the first ten callers who could correctly identify how many times Helen Reddy sang the phrase "leave me alone" during the song. I was busy counting. Just as I was near the end of the song with my count my brother came to announce that Aunt Betty was on the phone calling long distance from Ohio to wish me a belated Happy Birthday. "Damn it!" I shouted. "You made me lose count, you loser."

"   You're the loser," snapped my 18-year-old brother Bobby. "Now pick up the damn phone and say hello to your aunt," he said, leaving the room.

I was taking no chances; when I called the radio station I would give the correct answer, no willy-nilly haphazard guesses.   I was a regular listener to WBCW. During the summer when they held competitions for Pepsi for the caller who could identify a song first, I would win so many times during a week that I'd have to give my friends' names and have somebody drive us all to the station to pick up "our" winnings.   I wasn't taking any chances on this one. With Aunt Betty quickly off the phone, I counted out loud, "Thirty-three, thirty four, thirty-five, thirty…"

"I DON'T WANT TO HAVE TO TELL YOU BOYS AGAIN, NOW GET OUTSIDE AND SHOVEL THAT SIDEWALK BEFORE SOMEONE SLIPS AND FALLS. DO YOU HEAR ME?" my mom was on the first floor bellowing up the staircase.

"YES, WE CAN HEAR YOU AND SO CAN EVERYBODY ELSE ON SECOND STREET," I yelled back. Was she kidding? Of course we could hear her. I remember thinking, "This is what it would sound like if Godzilla attacked."

Helen Reddy could sure belt out a tune, but she was simply no match for my maniacal-sounding mom. The snow was several inches high on our sidewalk and until it got shoveled there was no doubt that my mother was not going to "leave *me* alone."

After braving the cold and removing snow from a few of the neighbors' sidewalks, I returned to the warmth of my bedroom and replayed "Long Hard Climb." I put on the giant headphones I had just gotten for Christmas, and was off to counting once more. I had the right number, I was sure, and quickly dialed in to the station.   "You're our tenth and final winner," the receptionist said. "We'll announce your name at the top of the hour. By the way, how many times did you have to listen to the song to know it was 43 times?"

"I wasn't counting," I said.

I listened to that song over and over again until I had memorized all the lyrics. Once I knew all the lyrics, I attempted to identify every instrument in the band. The more I listened to the song, the more mesmerized I became. Instead of liking the song less, I grew to like it more and more and more.

Back in those days, I'd buy an album based on the singer's or band's one or two hit songs, and then would often be disappointed by the other songs on the album. With Helen's album, too, I listened mainly to the two songs that were familiar to me from airplay. However, as I began to listen to the rest of the album, I found myself growing fond of her voice in general. Her pronunciation was impeccable; I'd listen to her music and would seldom need to check the liner notes for the lyrics because her diction was near perfect. I preferred it when Helen belted a tune — whether fast or slow — versus her softer renditions. I heard strength in her voice and was attracted to that.

Later that year, while I was shopping at the record store on Clay Avenue in Jeannette, I noticed another Helen Reddy album titled, *I Don't Know How To Love Him*. I bought it and found myself listening to it over and over again. I often did that, but I now found myself listening to Helen's two albums more than any others. I loved Helen's version of "I Don't Know How To Love Him," from the rock opera, *Jesus Christ Superstar*. I remembered hearing Yvonne Elliman's version on the radio. I later learned that this was Helen's first hit record. Yvonne had released her version first, which reached number 28 on the charts, and Helen's, coming a few months later, reached number 13.

At the record store, I noticed that Helen had another album, *I Am Woman*. I remembered hearing frequent airplay of that song on the radio. "I Am Woman" was Helen's first song to reach number 1. However, when it had been at the top of the charts, I had paid little attention. Although "I Am Woman" remained one of my least favorites on the album of the same title, I instantly found other gems that Helen had recorded and had even been hits prior to my discovery of her. There were songs penned by Graham Nash and Leon Russell, and there was Helen's version of Van Morrison's "Crazy Love," which was one of my favorites.

Listening to Helen's music became like a drug for me. I simply could not get enough of her voice, and I needed daily fixes. Thankfully, at that time, Helen was releasing two and three albums a year.

During the summer of 1974, Helen released *Love Song for Jeffrey*, an album dedicated to her family, and in particular, to her husband/manager Jeff Wald. The album cover opened like a book, and inside there were photos of Helen with various members of her family. She had two children — a daughter, Traci, and a toddling son, Jordan. There were also pictures of Helen with her father, mother, and Aunt Helen, for whom she was named. By the summer of 1974, Helen was one of Capitol Records' best-selling artists. She had been given her own television show during the summer of '73, and was becoming a regular on daytime talk shows like Merv Griffin, Dinah Shore, and Mike Douglas, as well as on The Tonight Show starring Johnny Carson. She hosted the American Music Awards and eventually became the permanent host of the Midnight Special, a Friday night rock and pop variety show, which featured top artists of the day. There was no shortage of Helen on TV or in print. The more I learned about her, the more I came to admire her.

I learned that Helen was a native of Australia and had won an American Idol-like contest in which she beat out more than 1,000 other contestants in order to come to the United States. The prize was a trip to New York and an audition with a record company. She arrived as a young single mother with only $300 to her name. After learning that the record company had been expecting a male group and had no interest in a female solo act, she sold her return ticket and stayed in the States illegally. She was determined to build a career in show business. I found her story inspiring.

It got to the point where I could no longer wait for the record store in Jeannette to carry a new Helen Reddy record. Now I was frequently calling the Record Mart in the Greengate Mall, inquiring about any new music from Helen. The Record Mart was hip, it was current. They would get new music days or even weeks ahead of the sad little record store in Jeannette. Whenever I was at the mall, I would pop into the Record Mart and ask the leprechaun-looking female manager about the next album. "Didn't you just call here this morning?" she once asked. I denied it. Not only was I embarrassed to admit that indeed I had just called that morning, but I wanted her to think there were numerous Helen Reddy fans who also needed their fix.

Unless Helen had specifically mentioned that she had a new album coming out, there was little way for fans to know when the next one would be released; at least, I didn't know how to secure that information. Therefore, I would wait a few weeks after a release and then stop by the Record Mart, go to Helen's section, and leaf through the past releases. I'd always make certain to move Helen's entire section of records to the front if she happened to be filed behind someone else with a last name beginning with "R" — sorry Leon Redbone and Otis Redding. For years, a group of my friends would hang out on some Friday nights at the Greengate Mall, where we'd spend hours playing pinball at the arcade. However, as soon as we were dropped off by one or another of our parents, I would head directly to the Record Mart for my obligatory search of the Helen Reddy bin. On those occasions when there would be a new release, I would feel pure happiness; nothing else in the world mattered. Helen's albums always had a photo of her on the cover; I had each cover memorized and would instantly recognize anything new. When her *Greatest Hits* album was released, I had to have that too, even though I already owned every song on it.

I would hold each new album very carefully on our rides home from the mall. These were the days before we were required to wear seat belts, and usually there were five of us plus a parent-driver squashed into a Dodge Dart or Buick Regal. My friends and I were into studio wrestling at the time and they would often mock a wrestling move or two in the car, pretending to put the album in harm's way. I couldn't get home fast enough, my heart beating with anticipation as to what the first track of side A would sound like. Helen always recorded a fast track for the first song on side A, and I almost always liked the faster songs. After two days I would have memorized every word of every song, even the ones I didn't like all that much.

In spring of 1976, following the release of *Ain't No Way to Treat a Lady*, Helen was scheduled to perform at the Syria Mosque in Pittsburgh. I was only a freshman in high school and could not drive yet. Both my brother and sister, who had driver's licenses, were operating in a parallel universe and could not have cared one iota about what I was interested in doing; I would not be asking either one of them to drive my friends and me to the concert. One day I stopped by to visit two of my neighbors, Gus and May Clemmons, an elderly couple who lived two doors away. I was a regular visitor to most of the neighbors who lived on and near our street. At a young age, I was just as comfortable interacting with adults as well as with kids my own age. I often went from porch to porch during the summers and was welcomed inside most of the homes during the winter. When I dropped by for a visit, May was playing Helen's new album on her stereo. "That's Helen Reddy," I said, surprised. "Yeah, I like this song," May responded, attempting to dance to "Ain't No Way to Treat a Lady." I didn't miss a beat before offering, "She's gonna be live at the Syria Mosque on April 2nd. We should go!"

"Yeah, we should," said May, an easygoing and attractive woman in her 60s. I knew it was a long shot. May didn't drive and her husband Gus drove her everywhere, including to and from her job as a dental receptionist. "Do you think Gus would want to go?" I asked, hopefully.

"I don't know, why don't you ask him," she replied. Before the words were out of her mouth I was on my way into their kitchen. Gus, a portly man, gruff yet kind, could only be found at the kitchen table or on the front porch. I never once saw him in their living room or dining room. Cooking, looking out the window, or reading the newspaper seemed to be his main activities.

"I don't think so, Danny, that doesn't interest me very much," he said when I asked him about the concert. I wasn't surprised.

"Maybe Penny could drive us," May volunteered after I informed her of Gus' response. Penny was one of her daughters-in-law.

On April 2, 1976, May Clemmons, three of my friends, and I were driven to the Syria Mosque in Pittsburgh by Penny Clemmons, another admirer of Helen Reddy. We were in the third row of the second balcony; it was the first concert I had ever attended. I had a camera that had a flashbulb and took so many pictures that a woman sitting in the row in front of us turned and angrily told me to stop. She was right to be angry; I didn't know concert etiquette. For months afterwards, my friends reenacted the scene of the woman growing angry with me during the concert. Although I watched the performance through binoculars most of the time because we were so far from the stage, the day following the concert I was in a dream state. I just could not get it through my head that I'd finally gotten to see Helen Reddy live. The experience only seemed to draw me further into my growing addiction.

Once I had my driver's license my life really began. I was a free man. The January blizzard of 1977, which blanketed much of the Pennsylvania and Ohio turnpikes, made my second sojourn to see Helen live more challenging than my six passengers would have preferred. When we were about a quarter mile from the theater, I put my foot on the brake as we approached a stop sign. I noticed that although my foot was where it was supposed to be, the car kept going. I was a new driver, yet experienced enough to know that the car is supposed to stop once the driver applies foot to brake. There was clearly something wrong with the brakes on the car. At the next stop sign, I asked my fellow passengers to observe the situation. It was unanimous; the brakes were not working correctly. We decided that since there weren't many cars on the road what with all the snow, we should keep going. In my mind, there was no choice. We had driven 150 miles for this concert. We'd worry about the brakes later.

After the show, my friends and I waited at the stage door. There were only a few others waiting. A comedienne named Elaine Boosler, who had been the opening act, came through the door first. "Are you all waiting for Helen?" she asked. "She'll be out in a minute." The door opened and out walked a petite Helen, bundled in a white winter coat. She looked stunning. "Helen, can I get an autograph?" asked the young woman standing next to me. Helen approached the woman and was now standing right in front of me, just a foot away. My hearing turned off. I was fixated on her, unaware of my friends or anyone else. It was just Helen and me in what felt like slow motion without sound. When Helen turned to go toward the waiting limo, I snapped back into real time, snatched the pen from the hand of the woman next to me, and pulled the program from my pocket, pleading, "Can I get an autograph, too?" Without stopping, Helen said, "That pen doesn't work." I was crushed. I had a camera, but didn't think to ask her for a photograph; I was dumbfounded. I stood staring as her limousine drove away.

As the years passed, my fanaticism grew. During the 1970s, rarely a few weeks passed that Helen wasn't on television. One of our neighbors had a weekly subscription to *TV Guide*, unlike my family, which consulted the simple guide that came in the Sunday paper. It was not as detailed as *TV Guide*, so I made it a point to visit my neighbor weekly, specifically to comb through the week's TV listings looking for Helen Reddy appearances. How I loved it when she would be co-hosting the Mike Douglas show for an entire week, or guest-hosting on the Tonight Show. I also looked forward to her annual appearances on the Carol Burnett Show.

I had two friends in high school who knew of my weekly ritual. To my surprise, they decided to become spoilers and began to get to the *TV Guide* before I did. They'd call me and say, "Did you know Helen's going to be on Merv on Tuesday?" or "Helen's filling in for Johnny on Monday."

By the 1980s, Helen's career had slowed. Her husband, Jeff Wald, suffered from a serious addiction to cocaine and one day Helen couldn't get a prescription delivered because her credit was no longer good. She was told she would have to go to the drugstore in person and pay in cash. Having accrued more than thirty million dollars in savings, she now discovered that most of it was gone. Jeff was a power in Hollywood and he had warned Helen that if she ever left him, he would bad-mouth her in the business. She divorced him and he kept his word.

Paula Poundstone joked about the Helen Reddy killer, the murderer who was killing Helen Reddy fans, because by the mid-1980s it was hard to find anyone who would admit to having ever been a fan. But Helen still had to earn a living. She still performed, although at much smaller venues; and she returned to her roots, the theater. As a youngster and young woman, Helen had mainly performed in vaudeville-like shows with her parents, who were well known throughout Australia.

When I made my first trip to California in July of 1985, my ultimate destination was to meet my aunts and uncle in Las Vegas for a few days of vacation. It was my first time west of Ohio. My aunt Betty was nervous about staying alone in a Vegas hotel room. She offered to pay my airfare if I would stay with her. I decided to fly to California first, and then drive to Las Vegas. Before flying to San Francisco, I discovered that Helen was going to be starring in *Anything Goes* at the Music Circus Theater in Sacramento. I bought a front-row ticket for a Sunday night performance. I got to say hello to Helen in the parking lot as she was getting into her car. That night, I met several other fans, who, upon hearing that I was driving all the way down to San Diego, mentioned that the following Saturday, Helen was going to be doing a concert in Santa Fe Springs, California. Although I had no idea where Santa Fe Springs was, I vowed to find out and get there. I spent the week driving the entire state before ending up visiting my childhood friend, Phil Albert, who was by then a naval officer stationed in San Diego. Phil was the son of Reverend Albert, the minister at Grace United Church of Christ in Jeannette. Phil and I became friends during my freshmen year of high school, so he was well acquainted with my fascination with Helen, and happily agreed to accompany me to her concert in Santa Fe Springs. It was an outdoor show. Afterward, we learned that Helen was at a private reception for some of the city leaders; the show was actually on the grounds of the municipal buildings. Phil and I pressed our faces up against the glass doors of the building where the reception was being held. Finally, one of the caterers came to the door to see what we wanted. "I've come all the way from Pittsburgh, Pennsylvania for this concert," I lied. "It would mean so much to me if I could come inside to say hello to Helen."

Phil quickly chimed in, "Yeah, Pittsburgh, and he's got to go back tonight. Please let him come in."

"Well," said the caterer, hesitating. Seeing that she was weakening and open to the idea, we both pleaded again, "Please, it would mean so much to me," I said. "Please, make this young man's dream come true," said Phil.

"Well, okay, but don't let anyone know I opened the door for you." And with that, we walked into a room filled with about 100 people milling about, drinks in hand, eating appetizers from trays being circulated by clean-cut servers in white jackets.

"Just act like we belong," said Phil with a knowing smile. We both laughed. It would be pretty difficult to pretend that we belonged. Everyone attending this reception was dressed semi-formally. The women were all in dresses or pant suits, the men wore suits or sport jackets, most with ties. Phil and I had come from the beach in San Diego and both of us were dressed in shorts and t-shirts. I was wearing a pair of JAMS — beach shorts with a psychedelic design — that were popular at the time. We clearly did not belong.

We looked around the room, but saw no sign of Helen. Before long, someone announced her name and out she walked, changed from her stage clothing, but dressed elegantly in a white pant suit. She was escorted to the center of the windows in the room and immediately began posing for pictures with various guests — the mayor, the vice mayor, then council members. I made my way to the photographer and, standing behind him, told him that I was a fan of Helen's from Pittsburgh. I had come all the way across the country just for tonight's show. Could I possible get a photo taken with her? I said all that into his ear as he was snapping pictures.

"I can't make that decision, son," he replied. "I'm employed by the city tonight. You'd have to get the permission from the mayor over there."

"Thank you, I'll be back," I said.

In short order I was back with the mayor, who gave his personal OK to have my picture taken with Helen. I stood in the line with the nicely dressed townspeople of Santa Fe Springs. When it was my turn, the photographer loudly announced, "Ms. Reddy, this young man has flown all the way across the country just to see your show tonight."

"It's true, Helen," I screwed up the nerve to say. "I've come all the way from Pittsburgh just to see you in concert tonight."

"That's nice," she said, unimpressed. I put my arm around her waist and, click!, time for the next person in line. It didn't matter that she could not have cared less. I was delighted. I left my name, address, and phone number with the photographer so he could send me a copy of the photo. Two months went by and I hadn't received the photo or heard a word. One afternoon in September, I called long distance from my Virginia apartment to inquire about the photo, and kept being transferred from department to department. I was growing nervous about the escalating cost of the phone bill. Finally, I reached a young-sounding woman, who seemed to know about the concert and the pictures that were taken. I described myself to her and she finally said, "Wait a minute, are you the guy in the SHORTS?" "That's me," I said, relieved. She laughed. "Oh, we had no idea who you were, but we sure got a laugh out of your outfit." The photo arrived the next week and has been a cherished possession ever since.

During the summer of 1986, Helen was appearing at the Inner Harbor in Baltimore. After the show, I walked onstage and chatted with her new husband and drummer, Milton Ruth. I told him I was a fan. He walked me backstage. He knocked on the door of Helen's dressing room and said, "Helen, a fan would like to say hello," and kept walking. The door opened. "Yes?" She had changed into jeans and t-shirt. "Hi Helen, I'm going to be moving to L.A. in September," I said. "I was wondering if you might have any jobs for an aspiring actor?"

"Oh, I can't think of anything at the moment. But it's nice to meet you. Good luck when you get to L.A. I hope you enjoyed the show."

"I did. It's nice to meet you, too."

"Well, I've got to run; my car is waiting to take me to the hotel. Goodbye."

"Bye."

Before moving to Los Angeles in September of 1986, I had written to Helen on a couple of occasions. The responses came from "staff of Helen Reddy Inc." The address was 820 Stanford Street in Santa Monica. I arrived in L.A. on a Monday, and on Tuesday, I was standing on the sidewalk of 820 Stanford Street. I was confused; it was a house, not an office building. Surely it couldn't be Helen's house, I thought. Prior to Helen's divorce, her Brentwood mansion was featured in magazines and on several TV shows. I knew what it looked like. But I had no idea what her current house looked like. Was I fortunate enough to be standing in front of the house where she was now living? It looked impressive enough to be the home of a star. I had gone to the address expecting offices. I was there to inquire about employment. In my naïve fantasy world, I had imagined that I would show up at Helen's offices and would be hired to work in a flexible job that would allow me to go on auditions and have plenty of access to Helen, who would eventually get to know me and decide to help me break into the business. Finally, breaking my reverie, a Sparkletts Water delivery person arrived on the scene.

"Excuse me; I'm looking for Helen Reddy Incorporated," I said.

"This is the address," he replied, unloading his delivery.

"But this is a house."

"She lives in the house. The business is in the back house."

I immediately grew nervous. Was she inside? I wondered.

I went to my car and got one of the horrendous headshots I'd had taken a month earlier when I was back in Virginia. At the time, I'd thought it was a great headshot. I wrote on the reverse, "Just arrived in L.A. Going to be an actor. Need to earn a living. Let me know of any jobs available." I also left the number of my new acquaintance, Jim Fleming, whose apartment I was staying at.

Two months later, in November, I received a phone call from Lucas Donat at Helen Reddy Inc. He was producing a show for Helen and was looking for someone to put flyers on cars.

"I'll do it!" I said, happily.

In December, Helen was performing for a week at the Westwood Playhouse near UCLA. I stopped at 820 Stanford Street and rang the bell. Helen answered the door. "Yes?" she said as though in a hurry.

"I'm looking for Lucas."

"He's in the back in the guest house."

"Is there a gate back there?" I inquired.

"No need, c'mon in."

I stepped into the foyer and she pointed into her living room and said, "Go that way and keep making rights. You'll eventually get to the backyard; then go up the stairs to the guest house." I was impressed that she let me, a stranger, go through almost the entire bottom floor of her home. It was not the grandiose home I had seen numerous times on television or in magazines. However, it was certainly grander than anything I was accustomed to. I was happy to know that Helen was still living in luxury.

I met Lucas, who, I would later learn, was married to Helen's daughter. Lucas handed me boxes of flyers for Helen's upcoming concerts. In a couple of days I got another call from Lucas asking if I would be available to help out at rehearsals. He said the position was that of a band runner. I jumped at it. It paid a grand total of nothing. I would volunteer my time, and I was happy to do it. I mainly ran errands, picking up sheet music and delivering it to the rehearsal stage or moving sound equipment. I was still working odd jobs for pay, and worked my paid hours around my volunteer job.

Now I was seeing Helen every single day. One day I received a message from Jonathan Tunnel, a second producer, on my answering machine, asking if I could be available for a certain errand. In the background, Helen was singing "Somewhere in the Night," one of my favorite songs. I was ecstatic and called many a friend and relative back east to play them the message.

I sat through several of the rehearsals. Once the show was underway, I was at the Westwood Playhouse all the time, either sitting in the audience or watching from backstage. It was seven days worth of shows. Helen was always friendly but distant. Once, when a band member and I were loading a heavy piece of equipment onto a truck, Helen was standing nearby. She saw us struggling and called to us to wait for her. She helped us push it into the truck and then jokingly commented, "See fellas, it takes a woman." Another time, during a rehearsal break, the subject of exercise came up. Helen, out-of-the-blue, placed a tissue on the floor and lowered herself backwards, yoga style, until her head was almost touching the ground, placed the tissue in her mouth and stood up to show the crew her flexibility. She would make casual conversation, but never asked my name or seemed interested in what I was doing there. With Helen, it was the show that mattered. She was dedicated to her craft. Each performance was the same, and her banter with the audience was largely unchanged each time. Despite that, I always looked forward to the next time.

Truthfully, had the roles been reversed, I probably would have been a bit nervous having this quiet adoring fan putting notes in my mailbox and then helping at rehearsals watching every move I made. However, as I grew to know Helen better, one thing was for certain — not many things seemed to frighten her. In fact, Helen never seemed afraid of anything. She was the personification of the strength I'd heard in her voice years earlier.

Once the series of shows at the Westwood Playhouse ended, I continued to keep in contact with Helen's crew. Soon after I became principal at St. Thomas School, I attended one of her concerts in a small club on Wilshire Boulevard in Santa Monica. Helen's husband Milt was back on drums. Mary Ekler, a lovely and artistic woman, was playing piano that night. Helen introduced a song she referred to as a "love song for the '90s," called "Here in My Arms." It was a beautiful ballad that had been written by Mary. After the show, the band members were having drinks in the club and I ended up having a drink with several of them, including Mary. Mary and I immediately hit it off and eventually become friends. When Helen appeared, she looked at me and said, "I know you." It was the first time I can remember that she showed any recognition of me. I took the opportunity to tell her about my new job as a principal at St. Thomas School. She wished me well but quickly dismissed the idea I proposed of her coming to visit the school to talk to the students about her native Australia. She was far too busy.

Once in a while I would drop by the offices on Stanford Street to extend the same invitation or to invite her to an event. Helen would always recite a litany of projects she was involved in and end by saying, "Keep in touch." Eventually, Mary Ekler, who continued to perform as Helen's pianist, agreed to come to the school to play for an event. Mary, like so many people, instantly liked our community, and recognized the value of integrating performing arts into the elementary school curriculum. Mary traveled a lot with Helen as well as with Little Anthony and the Imperials, but whenever she was available to play for one of our events, she accepted. In fact, Mary still plays for events at St. Thomas School.

One day in the spring of 1998, Mary called to ask if we would be willing to rent our keyboard to Helen for a week. Helen was about to host some guests from England, and one of them had need for a keyboard while he was there. By the end of the day, Joe Neeb and I were delivering the keyboard to Helen. A week later when we were picking it up, Helen asked if we would be interested in hearing a song from her upcoming CD, *Centerstage.* "Do you have time, Joe?" I asked, knowing with certainty that Joe would not say anything to deny me this moment. Helen turned the volume up loud as we listened to "Blow, Gabriel, Blow," from the Broadway show, *Anything Goes.* It had been more than ten years since I'd first heard Helen sing the same song on the stage of the Music Circus Theater in Sacramento on my first trip to California. As the CD played loudly, Helen sang along, obviously happy with her own recording.

"It's great, Helen," I said, when the song came to an end. "Is the rest of the CD as good as that?"

"You be the judge," she said, coyly, handing me a copy.

"What about me? I carried the keyboard, too, can I get one?" Joe asked, without feeling the least bit intimidated.

"Well, I suppose so," Helen said as she went to her office to get a CD for Joe.

By 1998, St. Thomas School had begun serious efforts to create and sustain a development office, and we had high hopes of erecting a new school building and leaving an endowment for the school. Knowing that the 1998-99 school year was going to be my last, I decided to do whatever was necessary to convince Helen to visit St. Thomas and perform a benefit concert to enhance our development efforts. Although she was a long way from the superstardom she'd enjoyed in the 1970s, she was still a well-known icon whose appearance at our school would give credibility to our marketing and development efforts. By now, Mary Ekler and I had formed a friendship. I knew that Mary was on the road a lot with Helen. I decided to propose the idea to Mary and have Mary do the ask. Mary returned from a concert they had done in Utah and said that Helen listened to her proposal to do the concert, but made no commitment. I decided I had nothing to lose by asking again myself. I knew I would get tongue-tied, so I wrote a letter to Helen in August of 1998. No reply. A few weeks later I got up the nerve to call her office to see if I could get her on the phone. When she answered, I said, "Helen, did you get my letter regarding the concert for St. Thomas?"

"Yes, Dan, you know I've been so busy. As you know, I'm on the road touring in *Shirley Valentine*, and I'm doing concerts all over the place. If I did it, it would have to be on October 2nd."

"Let's plan on it," I said without even checking a calendar. I didn't want to give her time to talk herself out of the possibility.

"All right then, I'll be in touch about the details," she said. "Give me your number."

I had not even given serious thought as to where we would hold this event. We didn't have a large enough auditorium. Eventually, we secured the social hall at St. Sophia Greek Orthodox Cathedral, which was across the street from our school. The community there donated the use of the space to us. Once we had the date and place, we were able to have tickets printed and begin advertising. However, while the pastor at St. Sophia, Father John Bakas, had led a successful campaign to revitalize our corner of Pico-Union and the neighborhood was now safer, cleaner, and much less intimidating than it had been in the early '90s, most people outside the area were not aware of all the changes that had taken place. Many potential concertgoers were put off by the idea of coming to the corner of 15th and Pico to attend a Helen Reddy concert.

I got an idea. I asked Helen to consider coming to the school to be interviewed by some local media to help get the word out that the neighborhood had changed. She agreed. We scheduled an interview with a local TV station for Saturday, September 26th at 11:00 a.m. Helen arrived early. I greeted her at her car saying, "Since you're early, let me give you a little tour of our school."

"Don't try to convert me," she responded.

I walked her around our school grounds and eventually we wound up in my office. As we were waiting, something unexpected happened. We began talking to one another on a personal level. As it turned out, President Clinton had made a "last minute" trip to L.A. that day and our reporter called to postpone until "next week." Helen didn't mind. Instead, we sat in my office and talked about my career in education, as well as Helen's recent dating life. She was now divorced from her third husband. As she was leaving my office, she offered to come back, saying, "Just give me two hours notice and I'll be here." Who was this woman? "You have my personal number don't you?" What would make her think that I had her personal phone number? Hesitatingly, I said, "No, you've never given that to me." Getting into her car she said, "Well, it's easy to remember, it's ..." I ran back to my office and quickly wrote it down.

The following week, two local TV channels agreed to come to help publicize our community's changed circumstances. Shaun Hubler wrote a column for the *Los Angeles Times* about the upcoming event and the changes in the neighborhood. As promised, with little notice, Helen visited the school two more times during the week of the show, both times when the students were there. That is when I saw a new side of Helen's personality. It was apparent that she loved children. She would stop and talk to the little ones, and at one point when some of the older students were practicing a dance number, Helen jumped in and joined the group learning their steps. Her appearances at the school worked; the phones lit up after the news reports and coverage in the *Times*.

By Friday evening, we were ready. Our neighbors opened their breathtakingly beautiful cathedral that night so our guests could stroll through on their way from the parking lot into the social hall.

Helen arrived earlier in the afternoon for a sound-check. She walked into the auditorium, hair in curlers wrapped with a silk leopard-print scarf. Joe and I were sitting at one of the tables watching students rehearse for their opening act. Joe greeted Helen, joking, "I almost wore the same scarf; good thing I chose something else." No reaction from Helen. She sat with us and watched the student performances. She called over one of the 7th-grade boys who was singing a solo to offer him a couple of tips. When it was her turn for the sound-check she chose the number, "Tell Me It's not True," from *Blood Brothers*. The song is my favorite number Helen has ever recorded. It is sung from the perspective of a mother who has just witnessed the murders of two sons. It starts slowly and builds to a booming finish; it takes a big voice to do it justice. Helen instructed, "I'm going to sing it the whole way through;

I need to clean out my pipes." Once Helen got going, even the people who didn't know her — the ladies working in the kitchen and the janitorial staff — came into the auditorium to see where this voice was coming from. She was stunning.

Later that evening, the sound man who accompanied Helen inquired if I would like to introduce her. I jumped at the opportunity. "Don't take all night," said Helen."

"Good evening, ladies and gentlemen, and thank you for coming," I began. "When Helen heard that I was introducing her she advised, 'Don't take all night.'" Turning toward the wings where Helen was waiting, I joked, "Helen, I'm the principal here, and I'm going to take all the time I please." (Laughter from the audience.) Turning back to the audience, I continued, "I began listening to Helen Reddy when I was in the 7th grade. I have loved her music for a long time. This concert tonight is to benefit a school that I have loved for a long time. It is a privilege for me to have a singer I have loved for so long performing at the school I have loved for so long. Welcome to St. Thomas the Apostle School, and please help me in welcoming Ms. Helen Reddy!"

She opened the show with "Blow, Gabriel, Blow." Helen was a knock-out. Her voice was seasoned, strong, and I must admit, better than I had ever heard it. She was a star doing a favor for a long-time fan.

The next week I was back at her house to drop off some thank-you letters from the kids. "I'm just about to eat," she said. "Have you had your dinner yet?" She set an extra plate at her kitchen table and we ate dinner together. We discovered that we were both movie buffs and decided that we would see a film together the next weekend. We were becoming friends, which included Helen getting to know my big black Labrador retriever/greyhound mix named Blue. Helen loved dogs and took a liking to Blue, who went almost everywhere with me. Whenever I visited her, Helen insisted that Blue should have the run of her yard instead of waiting in the car. But when we went out to a movie or a restaurant,

I preferred to have Blue wait in the car; I was concerned that if I left him in Helen's yard he might panic and make his way over the wall surrounding Helen's property.

One night after attending a movie in Santa Monica, we arrived back at the garage where we'd parked the car, but it was not there. My heart sank. I wasn't concerned about the car being stolen; I was worried about what had happened to Blue, who was in the car. Helen went one way and I went the other. We covered every floor of the parking garage in case I was mistaken about the floor we'd parked on. When we met up again I was shattered at the thought of someone having taken my dog. Helen suggested I talk to the attendant and that we summon the police. "Let me see your ticket," said the attendant, unimpressed by my pleas to call the police. Looking at the ticket, he said, somewhat annoyed, "You're parked in the garage a block from here." There were two identical parking garages one block apart. Blue was right where we had left him.

Shortly after I became principal at St. Genevieve High School, I considered going to Canada with Helen, who was scheduled to perform there in a concert with a symphony orchestra. Things were so hectic in my early days at St. Genevieve that I decided not to make the trip, knowing that I would be able to take advantage of a similar opportunity when it arose. Helen did not mention until her return that this had been her final public performance. She was retiring from show business and was putting her home up for sale. She had made a decision to move to Norfolk Island, a small island in the Pacific Ocean between Australia and New Zealand. I was saddened. Helen had been my idol for most of my life, and almost as soon as she had become my friend, she announced that she was moving to the other side of the world.

When I expressed my sadness to her, Helen, in her usual fashion, paid no heed, and simply said, "You'll get over it."

I helped her pack and received some of the furniture she wanted to give away. Before I knew it, Helen was gone from Los Angeles and largely from my life. She would return to L.A. once or twice each year. Sometimes I would get a phone call from her the night before she was leaving to go back to Norfolk Island. Eventually, she moved again to Sydney, where she had family and friends. On one of her trips to L.A., we were having dinner together and I told her about the speaker's series we had established at St. Genevieve. She seemed interested. I informed her that we invited various guests to lecture to an audience of both students and parents on subjects of leadership and character. I knew that Helen was now lecturing around the country on the subject of global transformation. I suggested that she consider stopping by St. Genevieve on her lecture circuit. No luck. When she was in the States promoting her autobiography, *The Woman I Am*, I suggested that she come by and talk about the book and her life's journey. No luck. Helen would not say a definitive no, but made it clear that it wouldn't be happening anytime soon.

It has become a St. Genevieve tradition to hold overnight retreats for our freshmen the first two weekends of the school year — the first weekend, the boys retreat is led by the boys of our senior class, and the girls retreat the following weekend is led by the senior girls. During the retreats, the freshmen learn some of the music that our school sings on a regular basis. However, one song that only our girls learn is Helen's "I Am Woman." I want them to learn it because it is so empowering for them to sing it. We also have added to the chorus so it goes, *"I am strong, I am invincible, I am Woman, I am smart, I am beautiful, I am powerful..."* The girls always have a lot of fun singing it. In the fall of 2009, the senior leaders were talking to the freshman girls about some of their recent personal experiences with boys.

One girl said, "Sometimes it takes him days to respond to my text, but when he texts me, he expects an immediate response." Another complained, "When we go out, he looks like a slob, but he expects me to dress up for him."

After I heard about some of these comments and subsequent conversations, I suggested that some of the girls write to Helen to invite her to be part of our speaker's series. They all decided to write letters and I sent them to Helen's Sydney address. Within weeks, I received an email from Helen saying that she would like to speak during her visit to L.A. in April. A few days later I received another email letting me know that she was making an earlier trip, in February, and if I preferred, she could speak in February instead of waiting until April.

On Thursday evening, February 11, 2010, I once again had the distinguished pleasure of introducing Helen Reddy to a community I loved and had been serving for years.

My introduction included numerous clips of Helen at the height of her show business career. We had a packed house of students, families, and friends, and I wanted to remind everyone of the amazing celebrity status Helen had achieved. When the clips were over, the student body stood and, accompanied by a live band, sang a rousing rendition of "Delta Dawn."

Helen then spoke on numerous topics, from the women's movement and the war in Iraq to current gender roles and the aquaponic garden she maintained on Norfolk Island. When Helen finished her speech, I invited her to stand with me on the Valiant crest at the gymnasium's center. I explained that our young ladies wanted to honor her by singing the song she had sent to number one on the charts almost 40 years earlier. When with great anticipation I handed Helen the microphone as the band and students belted "I Am Woman," she begged off singing.

The girls and women in the room sang the lyrics. When it came to the chorus, the boys joined in on the adjectives:

Girls: *I am strong!*

Boys: *Strong!*
Girls: *I am invincible!*
Boys: *Invincible!*

When the song finished, I asked Helen if she would accept a blessing from our community. She nodded her assent. Surrounded by the members of the senior class, she faced the audience in their chairs and the remainder of students in the bleachers. As the opening chords to the "Anointing" began to play, the students put their arms around one another and around Helen. As was usual, there was a gentle swaying in rhythm to the music. The students joyfully sang:

> *Anointing, fall on you,*
> *Anointing, fall on you,*
> *May the power of the Holy Ghost,*
> *fall on you,*
> *Anointing, fall on you.*

Several students had volunteered to pray verbally for Helen during the anointing. I would begin the spoken prayer and then pass the microphone. I faced Helen and the senior class who now stood with arms entwined around one another. I told Helen that she had been a moral compass for me throughout my life. I thanked her and thanked God for forging a friendship that had truly been a blessing in my life.

I'm not certain what else I said prior to passing the microphone. What I am certain of is seeing a look in Helen's eyes I had never seen before. Helen appeared humbled by this experience. I watched as she looked into the bleachers and at the faces encircling her. As she looked around the crowded gymnasium, her eyes kept darting back to me, but she did not look through me or past me — she looked straight into my eyes. She appeared to be soaking up the love and affection being offered by the senior class, who affectionately surrounded her. Her countenance said many things to me that evening, and each time our eyes met, I could sense her deep gratitude.

I had never before — nor have I since — felt the kind of connection to Helen that I felt that night. The performer I'd idolized for decades and who, for many years, seemed never to notice that I was even in the room, now kept glancing back at me during these anointing moments. Finally! Helen Reddy who had written and sung the iconic song, "I Am Woman," looked at me, Dan Horn, as though I was the only man standing in this crowded room. Her heart was full, and so was mine.

My first picture with Helen (I had crashed a private event in Santa Fe Springs, CA, 1985)

Helen with members of the St. Thomas staff following her benefit concert, October 2, 1998

Chapter 24. Oh So Blue

It was morning at St. Thomas the Apostle School. To be exact, it was Friday morning, May 13, 1994. As was typical of all mornings, things were busy. There were children being dropped off by parents, many of whom gathered on the schoolyard, waiting until the outside daily announcements were over and their children were safely inside and out of their line of vision. There was the excitement of the day ahead, especially among the younger students who looked forward to seeing their friends and teachers. And there was the hustle and bustle of the teachers making their last-minute copies and having a last cup of coffee.

This particular Friday morning had an added sense of excitement because a *dog* had wandered onto our grounds. Now, I knew for a fact that every one of our students had seen a dog before and that numerous families owned their very own dogs. Because of the presence of the little children as well as the food that frequently got dropped on the ground at this inner-city oasis, our elementary school was often visited by stray dogs as well as by neighborhood pets who had somehow gotten off their leashes.

This Friday morning, we apparently were receiving a visit from a stray; no one recognized him, but the principal received many reports and varying descriptions about this doggie: he was big, he was giant, he was huge, he was the biggest dog anyone had ever seen. He also was dark, he was black, he was blue, he was dirty, he was smelly, he was cute, he looked mean, he looked sad, he looked hungry. The final report was that he was hiding under Mr. O'Rourke's truck and wouldn't come out.

We had certain routines for dogs who wandered onto our campus, which depended on the visiting dog and its interactions. If the animal had a tag, we inevitably found a way to entice it close enough so that someone could read the number on the tag and we could then contact the owner. If there was no tag, we often called animal control. On occasion, a family would adopt the critter on the spot. On this particular Friday the 13th, the day had gotten off to a very busy start, and we quickly forgot about the lost soul under the truck. He was under the truck, after all, not in anyone's way. Fridays were half-days for the students, and the faculty had Friday afternoon meetings after the children left for the day.

Kevin O'Rourke, who was the fourth-grade teacher and by then a personal friend of mine, knew that I was a real dog lover. He also knew that I had recently purchased a townhouse and that in the coming months, once I moved in, I was considering getting a dog. As soon as our afternoon meeting was finished, Kevin quickly left for a weekend in San Francisco; he was driving up the coast and didn't have time to waste.

All of a sudden, as I sat at the secretary's desk opening mail, Kevin rushed back into the office holding a forlorn-looking black beast on the makeshift leash he had fashioned from his belt. Bringing the dog right beside me, he announced, "Here's your new dog." He took the belt from around the dog's neck, laced it back through the loopholes of his own slacks, and said, "See you Monday!"

Before I could react, Kevin had vanished through the office door and was already in his car bound for San Francisco. There was, however, a parade of young onlookers from our afterschool daycare program who had come in with Mr. O'Rourke and now dallied to giggle at their principal getting a new dog, and to ask a wide range of questions like: "Are you going to keep him?" "What will you name him?" "Do you like him?" "Can I pet him?" "I don't think he likes you very much, do you think he likes you Mr. Horn?" Then came the daycare supervisor, a small middle-aged Latina who didn't like the fact the children were out of her sight for even a moment. She entered speaking Spanish and pointing to the door to lead them back outside. A large chorus of "Bye doggie," was heard as they waved to him on their way back outside. The daycare supervisor gave a sour look and said, "*El perro esta feo*," meaning the dog is ugly, as she shook her head disapprovingly and followed the last of her charges.

I looked at this mess of a dog sitting beside me. All of the reports had been accurate. He was big, he looked sad, he looked mean, and he looked hungry...and boy was he ever dirty! I knew I couldn't keep him. I wasn't scheduled to move into my townhouse for two more months and the place I was currently living did not allow pets...period.

I looked at this scrawny animal whose every rib was visible, and was overcome with an *I don't know what to do with him* feeling. Up close, his black coat looked even more like the color of dirt, mainly because it was largely covered in dirt and gum with some tar thrown in. I could tell he had beautiful but sad eyes, but he refused eye contact. His body language mimicked how I was feeling. I sensed that he was tempted to run from me, but at the moment knew he wasn't being hurt in any way, so he just stayed put. He appeared largely perplexed by his entrapment. It was sad for me to realize as I sat staring at him, not wanting to get my hands or clothes dirty from his filthy coat, that this big ol' bag of bones was someone's garbage. He had no tags or collar and the fur on his neck was not at all indented, indicating that he had never worn a collar. He was as afraid of the children who followed him into the room as he'd been of Kevin, the adult who'd escorted him in. Knowing that he had spent the entire work day under a truck without moving, even after the engine started, I understood very quickly that this animal was experiencing extreme fear.

At that moment, I did not have it in my heart to take him to a pound. I would at least give him one night of peace, with food and water included. If anyone in my apartment building asked, I would say I was pet-sitting for a friend. I only hoped that no one would get too close.

It was a challenge just to get the big bugger into my car. I covered my seats with newspapers. The trip to my apartment was less than 30 minutes, and the entire time, this dog sat behind my seat attempting to melt into the corner, seemingly to get as far away from me as possible.

I'll always remember our three-block walk from my apartment to the neighborhood Trader Joes where I went to buy dog food. Two different individuals angrily chastised me on the way to the store because of the dog's appearance and frightened behavior. I'd made a makeshift leash and collar using a jump rope. The dog tried to stay as far as possible from me while also trying not to get too close to anyone we were passing on the sidewalk. He appeared to behave like one would expect an abused animal to respond. He did not know how to walk on a leash and didn't have the slightest interest in stopping to "smell the roses," as most normal dogs do. He walked with a sense of panic, rushing ahead of me, waiting for me to pass, and then rushing ahead of me again. After the angry greetings from the passersby, I decided to take a different way home; one far less busy than Santa Monica Boulevard.

I placed bowls of water and food in a corner of my living room far away from where I sat on the sofa. He kept his eye on me while he drank and drank and drank until the bowl was empty, and then he vomited. I cleaned up as he tried to make himself invisible in the corner. After that, he dug into the bowl of food while keeping his wary and weary eyes upon me the entire time. Somehow he managed to keep the food down. The blanket I had placed on the floor for him to rest on was the subject of his skepticism until his heavy eyes and head just got the best of him. Although he did his best to stay awake and to stand guard for his own safety, his head kept drooping, and eventually he allowed his front legs to give way and he rolled onto the blanket and went into a deep sleep. Every now and then he would awaken and jump a bit, listening to the voices coming from the television and see that I, his captor, was still firmly ensconced on the couch, and then sleep would again overtake him.

At some point during the evening, I quietly made the move to go to sleep on the futon in my small bedroom without disturbing the dog. When I awoke the next morning, the Saturday morning sun was beaming through the bedroom window, and I was in no hurry to get up and go anywhere. I was a little apprehensive about any possible messes my guest may have made during the night, but knew there was nothing I could do about it now. I just lay there.

Almost soundlessly, my visitor approached my open bedroom door. He was walking on top of the carpet as gingerly as possible so as not to make any noise. He was taller than my bed, which was a futon mattress atop a wood frame.

Perhaps it was the fact that he was looking down at me as I lay spread-eagled, head still buried in my pillow, or perhaps it was the fact that I had done him no harm and had fed him, but he now approached the bed, stared into my face, and made...eye contact!

I wonder if he has to go out, I thought. Well of course he does. I threw on some shorts and a t-shirt as he quickly backed away from me, fearful of my rapid movements. I managed to calm him down and noticed as we passed through the living room that all of the floor space looked dry — no messes. This dog is house-trained, I thought. He was someone's pet; someone very cruel, I surmised. We made it out of the apartment and back without incident.

After some breakfast for both of us and a little morning TV, I decided he could spend the entire weekend without me getting into any trouble. He had not made a sound — not a growl, not a bark, a woof, a sigh, nothing. My neighbors would never know he was there. Fortunately, there were only 10 units in my building and we all entered from the outside. I was in number 10, so all I had to do was take him down my stairs, and the entrance to the garage was just around the corner. I could load him into the car and take him to a park for exercise. However, first I had to get him to agree to a bath.

Once I lifted him into my bathtub, he knew the cruel treatment was about to come back into his life and he panicked. However, I could not keep this stinky, mangy mutt in my apartment a minute more without giving him the benefit of some baby shampoo and water. I closed the shower door as we took our turns getting clean for the day. As the shower spray hit his fur, it seemed as though the dirt was part of him, but it gradually got washed away after repeated shampooing. Afterwards, as I rubbed his coat with towels to help him dry, he realized I was not going to hurt him, and I realized we were starting to bond. I'd better get him to a pound first thing on Monday, I said to myself.

By the time he was lying on his side across the middle of my futon, allowing me to gently stroke his beautiful sun-drenched blue-black coat, I knew I was falling for this big puppy. As I tilted my head to better view the blue sheen of his newly coiffed coat, I heard myself asking, "Why are you so blue?" He lay very still, and I realized that he had not made a sound and seemed to always be trying to just melt away into some corner to avoid any more suffering. I said again, softly, "Huh fella, why are you so blue?"

Oh no, I've named him, I thought. I realized that I had crossed a line and would not be able to take Blue to a pound. In an instant, Blue was mine, and I was his.

My new, fully-grown pup stood the approximate size of a baby colt, or at least that's how it often seemed. When I took him in for a check-up and appropriate shots, the vet told me he was about 11 months old. She also said that he was most likely a mixture of Labrador retriever and greyhound. She said his long legs and pointed nose indicated greyhound; he was taller than a Lab.

As it turned out, Blue was the perfect name for him. Not only would this sad critter with his worried eyes embody the name, he also caused me to feel more than my fair share of blueness over the years to come.

About two weeks after I adopted Blue, he became very sick. Since I was not allowed to have pets in my apartment, I was taking him with me to school each day. Soon after arriving at school one morning, Blue began to breathe heavily and his body began to convulse as though he were doing doggie push-ups. My instinct told me that he was about to vomit. We rushed outside to the small piece of grass right outside the neighboring convent. Once in the grass, he vomited everything he had eaten that morning, then sat still until the push-ups started again. More vomit; then came the other end, diarrhea. Scared that he might be extremely ill, I took him to the same nearby clinic where he had recently been vaccinated and neutered.

Parvo virus? It didn't sound good, and it sure sounded expensive. They explained that although he was a rather large dog, he was still less than a year old and was considered a puppy; this condition usually affected pups. Often, it was fatal. Fortunately for him, he was an older puppy and had recently been vaccinated for the disease, which could possibly help his fight. Unfortunately for me, the disease would require him to stay at the vet's and received costly care if he were going to survive.

Now let me get this straight, I thought. This mutt, whom I barely knew, was now going to cost me, a guy who had just put every penny I had toward a down payment on a townhouse, hundreds of dollars of medical care. And after a hefty sum was placed on my credit card, the dog may not even survive the ordeal. I breathed heavily not knowing which one of us deserved more sympathy. I thought of his long greyhound snout and his sad eyes avoiding any contact with mine on the day he was found at St. Thomas. I didn't even want to imagine the cruelty he must have suffered to make him so afraid of the world. Now, just as he had begun to trust someone, a disease was waging war on him. Not knowing how I would deal with the credit card payments or the stress, I decided that I had to give Blue Horn a shot at a good life. I surmised that he had come into my life at that particular point for some reason. Obviously, I had some lessons to learn from him.

Lesson number one: patience. I would become a more patient person because of this dog. Once he was home from the hospital, I foolishly thought that I could go out in the evenings and he would quietly convalesce. For several evenings, I thought that was exactly what he was doing. No chance. Apparently, he was giving a concert to all my neighbors. My downstairs neighbor angrily confronted me one evening upon my return home. "What are you doing with a dog? You know you can't have a dog here don't you? I'm calling the landlord and letting him know you have a dog and that he howls all the time!"

Howling? Not my sweet quiet dog who is supposed to be healing from his recent disease and hospital stay. I was sure my neighbor was exaggerating.

I decided to do a test. I left the apartment and waited outside for a few minutes. Nothing. Thank God, I thought. Just as I had thought, my neighbor was exaggerating. Just to be sure, I took a walk. Ten minutes later, phew, still nothing. I got in my car to head for an appointment. Roof down on my convertible, I drove around the block just for good measure. My stomach fell as I was on the street opposite my back-unit apartment. Blue was howling all right, and it was loud!

The landlord had no patience with me and took no pity; I had broken the lease. I moved into Joe Neeb's apartment for the next two months until my townhouse was ready. Joe was studying for a month in Boston and his landlord loved Blue. Even after he tore a large hole in the drapes while I went grocery shopping, she still loved Blue. Even after he ripped the curtains and the rod off the wall, she still loved Blue. I, on the other hand, after racking up more credit card debt, wasn't so sure.

After Blue tore up some of the new carpeting in my brand new townhouse and chewed up a pair of prescription glasses, I simply wasn't sure if I would have either the patience or the pocketbook to be able to raise him into a responsible adult dog. But I decided that I had to try.

Shortly after our move into our Glendale townhouse, Blue contracted a serious problem with his ears and had to have surgery on both of them. I began looking for additional part-time work. After being a principal all day, I would then head over to Evans Adult School in downtown L.A., where I taught English as a Second Language and citizenship to adults for several hours each evening. This solved a couple of problems. I was now making enough money to help offset the rising cost of caring for a dog who seemed to have physical and emotional ailments, and since I would be gone from my new townhome for 12-14 hours a day, the dog would have to come with me and couldn't do any more damage. He had the run of the school when he was with me all day at St. Thomas School. However, when I went to teach my evening class, he was relegated to the back seat of my Chrysler LeBaron convertible. The back seat of the car actually became somewhat of a third home for him.

Night after night, it was the same ritual. After an enjoyable day of being my shadow at St. Thomas, Blue would guard the LeBaron's back seat, watching and wondering if I would ever return. After the three hours of my ESL class, he would spot me coming down the same sidewalk I had disappeared from earlier, greeting me as his long-lost prodigal savior. Each time I returned to the car I would have to push him away or else the licking would devolve to where both paws would be around my neck and my ears would be examined by his protruding wet tongue as though some Alpo dog food had been buried next to my brain and Blue was determined to feast on it.

Someone told me once that each time a dog's owner leaves, the animal's brain tells the dog that its person may never come back. Every time the owner returns, it is a celebration in the canine's mind. That certainly proved true with Blue. Whether it was three hours of teaching night school, or three minutes to pick up my dry cleaning, I received the same hero's welcome.

Speaking of dry cleaning, my once-friendly neighborhood dry cleaner and I became enemies because of my protective pup. Imagine my anger when I was dressing one morning and noticed tiny holes on the front of one of my favorite shirts. What kind of crazy outdated machinery must that dry cleaner be using, I wondered. Later that day when I aggressively confronted the woman behind the counter, she had the nerve to tell me that the shirt had come in with the tiny holes. A nosy customer had the temerity to poke his head into our heated conversation, and after a quick examination of my shirt, passively said, "Looks like a dog did that." I gave him the kind of look that said "mind your own business, you fool," and as my head swerved back to the counter I chanced a quick glance at the big black dog sitting in the back seat of my convertible, big floppy ears perched at attention as though he were listening to the conversation and hoping I would not discover his guilt. I admit, I was too embarrassed to tell them I was wrong, but by the time my eyes again met those of the woman at the cash register, she and the man standing behind me weren't the only ones who knew what had happened. Turns out, I was the fool, thanks to the culprit sitting pretty in my backseat. I quickly let the dry cleaner off the hook and slunk out, never to return — not out of anger, but embarrassment.

Did I say embarrassment? Let's just say that once my puppy grew up and overcame his fear of the world, he became bolder than I ever could have imagined. He also became quite clever. He learned to turn doorknobs with his longer than usual and incredibly determined snout. Because of his penchant for running, he never seemed to get enough of it, and he remained quite thin. Sometimes when Griffith Park was near closing and no other cars were around, I would zoom off and have him chase my car wildly. I would do this not to scare him, but to tire him out, or at least attempt to. I'd use a particular leash when we were heading off to the park. Whenever he saw the park leash, he became so excited that he would literally spin in circles as we walked to the car. His spinning always reminded me fondly of the Warner Brothers cartoon character of the Tasmanian Devil.

Although there were leash laws in L.A., it always pleased me when no one was around and I could set Blue free, watching him run up and down the hillsides as though he were on fire and attempting to find water. Once, he disappeared into some brush and quickly flew back into sight, throwing himself down on the dirt path, writhing around in the dirt, and exuding a toxic smell. As I ran to him, I quickly realized that he had been skunked. As much as I wanted to leave him behind at that moment, I knew he would only chase my car onto the freeway, probably attracting some unwanted attention, or something far worse. I threw whatever blankets and clothes I had in my car over the back seat, put the roof down, and drove immediately to the vet, where they kept him for several days, bathing him in tomato juice.

In my years of studying under the direction of metaphysical teachers like Marianne Williamson and Louise Hay, I learned that certain people and circumstances are often made part of our lives to teach us lessons. In fact, sometimes it's the most frustrating people and circumstances that teach us the most. Since we frequently had stray animals showing up at our door at St. Thomas, I believed that the timing of Blue's arrival just as I had purchased my own home, combined with Kevin's certainty that this was the dog for me, meant something deeper. Blue had more to teach me beyond patience.

Although it took months before Blue overcame his fears, once he did, he began to exhibit the opposite behavior — he embraced life fully. And he helped me do the same. He taught me to appreciate and even love the simple pleasures of life that only an animal can, such as love for an open field. How many thousands of open fields must I have passed in my life that meant nothing to me until I met Blue? Now, it was impossible for me to pass a grassy field without my backseat companion whining and getting excited. He wanted me to stop so he could get out and run and smell all the scents. There were many times when we did stop and both of us would run and one of us would smell all the scents. There was little else in the world Blue loved more than a wide-open field. Because I was primarily the focus of his life, I never worried about taking his leash off and setting him loose; he would always come back. The sight of seeing the jet-black streak running through a field or up and down a hillside made me feel utter joy.

The day he discovered that his webbed Labrador paws were made for swimming was quite by accident. It was a hot summer early evening, the sun had just set, and I was walking Blue through Balboa Park. I waited until it was late enough to not be too hot and when most people would have already gone home. I decided to allow this pent-up pup some freedom, and let him off the leash so he could explore, and hopefully, burn some energy. Because he was so black and it was after dark I depended on hearing him rather than seeing him. I also knew that he rarely let me out of his sight for more than a minute at a time; my little stalker insisted on knowing where I was at almost every moment. Every once in a while I could hear him running toward me. The ground was dry, and his paws rapidly thumping against the dry dirt sounded like a stampede coming at me. His eyesight was excellent and I knew that he knew where I was and that he would not run into me, so I kept walking, only to hear the stampede grow louder, loudER, louDER, until voooooooooooooooom and swishhhhhhhhh! The black streak came within inches of my body and ran past me...a few minutes later, and another stampeding voom and swish, there he would go again in the other direction.

Wait a minute; maybe his eyesight wasn't as excellent as I thought. The next sound I heard was not the stampeding voom and swish, it was a giant SPLASH! Ducks were quacking wildly. The foolish dog, who had always been terrified anytime he got near water, apparently thought that manmade Lake Balboa was different. As I ran in the direction of the lake, I could hear the wild paddling of four long legs as Blue discovered he knew instinctively how to swim. However, he could not get his big puppy body out of the water due to the man-made rim around the lake, which is really more like a swimming pool than a lake. He splashed around feverishly until his new love, me, came and pulled him out, saving his life. I didn't realize until later that this heroic act on my part only caused his obsession with me to grow that much stronger.

At school, Blue quickly became the ruler of the roost. Whenever I went off to do various things around the school, I would close my office door behind me, leaving Blue safely inside. He would wait the proper amount of time until I disappeared, then turn the knob and let himself out. The first-grade classroom was right across from my office. Marisa, our first-grade teacher, was a young, vivacious woman of Cuban descent who happened to love dogs. She usually left one of her classroom doors open and Blue loved to visit the first graders, not only because of Marisa, but also because the little kids did not always wash their hands after lunch and Blue enjoyed the occasional lick of peanut butter or whatever happened to be on the menu that day. Eventually, he became so bold that when his little friends were outside sitting on a bench enjoying a snack, he would cuddle up beside a couple of them and take their snacks in a manner that almost made them think they had offered them up freely. Sometimes, when he was on an energy high, perhaps after a game of catch with the older students, he would swoop by and take a snack right from someone's hands, and all anyone would see was a black streak whizzing by with a tamale in its mouth. Most of the time, the kids would laugh and borrow part of someone else's snack. They too, loved Blue. The entire student body thought Blue belonged to them.

Something that's a funny memory today but was horribly embarrassing at the time occurred on Marisa's wedding day. Marisa and Vince, our eighth-grade teacher, had fallen in love and had planned a large and elegant wedding. It was a beautiful fall day. As usual, I took Blue with me and kept him in the car during the wedding. Over the years, he had grown accustomed to sitting in the backseat of my open convertible, sometimes waiting hours for me to return. His fear of losing me always kept him right there in the backseat; he never left the car. Because of his size, most people mistook his serious, sad-looking eyes for menace, and no one bothered him. After the wedding, we drove to the reception and I parked in a large public lot next to the event venue, a swanky and formal Victorian house in downtown Santa Monica.

I'll never know what the trigger was. Perhaps he studied which building I entered. Perhaps he recognized so many of the faces going into the same building. Perhaps he saw Vince arriving with Marisa, another object of Blue's affection.

As I sat in my assigned seat at the elegantly decorated table with fine linens and silverware and glassware, I watched as the bridal party was introduced, couple by couple. Finally, Marisa and Vince were introduced and came to the center of the room for pictures. Just as they arrived at the center of their bridal party and flashbulbs commenced, I saw the black streak zoom past my table bounding toward the newlyweds.

The first thought that crossed my mind was, what kind of a place is this that has animals freely running about? My brain would simply not allow me to register what was actually happening. I sat, relaxed, as this animal made its way to Marisa, until Joe, our kindergarten teacher, shouted, "DAN! THAT'S BLUE!"

My instincts kicked in and my body sprung into action, all while my psyche suffered deeply the embarrassment I deserved at that moment. The giggles barely registered but the horrified looks from some of the guests penetrated my existence as I grabbed Blue by his collar and pulled him away from the bride, who was holding a bouquet of flowers with one hand while petting her adoring fan with the other. "Sorry Blue, I've married another," Marisa said, laughing, while I dragged the dog out of the building to secure him in the car this time. After dinner Marisa and Vince insisted on a formal picture with Blue; they obviously got a kick out of their wedding crasher.

That night Blue had taught me another lesson; no more would I be able to leave him in the car with the top down. From that point on, the top stayed up with the windows partially down.

At the end of that school year, I accepted the job of principal at St. Genevieve High School. During the interview process, the pastor of St. Genevieve, Monsignor Van Liefde, came to visit me at St. Thomas. He didn't seem fazed that a big black dog was in my office. As we walked around the school, he laughed when Blue attempted to bite the jump rope or chased a basketball as it was being dribbled across the outdoor court. The students took it in their stride and so did he. Therefore, I knew he would be fine with Blue being part of the package when I took over at St. Genevieve.

Adjusting to high school life is not always easy for kids and it was not the easiest transition for Blue either. The kids were so much bigger than the ones he was used to. In fact, he would sneak next door to St. Genevieve elementary school only to have the little ones cry upon seeing him, requiring the ever-vigilant adults to bring him back across property lines.

Within weeks of our arrival at St. Gen, Blue became somewhat of a celebrity. He was quite accustomed to having his school picture taken each year, but seemed a bit shy the day the *Los Angeles Daily News* was on campus for a story. The reporter and photographer found it delightful that Blue had the run of the campus, but for some reason he did not cotton to the idea of posing for them. Eventually, I crouched down and he came right over, but kept turning his head away from the photographer. We ended up taking the picture together and it remains among the many of my favorite photos of Blue.

Eventually, he adjusted to his routine. It wasn't as easy to snatch food out of the hands of high school kids, but they often left food on the ground and were usually more than willing to push the button that made the water come out of the fountain so he could get a drink. Rarely did a student find it disgusting that the dog drank out of the same fountain that the students did. In fact, it was some of the students who actually taught him to drink from the fountain, and then he would just wait staring at the big white porcelain water bowl until someone pushed the button for him; if one of the kids had to go, another one would come along until Blue got his thirst quenched — an excellent method, particularly after scavenging in the sun for his daily snacks. I never encouraged his fountain drinking, however, and always had a fresh bowl of water waiting for him in my office.

I also always tried to clean up his messes, though of course I couldn't be with him constantly. Some of the football players from back in those days laugh today about sliding into a pile of Blue's making. I'm fairly confident that the holes in the fence allowed other dogs from the neighborhood to wander onto the field and make contributions for which Blue mostly received the blame. Blue liked to wander the grounds in search of food and attention, and would often be searching for me. But I rarely saw him wander onto our practice field.

However, there was one incident involving Blue and a football field that I will unfortunately never forget. It was during a regular season league game against Daniel Murphy High School. It was our home game, which was held at Polytechnic High School, approximately two miles from St. Genevieve. As was my usual custom, Blue traveled with me. By this point, I'd not only learned my lesson about not having the top down, I no longer even owned a convertible. Blue was left safely and securely in my car with the windows partially down. To this day I'm not certain how he escaped from the car. Nor will I ever know how he got through the closed stadium gates, or how he gained access to the field itself. I'm guessing that he must have studied me when I left the vehicle and watched as carefully as possible until I disappeared into the crowd in the stands. Perhaps that is how he knew on which side of the field and where in the bleachers I was sitting.

Mr. Van, our vice principal, was announcing the game. As the crowd sat waiting for the next play to begin, I heard him announce, "It seems we have a dog on the field. Could someone assist in removing the dog from the field?" Mr. Van knew Blue. It just didn't register on him who this errant dog was. I, too, was again in my oblivious fantasy world imagining that one of the yappy neighborhood dogs had squeezed through the fence and was interrupting our game. Why don't people take better care of their animals? I thought to myself. As I looked down on the field expecting to see a little runt of a dog being chased by those wanting to get the game underway, I instead witnessed the deliberate gallop of a determined stalker dog looking for his prey. It didn't fully register, though, until I heard Marlon, our athletic director, say, "DAN! IT'S BLUE!

Blue suffered numerous ailments and illnesses during our years together. Through it all, he taught me to love and appreciate life and nature more than I ever had. He certainly taught me patience, and encouraged me to exercise right along with him. There came a time when he became ill but he didn't snap out of it after a day or two like he normally did. His illness lingered for days, then weeks. Trips to the vet yielded nothing tangible. Blue was at least 13 years old by then. His personality began to change. He began to wander off and not come looking for me. After he wandered out into the busy street in front of our school on a couple of occasions, I realized I could not allow him free rein of the campus any longer. For his own safety, I began to leave him at home during the day, something he wasn't accustomed to. At night he began to frequently use the living room as a bathroom, creating messes that caused him shame and me stress. One day a neighbor dropped by to inquire about him, saying that she hadn't seen him riding in the car with me lately. She and her husband were animal lovers and had taken a great liking to Blue. I described what was going on. I told her that Blue's doctor thought these were signs of him aging. She suggested I consider doggie diapers. After much thought, I made the decision to release Blue's spirit from his body.

Blue had grown to trust me. He'd had a great life, and I loved him. I especially loved his lust for life. I did not want the end of his life to be that of a confused spirit wandering into traffic having to wear a diaper in order not to make messes in our home. I wanted for us both to only know of the soaring spirit of a dog who loved going to school. It was time for Blue to graduate.

The next morning, I helped him get into the back of my car. I drove to the spot at the bottom of the Santa Gabriel Mountains near our home where we often hiked. There was not a spark of remembrance. I lifted him out of the car and we began our final walk up the hill. He lagged behind me, following out of duty rather than being sparked by his usual excitement. I turned and watched him slowly walk in my direction.

Then we drove to the vet's office. Blue and I both sat on the floor. As usual, he was trusting me to take care of him. My arms were wrapped around his large rib cage. As the needle was inserted, I could not look, but kept my head pressed against his, knowing how much he loved that. At the moment his heart stopped, mine broke with sadness. I could literally feel his spirit leave his body. His muscles let loose and he collapsed onto me. The vet expressed her sympathy and told me to stay with him as long as I wished. I stayed another ten minutes or so, petting his beautiful black coat for the last time.

As I left his body on the floor of the vet's office, I felt about as blue as I had ever been. It had been a fiercely loyal friendship and it was over. I left knowing that I had made it possible for a forlorn and abused stray pup to live a happy and wonderful dog's life. I also knew that I had been loved magnificently and that I and hundreds of students from St. Thomas the Apostle School and St. Genevieve High School would forever have fond and funny memories of a dog named Blue.

Me and a dog named Blue

Blue enjoying the snow during his travels to Big Bear, CA

Marisa and Blue after his unexpected appearance at her reception

One of my favorite pictures of Blue as he staked his claim in his beloved back seat of my Chrysler LeBaron convertible as my two nieces attempt to enjoy a drive up Pacific Coast Highway at dusk.

Chapter 25. Just the Beginning

Although this is the end of this book, my outlook is that we are always at a beginning. So as I complete this manuscript during the Christmas vacation of 2013, we at St. Genevieve are, as usual, in an expectant and ongoing state of renewal, and experiencing anointed moments.

This is my 15th year at St. Genevieve High School. Recently, I was asked by two separate parties to consider applying for positions that are rather different from what I currently do. Both offered unique, and what I would term enticing, challenges. At first, I was eager to apply for both, as I'd gotten to the point where I felt I was ready to move on and try something new. As with most jobs, mine included days when I thought I couldn't take it for a minute more and I longed to try something completely new and different. Toward the end of this last school year, it seemed as though I was having more than the usual number of those kinds of days. But once I indicated my interest in these other possible positions and the parties began to actively pursue my candidacy, something kind of strange and wonderful happened: I realized that I actually wasn't through quite yet.

As I imagined myself doing something new, I saw that I really was still enamored with my work and my community at St. Genevieve. The thought of moving on became totally unappealing, and I formed a deeper appreciation for how blessed I already was.

And while some change is good, it also can be good to approach some things that don't change in new and different ways. Not long before the end of last year's spring term, our school took another trip to Plains, Georgia to visit the Carters. More than 80 students staged Jimmy Carter's favorite Broadway show, *Carousel*, at the historic Rylander Theatre in Americus, Georgia. We invited Shirley Jones to come along, and to our surprise and delight, she accepted. Shirley had starred in the motion picture version of *Carousel* and had, until she joined us, already sung for six U.S. presidents. Shirley opened the show by singing "If I Loved You," and by doing so, could now say that she has sung for seven U.S. presidents.

After the show, former president Carter remarked that when he proposed to Rosalynn, he had just seen *Carousel* on Broadway as a midshipman at the Naval Academy, and had been so inspired that he sang "If I Loved You" as part of his proposal. She said "no." But we all know that wasn't the end of that story; the Carters recently celebrated their 67th wedding anniversary!

On February 19, 2013 both President and Mrs. Carter visited St. Genevieve in what will remain one of the great highlights in our school's history. Knowing they were coming to southern California for a Carter Center event, we invited them to come and celebrate a Mass with us. After all, we have attended many Baptist services at the Maranatha Baptist Church in Plains. The Mass the Carters attended at St. Gen's was one of the most beautiful ones we ever celebrated. Following the Mass, we hosted a dinner for the Carters with our faculty, staff, and many of the friends of our school. Chuck D, one of our former motivational speakers, read a poem he had written for the evening called, "The White House Gets a Heart Transplant," which referred to the unique administration of Jimmy Carter. Shirley Jones performed a medley of songs from movies such as *Oklahoma*, *Carousel*, and *Music Man*. Helen Reddy, who in July of 2012 came out of a 10-year retirement right here at St. Genevieve High School, also sang for the Carters that night. Previously, Helen had honored us with a two-night benefit concert engagement to raise money for the arts. Our Valiant Voices choir and our jazz band were her opening acts. Fans of Helen traveled from 18 states and three countries to see her performances at our school. It was in relaying this story to former President Carter that I discovered that he, too, is a fan of Helen's. So at the dinner on February 19th, Helen sang "Delta Dawn" for the first time in 10 years, and then dedicated "You and Me Against the World" to Carter's mother, Miss Lillian.

Once again, the St. Genevieve students made me so proud with their great attention to all of our visitors. They celebrated grandly during the Mass, and both the choir and jazz band performed at the dinner. As the evening came to a close, I had a touching experience of recounting to our gathering how this historic and unique relationship with the Carters had come into being. I held up the original letter I'd received from Rosalynn, where she herself had included a short handwritten note. Rosalynn came onto the stage and hugged me. She gave a heartfelt and beautiful speech about the work of the Carter Center as well as the relationship our school has with her and our former president. She ended her remarks by saying: "What if all the schools in our country were like St. Genevieve? We'd be friendly and peaceful and just a totally different world."

In spring of 2013 our pastor, Father Alden Sison announced a restructuring of our two schools. For the first time in the two schools' histories we now have one principal and I have the honor and pleasure of serving in that role. Oh, and remember my friend Vince? He joined the St. Gen staff this year after years of us talking about how great it would be to one day work together again. Both of us keep in touch with many of the faculty and staff we worked with at St. Thomas school, most of whom have moved on from there as well. When any of us get together we marvel at how bonded we still feel by the unique and heart-tugging experiences we shared way back then.

On December 17, 2013 in my new role as principal of both St. Genevieve Elementary and High School, I wrote and directed my first elementary school Christmas program since December of 1998. It was an extraordinarily satisfying experience for the students, and especially for me. The days leading up to the actual event had my mind working overtime, bringing forth the many fond memories of my days at St. Thomas the Apostle School. It was — and is — wonderful to be back working with elementary school students again. Two nights later we celebrated a stunningly beautiful Advent Mass with our high school students and their families. Our dear friend Sister Clare Fitzgerald provided the exegesis and had our students and guests spellbound. That night during our opening hymn, "Prepare Ye," from *Godspell*, we paid homage to our new pope, Francis. During the opening chords of the song a student from each grade stood one at a time as a spotlight shone on them in the bleachers. The rest of the gym was darkened, and each student, alone, sang the words, "Prepare Ye the way of the Lord," just as in the play *Godspell*. It is a lovely and haunting call to worship. When the first student finished, the spotlight moved to the center of the gym floor as another student, dressed as Pope Francis, tells a would-be limousine driver, "No thank you, I'm going to ride on the bus with my fellow priests," just as Francis was reported to have done following his election. Then, dramatically, the spotlight moved back into the darkened bleachers, finding the next soloist who again sang only the words, "Prepare Ye the way of the Lord." Back on the gym floor we then watched more of the widely reported actions of our new pope, his washing the feet of a Muslim woman...his embrace of a disfigured man.

Anointed moments, right?

Francis is shaking up the entire world! Why? He is a steady reminder to us all about what it means to be Christ in a modern world. Those are the lessons that my colleagues and I have been trying so hard to teach our students at both St. Thomas the Apostle and St. Genevieve schools. When we strive to be our best every single day, when we treat others with kindness and compassion, when we welcome others, and most of all, when we love, we become Christ to our modern world. We each have the power to be a burden

Anointed Moments

or a blessing to this great world in which we live. When we choose to be a blessing, *our* lives become blessed and our time on this earth becomes anointed.

None of us know what the future holds for us. If I have my way, St. Genevieve will one day have a new campus, which will allow us to have much needed athletic facilities, improved classrooms, band rooms, and a theater. We accomplish a lot with little resources.

Our greatest accomplishment has been building a community where so many people have had the opportunity to experience the divine presence of God. I've had a front-row seat and have had experiences that have touched my heart and changed my life forever.

When I arrived in the City of Angels in September of 1986, I was certain I would soon be a movie star. Little did my wannabe "star mind" realize that God had other plans for me. I was soon to be cast as a Catholic school principal and it would become my dream role of a lifetime.

Serving these more than two decades as principal, first at St. Thomas and then at St. Genevieve, has provided my life with a joy and fulfillment I could not have imagined possible.

My life is forever blessed, and yes, even anointed by the two schools I've called home, and all the wonderful people who have become my family.

I do my best to live without regrets, strive to grow spiritually, and can honestly say that *I love my life.* So while this is the conclusion of this book, for me, personally, it really is just

The Beginning...

Acknowledgments

In all circumstances give thanks, for this is the will of God for you in Christ Jesus.
- Thessalonians 5:18

Love is the way I walk in gratitude.
- Course in Miracles, Lesson 195

It makes me nervous attempting to thank and acknowledge everyone connected to this book. The spectrum is wide and far-reaching. I will certainly leave someone out and if you are among that group I ask for your understanding. This list is in no particular order.

Howard Anderson for his cover design. The saying goes that you can't judge a book by the cover, but in this case, I hope you enjoy the book as much as the cover.

Kathy Parker for her editing skills and for encouraging me to self-publish.

Tom Parker for many insightful questions and suggestions on writing this book.

Craig Udit for his lasting friendship, constant encouragement, and for pulling it all together to make this book happen.

Father Paul Wolkovits for his time spent proofreading, offering suggestions, and providing encouragement.

Kathy Anderson for some great advice during the edit.

Sister Clare Fitzgerald for being part of so many anointed moments in my life.

Our wonderful friends from Plains, Georgia, who have provided numerous and memorable lessons to our Valiant Community on the true meaning of Southern hospitality: Betty and Boze Godwin; Dan and Nelle Ariail; Jill Stuckey; The Fuller Family; and Jan and George Williams.

Fr. Ken Deasy for being a great teacher and friend.

Sister Mary Elizabeth Galt for standing by my side for more than 20 years, even when the bullets were flying.

Ken Skinner and Joe Rawlinson for believing in St. Genevieve High School when few people did.

Father Alden Sison for going through the fire.

Mary Bailey for constantly applauding and encouraging everything I do.

Aldene Horn for being a great anchor in my life.

Rosalynn Carter for a friendship spanning 28 years.

President Jimmy Carter for all he has done for our school, for me personally, and for our world.

Helen Reddy for your music and friendship.

Chuck D and Gaye Johnson for your encouragement and for always uplifting our community when you visit.

Edward James Olmos for your passion and always making us think.

Shirley Jones for creating memories none of us would have imagined possible.

Monsignor Michael J. Ryan for having the vision and fortitude to build St. Genevieve Parish and Schools.

The Sisters of St. Joseph of Peace for all you did to form our foundation.

The Salesian Sisters for continuing to build upon that foundation.

Father Jarlath Cunnane, Monsignor Van Leifde, Father Marcial Juan for being great pastors!

Monsignor Lloyd Torgerson and Monsignor John Barry for the founding gifts of St. Thomas Heritage.

Christian DeGuzman, Gabe Cheng, and Lance Hollandsworth for photographs.

Juan Jasso for attempting to keep me organized.

Rose Corpuz, Allan Shatkin, Dennis Yumul, Lynn Muro, and Kelley Endreola for helping create the Anointing experience.

The many men and women who have been part of the St. Genevieve Character Education Speakers Series.

All of you who said, "you ought to write a book about your experiences."

The Benedictine Priests and Nuns who dedicated their lives to God and served Sacred Heart Parish in Jeannette, PA.

My teachers at both Sacred Heart in Jeannette, PA and Greensburg Central Catholic.

The Bob Horn Family

Father Ed McDermott S.J. and Sister Mary Peter Travis for introducing me to Moral Development and Character Education.

Dale Hoyt who encouraged my attendance at my first symposium on Moral Development and Character Education

Michael Josephson for creating Character Counts and all your contributions to our mission.

The Character Education Partnership (CEP)

Carl Masciantonio for letting the Valiants borrow the Jayhawk Fight Song.

My hometown of Jeannette PA. I still call Jeannette home.

The United States Parks Service, Plains Division for always supporting and helping with our school projects.

The United States Secret Service Officers for having worked so professionally with our school both in Plains, Georgia and in Panorama City, California.

Heather Stanley and her crew at the Rylander Theater in Americus, Georgia for always welcoming our community to your beautiful theater.

The Windsor Hotel and Staff in Americus Georgia for always taking such good care of our students and staff each time we visit.

Foundations and individuals which have supported St. Thomas the Apostle and St. Genevieve Schools, including:

John and Dorothy Shea for our Field of Dreams.

Joan Payden for our library and multiple blessings.

Sarah Arias and the Arias Family

The Catholic Education Foundation

The Fritz B. Burns Foundation

The Willam H. Hannon Foundation

The Bill Hannon Foundation

The Dan Murphy Foundation

The Ahmanson Foundation

The Carrie Estelle Doheny Foundation

The Specialty Family Foundation

The Rose Hill Foundation

The Weingart Foundation

The Thomas and Dorothy Leavey Foundation
The William R. and Virginia Hayden Foundation
The Centofante Family Foundation
The Frank McHugh - O'Donovan Foundation
The Seidler Foundation

And special thanks to:
The proud community of St. Thomas the Apostle Parish and Schools for having made me a better man.
The founding parishioners of St. Genevieve for a creation of beauty in Panorama City.
The current parishioners of St. Genevieve for supporting our schools.
Our alumni at St. Thomas the Apostle and St. Genevieve.
The Class of 2000 for sharing the vision and leaving a lasting legacy.
Our alumni of principals, teachers and staff at St. Thomas the Apostle and St. Genevieve.
The students of St. Genevieve High School for their enthusiasm and spirit, which makes for a daily reality that is filled with anointed moments.
The students of St. Genevieve Elementary School for their welcoming kindness; I look forward to having many cherished moments with you.
The faculty and staff of St. Genevieve High School and Elementary School for their continual giving of themselves, their time, and their talents. I'm blessed to work with you.

And thanks to you, the reader, for sharing this journey.

- Dan Horn

The Author

Dan Horn

*What you can't see in this photo are the
37 kindergartners laughing joyfully as their
principal poses proudly with the crown
celebrating the 100th day of school!*

Made in the USA
Charleston, SC
16 April 2014